AI for People and Business

A Framework for Better Human Experiences and Business Success

Alex Castrounis

Beijing · Boston · Farnham · Sebastopol · Tokyo   O'REILLY®

AI for People and Business

by Alex Castrounis

Copyright © 2019 Alex Castrounis. All rights reserved.

Published by O'Reilly Media, Inc., 1005 Gravenstein Highway North, Sebastopol, CA 95472.

O'Reilly books may be purchased for educational, business, or sales promotional use. Online editions are also available for most titles (*http://oreilly.com*). For more information, contact our corporate/institutional sales department: 800-998-9938 or *corporate@oreilly.com*.

Acquisitions Editor: Rachel Roumeliotis

Developmental Editors: Mike Loukides and Jeff Bleiel

Production Editor: Nan Barber

Copyeditor: Octal Publishing, LLC

Proofreader: Christina Edwards

Indexer: WordCo Indexing Services, Inc.

Interior Designer: Monica Kamsvaag

Cover Designer: Karen Montgomery

Illustrator: Rebecca Demarest

July 2019: First Edition

Revision History for the First Edition

2019-07-01: First Release

See *http://oreilly.com/catalog/errata.csp?isbn=9781492036579* for release details.

978-1-492-03657-9

Praise for *AI for People and Business*

A must read for business executives and managers interested in learning about AI and unlocking its benefits. Alex Castrounis has simplified complex topics so that anyone can begin to leverage AI within their organization.

—*Dan Park, GM and Director, Uber*

Alex Castrounis has been at the forefront of helping organizations understand the promise of AI and leverage its benefits, while avoiding the many pitfalls that can derail success. In this essential book, he shares his expertise with the rest of us.

—*Dean Wampler, PhD, VP, Fast Data Engineering at Lightbend*

With the enormous impact AI is having across many different industries, it's imperative for all organizational leaders to develop a baseline understanding... and this book provides just that.

—*David Bledin, Director at Google*

A long-overdue deep dive into how AI changes organizational ecosystems and the lives of people who inhabit them. The AIPB Framework is the essential roadmap for every businessperson on the AI journey.

—*Mark Fetherolf, CTO of Numinary Data Science, Coauthor of Real World Machine Learning (Manning)*

A well organized, very readable, non-technical survey of the often misunderstood science of AI and machine learning. I highly recommend this book for business leaders and curious consumers aspiring for literacy in this important field.

—*Richard B. Noyes, Angel Investor and former CFO,*
Astra Pharmaceuticals NA

Contents

Preface

The Motivation Behind This Framework and Book

After earning my master's degree in applied mathematics (awarded with distinction), I became an IndyCar race car engineer and race strategist who competed in more than 100 races worldwide, including many times in the Indianapolis 500. I also ran the vehicle dynamics and data science department at Andretti Autosport, which helped drive results for a four-car IndyCar racing team.

In American professional motorsports, winning the Indianapolis 500 is the ultimate goal. I attended my first Indianapolis 500 when I was still in high school. If you've never been, I highly recommend it. This event is truly the greatest spectacle in racing and is the largest single-day sporting event in the entire world. The track itself is the largest sporting facility in the world (*http://bit.ly/ 2Wzjoa2*) in terms of capacity.

The first year I attended, 1992, turned out to be the closest Indy 500 finish in history (and still is), and ended with Al Unser, Jr., beating Scott Goodyear for the win by 0.043 seconds! Think about that! That's less than half of one tenth of one second after racing for almost three hours, at an average speed of 220-plus mph, and for 500 miles (the equivalent of driving from Chicago to Toronto)!

I was so blown away that I walked out of the Indianapolis Motor Speedway (IMS) that day telling those with me that I would someday work in IndyCar racing, and the rest is history. Additionally, and very serendipitously, my racing career began with me working for Al Unser, Jr., the driver who won that very same Indy 500 that I attended as a kid. I came on board as chief assistant engineer to Alan Mertens, the engineer who designed the car with which Unser won in 1992!

Figure P-1 shows an image of an article in *Racer* magazine following the 2007 Indianapolis 500, where I was the race engineer and strategist for Davey

Hamilton. I'm shown on the right celebrating a ninth place finish after starting 20th, this was Davey's remarkable comeback race following 23 surgeries to reconstruct his legs and feet after a horrific and massive crash at the Texas Motor Speedway in 2001.

DAVEY'S ON THE ROAD AGAIN
Six years on, Hamilton's return reaps reward

Not long ago, Davey Hamilton was declared disabled and allowed to collect disability benefits. That's how severe his foot injuries were. It also illustrates the depth of his comeback from injuries so severe, doctors initially thought they would have to amputate. Instead, they saved his feet through a series of complicated surgeries that included rebuilding tiny blood vessels and skin grafts.

It was a long and painful path for Davey Hamilton, but his ninth-place Indy 500 finish was a worthy reward for his 23 surgeries.

Six years after a frightening crash smashed his feet, Hamilton returned to a race car for the 91st Indianapolis 500. He finished ninth, a remarkable result given the circumstances.

"It was a long, tough road," Hamilton said. "The first two years, it was definitely a life-changing experience for sure. I had a lot of mental anger, really just wanting to know why, then not knowing if I was going to keep my legs, if I was going to be able to walk, and if I could, how well, how much pain. Mentally, that plays on you. Racing drivers do whatever it takes to make it to the next race. We're always busy. To be lying in a hospital bed with those injuries, it was tough mentally."

The deal with Vision Racing and Hewlett-Packard only involved Indy, but Hamilton wants more. "I'm trying to put something together," he says. "We'll see where it leads, but I definitely have more left."

Considering that little more than four years ago he was in a wheelchair, Hamilton's story astounds even the primary character.

"I did feel at times it wasn't going to happen," he said. "But I just couldn't talk myself into that."

Figure P-1. Racer Magazine 2007 Indianapolis 500 article (reprinted from RACER Magazine with permission)

As my racing career progressed, I quickly learned that professional motorsports involves generating competitive advantage on steroids. Racing at that level requires intense innovation, continuous optimization, perfection, advanced analytics of inordinate amounts of data, rock-solid teamwork and collaboration, and the ability to execute and adapt on the fly at an often unrealistic pace. All of this while under intense pressure and accountability. Ultimately, professional motorsports is all about maximizing insights to drive—and benefit from—decisions, actions, and outcomes in the least amount of time possible. This is how competitive advantage and top results are produced.

As an IndyCar race car engineer and race strategist using AI, machine learning, and data science to optimize race car setups and race strategy for a given combination of driver, track layout (super speedway, short oval, road course, street course), and conditions (weather, track surface), I was able to help my teams win many races and podium finishes, including winning the historic final Champ Car (formerly CART) race in Long Beach, California. I worked directly with many notable drivers and team owners, including Michael Andretti, Al Unser, Jr., Jimmy Vassar, Will Power, Tony Kanaan, Danica Patrick, and Ryan-Hunter Reay to name a few.

You might be wondering what this has to do with this book, the framework it's about, and AI in general? The answer is everything! Let me explain.

After about 10 years in racing, I decided to transition into the tech industry. I quickly realized that, much like in racing, companies are also constantly trying to beat their competitors to win. One thing that quickly became clear to me is that what it takes to win races doesn't apply only to racing, but also to companies, regardless of industry or size. Although the definition of winning might be different for every company (e.g., achieving specific business profit and growth goals), what it takes to win is the same. In both racing and business, winning, and especially winning consistently, requires competitive advantage, which is the ability to understand, act, and achieve performance levels in ways that your competitors can't.

Based on my professional experience in both racing and business, competitive advantage comes primarily from two areas. First, for products with some form of user interface (UI), competitive advantage comes from superb design, an optimized user experience (UX), and from features that delight. Second, and most important in my opinion, it comes from having the "right" data, creating a winning strategy to take advantage of it, executing that strategy, and then using data to continuously improve and optimize things over time.

Since leaving racing, I have leveraged my expertise in business, analytics, and product management to help companies of all sizes in many industries to benefit from technological innovation and digital transformation, and to build great data products. Through speaking and teaching, I have also helped thousands of people grasp the details and benefits of data science and advanced analytics.

I am the founder, CEO, and principal consultant of InnoArchiTech, a data and analytics consulting firm that helps business leaders know what to do with their data. My primary goals are to help business leaders develop a vision and strategy to benefit from their data and also build great data products and solutions. I have a strong interest in helping to eliminate confusion associated with data science and advanced analytics.

This book, and the framework that it presents, is based on these goals and my nearly 20 years of real-world innovation, experience, and expertise; it is intended to guide the creation of better human experiences and business success through end-to-end AI-based innovation built on a winning AI vision and strategy.

Navigating This Book

The book is divided into four parts. Part I introduces and details the AI for People and Business (AIPB) Framework, its North Star, benefits, and components. It ends with a nontechnical overview of AI and machine learning, as well as an overview of real-world AI applications and opportunities. This will help spark ideas, and provide the context required for developing a vision and strategy around relevant AI applications and use cases.

Part II is about developing an AI vision. It begins with an in-depth discussion of *why* to pursue AI, followed by defining AI vision-aligned goals for different stakeholders such as businesses, customers, and users. We then go over what people need and want, and how to turn that into great AI-based products and better human experiences.

Part III is about developing an AI strategy. It is focused on concepts such as scientific innovation, AI readiness and maturity, and key considerations for achieving success with AI. You should use these concepts to perform appropriate assessments as defined by AIPB to develop a strategy to fill gaps and address key considerations, as well as for developing a vision-aligned AI solution strategy.

Part IV concludes with a discussion of the potential impact of AI on jobs, final thoughts, and the future of AI, particularly what to expect and watch out for.

Please feel free to visit *https://aipbbook.com* any time for the latest AIPB information and resources. Thanks for picking up a copy of this book. I hope you enjoy it!

O'Reilly Online Learning

For almost 40 years, *O'Reilly Media* has provided technology and business training, knowledge, and insight to help companies succeed.

Our unique network of experts and innovators share their knowledge and expertise through books, articles, conferences, and our online learning platform.

O'Reilly's online learning platform gives you on-demand access to live training courses, in-depth learning paths, interactive coding environments, and a vast collection of text and video from O'Reilly and 200+ other publishers. For more information, please visit *http://oreilly.com*.

How to Contact Us

Please address comments and questions concerning this book to the publisher:

O'Reilly Media, Inc.
1005 Gravenstein Highway North
Sebastopol, CA 95472
800-998-9938 (in the United States or Canada)
707-829-0515 (international or local)
707-829-0104 (fax)

We have a web page for this book, where we list errata, examples, and any additional information. You can access this page at *http://bit.ly/ai-for-people-and-business*.

To comment or ask technical questions about this book, send email to *book-questions@oreilly.com*.

For more information about our books, courses, conferences, and news, see our website at *http://www.oreilly.com*.

Find us on Facebook: *http://facebook.com/oreilly*

Follow us on Twitter: *http://twitter.com/oreillymedia*

Watch us on YouTube: *http://www.youtube.com/oreillymedia*

Acknowledgments

I would like to thank you, the reader of this book. Writing it was a major and very difficult undertaking that is made 100% worth it if you read it and learn something new and valuable.

I would like to thank Alan Mertens and Chris Mower for taking a risk on hiring an unknown and relatively inexperienced race car engineer and race strategist. It is because of them that I have worked and competed at the highest level of professional motorsports, traveled the world, worked with some of the greatest names in the sport's history, and experienced the indescribable thrill of winning races. All of this helped build the foundation for my post racing professional successes.

Thanks to all of the teachers, experts, colleagues, and mentors who have helped me throughout my professional journey. People who share knowledge and expertise for the purpose of benefiting others are certainly helping to make the world a better place.

Thanks to Matt Mayo for being a great collaborator, and for putting me in touch with Marsee Henon.

I would like to thank my book reviewers, Beth Partridge and Matt Kirk. Both provided invaluable insights and ideas, and my book is better because of their help. Additionally, I would like to thank all of the people whose high-quality work and ideas are referenced in this book, and anyone else who provided advice along the way.

Thank you to all of the people at O'Reilly Media with whom I might not have interacted directly or in a significant way, but who helped produce this book. I would also like to thank O'Reilly Media for publishing my book. I have read many O'Reilly books, attended conferences, benefited from its online learning platform, and am a fan in general. It is an honor to put my name alongside O'Reilly Media on this book.

Specifically at O'Reilly, I want to thank Marsee Henon for introducing me to Mike Loukides, who was my Acquisitions Editor. Thank you to Mike as well as O'Reilly's Nicole Tache for sharing my vision for this book, for providing excellent ideas, and for helping to make this book a possibility. I would also like to thank Nicole for her editing work, which helped me make many needed improvements.

I would like to thank all O'Reilly production staff members who worked on the book, particularly Rebecca Panzer and Nan Barber. I would also like to thank Bob Russell for his copyediting expertise.

I would especially like to thank my development editor, Jeff Bleiel, for all of his great ideas and improvements, and for putting up with the loud music and espresso machine noises during our meetings when I was working from coffee shops. Most important, I would like to thank Jeff for being a great collaborator and for helping to make my book so much better.

I would like to thank Kate Shoup, a dear friend and fellow author. Her extensive professional writing and editing experience and advice has proven to be invaluable. She is also an amazing host at race events. Thank you to all of my other good friends who have supported me throughout my life.

A special thanks to my family and friends, who have provided ongoing love and support. In particular, I would like to thank Nancy and Richard Noyes and Lourdes and Alain Weber for their interest, check-ins, and encouragement throughout the book-writing process. I would like to thank Richard specifically for immediately offering review assistance and then providing great insights and advice.

Finally, this book is dedicated to my beloved wife, Stephanie, and mom, Linda. I would like to thank my mom for her unwavering love, support, and the sacrifices she made for me throughout my life. This, and her emphasis on education as well having multiple options has largely helped get me to where I am. Lastly, I would like to thank my wife for her strong and steadfast love, support, and patience throughout the book-writing process and in general. Her intelligence, perspective, and assistance helps make everything I do better. I couldn't have written this book without her.

The AI for People and Business Framework

Artificial intelligence (AI) is exciting, powerful, and game changing. The mainstream hype machine has generated gail-force winds behind its sail, to the point that AI is on virtually everyone's radar and is part of the vernacular and yet is barely understood by the majority of people.

Do you ask yourself any of the following questions?

- What is AI, and what value can it bring to my business? What value can it bring to my customers, users, or even me?

- How do I develop a vision and strategy around AI and my data in general?

- How do I determine whether I'm ready to pursue AI initiatives and what should be my key considerations?

- How do I identify specific opportunities, use cases, and applications of AI for my business?

- How can I apply AI to solve real-world problems that are aligned to my goals?

- How do I measure the success of AI initiatives?

- How is AI different from machine learning, data science, neural networks, and deep learning?

- What data do I need to power AI applications?

- How do I take advantage of AI in an ethical, unbiased, and regulatory compliant way?

- Is there a framework that I can use to get the most value from AI, while mitigating risk and ensuring the best chance of success?

This book was written for you if you answered yes to any of these questions. Also, a hint on the last question—the answer is yes, and it's called the AI for People and Business (AIPB) Framework, which is what this book is about! The goal of this book is to hopefully answer all of these questions with the assistance of AIPB, at least at a high level. This is also a book about innovation, and another primary goal of the book is to help executives and managers develop a vision and strategy for building great, highly successful AI-powered products and services that create better human experiences and business success.

With that, welcome to Part I of the book. Part I begins with a discussion of what success with AI looks like, and also challenges to achieving it. This is followed by covering AIPB, the framework on which this book is based. This discussion includes what makes AIPB unique and powerful based on its North Star, benefits, structure, and approach.

Part I concludes with a nontechnical overview of AI and machine learning, as well as an overview of real-world AI applications and opportunities. This will help spark ideas and create the high-level context and understanding for you that is required for developing a vision and strategy around relevant AI use cases and applications.

Part II of the book is dedicated specifically to developing an AI vision, and Part III to developing an AI strategy.

Let's begin by learning about success with AI.

Success with AI

This book is for you if you are an executive or manager interested in engaging AI within your organization. This book is for you if you want to understand exactly what AI is, why AI is able to provide value for your business and the people who interact with it, how to identify AI opportunities, and how to develop and execute a successful AI vision and strategy.

Reading this book should help dissolve the often nebulous and mysterious perception of AI and give you the right assessment tools, processes, and guidance so that you and your business can gain the requisite, level-appropriate understanding and begin using AI today. This book will also benefit data and analytics practitioners (e.g., data scientists) and anyone else who is interested in learning more about AI from a strategic, business-level perspective.

This book, and the AIPB Framework that it introduces, will hopefully help answer your AI questions and guide your journey to success with AI.

Racing to Business Success

As I mentioned in the preface, the ultimate goal in American professional motorsports is to win the Indianapolis 500. And in this event, where anything can happen, the timely advanced analysis of data—including historical events, sensor data, telemetry, computer simulation, driver feedback, and more—makes all the difference. Since shifting to tech from working as an IndyCar engineer and race strategist for various teams, I've discovered that the same goes for business. In the age of big data and advanced analytics, developing and executing a vision and strategy to turn your company's data into top results might be the only way to win.

Making decisions and taking action based solely on historical precedent, simple analytics, and gut feel no longer gets the job done—nor does pursuing nearsighted goals or commoditized technologies. And yet, too many businesses remain mired in the status quo. More and more, it's those that effectively use analytics who succeed; that is, those that extract information such as patterns, trends, and insights from data in order to make decisions, take actions, and produce outcomes. This includes both traditional analytics and advanced analytics, which are complementary.

I use the umbrella term *advanced analytics* in a way similar to a definition given by Gartner (*https://gtnr.it/2Rcb513*): "Advanced Analytics is the autonomous or semiautonomous examination of data or content using sophisticated techniques and tools, typically beyond those of traditional business intelligence (BI), to discover deeper insights, make predictions, or generate recommendations." Advanced analytics techniques include those associated with AI, machine learning, and others covered in this book.

Data is a core advantage if, and only if, you know how to use it. All companies should begin to think of themselves as data and analytics companies, regardless of what their core offerings are. As long as data is involved, this is a critical step in getting ahead of the competition while also gaining an increased ability to create huge benefits for both people and business.

Many companies increasingly know this and want to undergo a data and analytics transformation, but struggle to identify real-world AI opportunities, use cases, and applications, as well as create a vision and strategy around them.

Turning an AI idea into actual benefits that are realized by people and businesses is difficult and requires the right goals, leadership, expertise, and approach. It also requires buy-in and alignment at the C-level. All of this is what I call *applied AI transformation*; it is what this book, and particularly the framework that it presents, is all about. Note that I call it *applied AI transformation*, and not digital transformation. I think this distinction is critical and I'll briefly explain why.

Terms like innovation, transformation, and disruption are thrown around all the time, and usually in a broad context. Similarly, the phrase digital transformation is equally as broad and therefore its meaning isn't necessarily clear. Don't get me wrong—there is value to the phrase and its intended meaning, and there are many companies that absolutely need to undergo a digital transformation, and the sooner the better. But simply saying you need to undergo a digital transformation may generate more questions than answers. Some of these questions include: what does digital transformation mean exactly? What specific technologies or technology systems (e.g., AI, blockchain, Internet of Things[IoT]) should we be using and which should we choose first? How do we prioritize between different digital goals and initiatives? How will digital transformation meet our goals and by how much? How much will it cost and what's the potential ROI? When will we realize that ROI?

All three words in the phrase "applied AI transformation" have a specific and intended meaning. Due to the relative infancy of AI and its limited use (so far) in real-world applications, AI is widely viewed as being largely theoretical. The term applied is intended to distinguish between theoretical AI and AI that is applied to real-world use cases, something for which we're now seeing a significant and diverse proliferation. The term transformation is as expected, and in the case of AI, means harnessing AI to generate certain benefits or outcomes not attainable through other methods, or in other cases, to produce high-impact outcomes much more efficiently (time and cost) and with greater value. In this context, applied AI transformation leaves no room for ambiguity—it means applying existing and emerging AI techniques to build real-world solutions that can transform businesses and people's lives. Whether pursuing a digital transformation or applied AI transformation, both require a vision and strategy. AIPB helps guide this in the case of an applied AI transformation.

Why Do AI Initiatives Fail?

There are many reasons why AI initiatives might fail. One reason is that AI is still generally not well understood. Few executives and managers truly understand what AI really is (*https://tek.io/2XbQgZo*), the current state of AI and its capabilities, the value it represents, what's required for AI success, the difference between AI hype and reality, the differences and unique benefits of AI as compared to alternate forms of analytics, the differences between AI and machine learning, and much more. AI can have tremendous benefits for companies, customers, users, and/or employees, but it's not always obvious how, nor is it obvious what data, techniques, time, cost, and trade-offs are required. It's also not always obvious how to measure the success of AI solutions after you build them.

Companies also might not have the "right" data and advanced analytics leadership, organizational structure, or talent in place. AI is an extremely technical subject area and requires translators between management and advanced analytics experts, a responsibility usually held in the context of software by business analysts and product managers. Like their executive counterparts, very few of these folks understand AI either, thus spawning new data-centric versions of these roles (e.g., data product manager), although that's relatively new and talent is scarce. Also, due to the relative infancy of data organizations within companies, real-world data organization structures (e.g., leadership, reporting, functional alignment) are all over the place. Most important, these data organization structures might not be optimized for cultivating internal adoption, alignment, and understanding around AI initiatives, nor for successful delivery of AI initiatives in general (e.g., roles, responsibilities, resources).

When considering investments in technology, executives are rightfully concerned with understanding final outcomes, costs, time to value, ROI, risk mitigation and management (e.g., bias, lack of inclusion, lack of consumer trust, data privacy and security), and whether to build or buy. Unlike traditional technology investments associated with undergoing a digital transformation—for example, building a mobile app or data warehouse—AI is better characterized as scientific innovation, a concept that implies an inherent amount of uncertainty in a way similar to that associated with R&D.

AI is a field based in statistics and probability and is rapidly advancing in both state-of-the-art and potential applications. It might be impossible to avoid some amount of appreciable uncertainty with AI. Not understanding this or incorrectly setting expectations is another potential cause of failure. So is not pursuing AI in an Agile and Lean way and appropriately respecting the exploratory and experimental nature of AI. Appropriate assessments should be performed as part of a broader approach tailored specifically to the unique characteristics and potential challenges of AI. The AIPB Framework is intended to help companies address and avoid potential points of failure and maximize their chance of success with AI.

Lastly, building successful AI solutions that benefit both people in addition to business requires a basic understanding of what people need and want, and also what the ingredients are for making great products and user experiences given that many of these ingredients will apply to making great AI solutions, as well. Fundamentally, people use products and services that are useful, better than the alternatives, are enjoyable and delightful, and that result in a good experience. AI solutions that are able to deliver on all of these will succeed, whereas those that miss on just one ingredient can fail.

Why Do AI Initiatives Succeed?

AI initiatives (and undergoing an applied AI transformation) succeed when decision makers like you try to better understand AI, including its benefits, opportunities, potential applications, and challenges. AI initiatives also succeed when the *why* behind them is clearly and concretely established, is aligned to goals for both people and business, and is used as the North Star that guides everything else.

Further, AI initiatives succeed when the appropriate data and analytics organization is prioritized and built (some recommendations for which we cover in this book). This includes leadership, organizational structure, and talent that fills strategically appropriate analytics roles and responsibilities. This type of organization is able to do the following:

- Identify and prioritize AI opportunities.
- Help prioritize company-wide investment in AI.
- Cultivate AI adoption and alignment.
- Properly set expectations around AI initiatives.
- Generate a shared vision and strategy around AI.
- Help break down silos.
- Democratize data and analytics.
- Help continually advance the organization's data and analytics competency.
- Foster a cultural transition from a gut-driven, historical precedent–based, simple analytics–based organization to a data-driven and/or data-informed organization.
- Build, deliver, and optimize successful AI solutions.

Additionally, successful data and analytics organizations are able to properly assess their AI readiness and maturity level and identify gaps and develop a prioritized strategy for filling in those gaps. They are also able to analyze specific key considerations and any associated trade-offs on an initiative-by-initiative basis, similarly identify gaps and prioritize filling them, and also make the right decisions as needed throughout the initiative's life cycle.

Data and analytics organization members must be able to work cross-functionally and collaboratively with experts from all functional areas of an organization in strategic ways, and as needed. AIPB uniquely defines a high-level set of cross-functional experts who must work together during certain phases of AI initiatives to ensure successful outcomes.

Creating a real-world deliverable that delivers on its intended benefits requires an effective sequence of iterative phases, which the AIPB Framework uniquely defines in the context of AI. Each of these phases has a related output defined by AIPB as well, all of which are key ingredients of successful AI solutions. Understanding concepts that we discuss, such as scientific innovation, particularly in the context of AI, contributes to success, as well.

Harnessing the Power of AI for the Win

To help answer the questions and accomplish the goals discussed so far, this book presents the AIPB Framework that I have created based on my nearly 20 years of innovation experience and expertise. It is a formalization of the real-world strategies, approaches, and techniques that I've used successfully throughout my professional career, with companies spanning many industries and ranging from IndyCar racing teams, to early-stage startups, to large corporate enterprises. It also represents a unification of my expertise, knowledge gained from experience, and what I've found works best in the areas of business, analytics and product management and pursuing innovation in general.

I call it AI for People and Business (AIPB), because it is specifically focused on creating successful AI solutions for better human experiences and business success. AIPB will help executives and managers due to its unique and purpose-built North Star, benefits, structure, and approach. It is an end-to-end framework to guide pursuing AI initiatives, including everything from performing appropriate assessments, to developing an AI vision and strategy, through to building, delivering, and optimizing production AI solutions.

The intention of this book isn't to say that AIPB is *the* definitive framework that should replace everything else. In fact, as we will soon discuss, AIPB is high level and modular. This means that for your initiative or project, your team should use whatever subframeworks that it thinks work best (or those that I recommend, if preferred).

In explaining the framework that I've developed, my intention is to help guide your thinking at a high level so as to help eliminate some of the confusion that comes with trying to innovate with AI. Whether or not this particular framework is implemented, I think this discussion of AIPB and other topics covered in this book will provide a conceptual way of thinking about successfully using AI in an organization.

We cover the comprehensive, end-to-end AIPB Framework in detail in the next couple of chapters. The remainder of the book will cover almost everything that any executive or manager should understand about AI at the appropriate level, with a primary focus on developing an AI vision and strategy. In my experience, developing an AI vision and strategy is what the target audience of this book tends to struggle with most.

This focus should help decision makers better understand AI and more confidently make decisions and investments around AI initiatives. If, by simply understanding the concepts presented by AIPB and the contents of this book, executives and managers are able to progress further ahead with advanced analytics than where they are today, that's a win.

For the latest information and resources and to sign up for the AIPB mailing list, visit *https://aipbbook.com*.

2

An Introduction to the AI for People and Business Framework

AI is a set of concepts, tools, and techniques that represents huge disruptive and transformative potential. Definition-wise, we can think of AI simply as intelligence exhibited by machines that can be used in a beneficial way (e.g., carrying out tasks, making decisions, assisting humans, saving lives). Specific highly beneficial and advanced applications include helping blind and visually disabled people "see" (*http://bit.ly/31vKTmP*) and cardiovascular disease assessment and prediction of risk factors (*http://bit.ly/2KdmflG*) from retinal scan images.

Developing and executing an AI vision and strategy guided by the AIPB Framework is the key to AI-based innovation that's beneficial to both people and business; that is, innovation that creates better human experiences and business success. This framework and the information covered in this book will be valuable to any business interested in ensuring successful delivery of AI-based products with maximum value and benefits.

The goal of this chapter is to introduce the AIPB Framework and the more general for People and Business Framework (FPB) on which it is based. This chapter provides an in-depth discussion of the benefits of AIPB while briefly covering the other components that are built on top in a foundational way—in other words, assessment, methodology, and output components. We discuss those in much greater length in the next chapter.

Note that for the remainder of this book, I use the simplified and encompassing term "product" to describe any AI-based business, product, service, or solution.

A General Framework for Innovation

The AIPB Framework is a specific application of a more general FPB innovation framework that I've developed. FPB is more general because we can apply it to any form of innovation or emerging/state-of-the-art technology, such as Innovation for People and Business, Blockchain for People and Business, IoT for People and Business, and Robotics for People and Business.

The FPB Framework consists of a North Star, a benefits pseudocomponent, and four core components, as shown in Figure 2-1. The FPB Framework is unique in its North Star, benefits, structure, and approach.

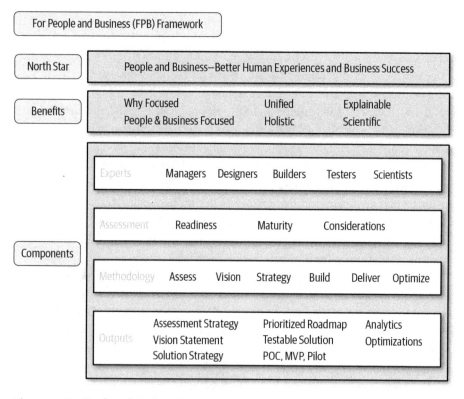

Figure 2-1. For People and Business Framework

As indicated by the top of the diagram, the purpose of FPB is innovation with both people and businesses in mind, and with the goal of creating better human experiences and business success. This serves as the North Star. The unique benefits of the framework are represented by the benefits pseudocomponent, as shown below the North Star, which we discuss in detail shortly.

The parts of this more general framework that are customized to AI in order to create the AIPB Framework are the experts involved (e.g., data scientists and machine learning engineers), the AI-specific assessments, the AI-specific details involved in the various phases of the methodology component (e.g, developing an AI vision and strategy), and some of the outputs (e.g., actionable insights, augmented intelligence, and automation). Blockchain for People and Business would analogously be customized with cryptography experts, different assessments, a different vision and strategy, and different outputs. The rest would be more or less the same. For the remainder of this book, we will refer only to AIPB, but you're encouraged to keep in mind that the FPB Framework can be generalized to other forms of technology-based innovation.

You can say in the style of an elevator pitch that AIPB as an AI-based innovation framework is able to create better human experiences and business success (*why*) through its unique value proposition (North Star, benefits, and key differentiators), which requires the participation of experts working collaboratively through a unique process (assessment and methodology) in order to produce desired deliverables and outcomes (outputs).

The AIPB Benefits Pseudocomponent

Perhaps you're wondering why I've included a benefits pseudocomponent. Normally, framework benefits are discussed when introducing or teaching about a framework, but not actually baked into the framework. The reason is that the benefits of the framework, like the framework's North Star, are the *why* behind the framework; that is, the entire reason for using it, or put another way, its value proposition. What's the point of remembering everything else in a framework or model if we don't remember why it benefits us and why we should use it in the first place?

Before diving into specific AIPB benefits, let's discuss the actual AI and machine learning process and related models. You might already be familiar with CRISP-DM, a common process used for data mining, data science, and machine learning. I've created my own process model that I call the GABDO AI Process Model, as shown in Figure 2-2, and which I cover in depth in Appendix B.

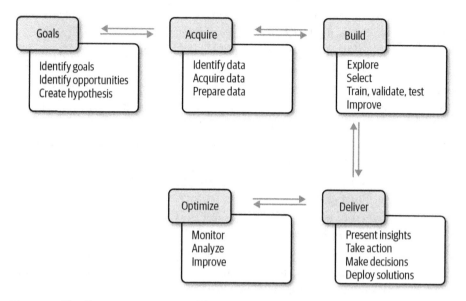

Figure 2-2. The GABDO AI Process Model

Most machine learning process models, including this one, omit the work that should occur upstream; that is, the definition and development of an AI or machine learning vision and strategy. At best, some of these models mention the need to ask the right questions and identify goals and opportunities, but not much beyond that. Most executives and managers that I've spoken with really struggle with knowing how to develop a real-world applied AI vision and strategy, and to figure out where to start. They're not particularly concerned with tactical-level, machine learning processes such as CRISP-DM and GABDO, and right-fully so. A primary goal of mine when I was developing AIPB was to fill this upstream gap. AIPB does that, and much more as you'll see.

Existing Frameworks and the Missing Pieces of the Puzzle

One way to view AIPB's unique approach is by comparing it to most existing business and product development frameworks, models, and methodologies. There are many popular frameworks that are used to help develop a business strategy, maximize product development success, and/or facilitate the innovation processes. I break these into the following process categories (with some of my recommended specific methods), which, moving forward, we'll refer to as the AIPB Process Categories:

- Assessment (e.g., gap analysis, competency analysis)

- Ideation and vision development (e.g., design thinking, brainstorming, five *whys*)

- Business and product strategy (e.g., Strengths, Weaknesses, Opportunities, and Threats [SWOT], Porter's five forces, cost-benefit analysis (CBA), the Product-Market Fit Pyramid)

- Roadmap prioritization (e.g., cost of delay, CD3, Kano model, importance versus satisfaction)

- Requirements elicitation (e.g., design thinking, interviews)

- Product design (e.g., design thinking, UX design, human-centered design)

- Product development (e.g., Agile, Kanban, GABDO, continuous delivery)

- Product evaluation, validation, and optimization (e.g., minimum viable product [MVP]/prototyping, success metrics, key performance indicators [KPIs], usability testing)

All of these process categories and specific methods can be very useful (including in AIPB, which is meant to be modular!), and many of them share common gaps that AIPB intends to fill. These gaps include the following:

- Not *why* or goal focused (focused more on details, how, and what)

- Business focused (instead of people focused)

- Siloed (involving a limited group of participants and breadth of expertise)

- Not holistic (focused on a subset of a much larger process)

- Documentation focused (bullet point lists, filled-out canvases, white boards)

- Not explainability focused (do not help generate a shared vision and understanding across all stakeholders)

- Deterministic (assumption that everything can be known and planned on in advance)

- Assembly focused (simply build the solution by following a linear process or set of steps to get to the end result)

AIPB fills all of these gaps as a *why*-driven, people- and business-centric, unified, holistic, collaborative/interactive, and scientific innovation framework that provides many significant benefits as a result.

AIPB Benefits

My ultimate goal for AIPB is to help people understand how to build an AI vision and strategy, apply AI to real-world use cases, and, finally, execute their AI strategy for maximum success. As you'll see later in the book, AIPB also helps guide gap identification as well as plan for pursuing AI initiatives by conducting critical assessments around AI readiness, maturity, and other key considerations.

AIPB fills gaps by providing the following benefits:

- Why focused

- People and business focused

- Unified and holistic focused

- Explainable focused

- Science focused

Let's discuss each of the unique benefits of AIPB and how they provide an end-to-end foundation for AI-based innovation. These ideas will be developed further throughout the book.

WHY FOCUSED

Traditional approaches to understanding markets and opportunities consist of initial market research, but I would argue that you're not innovating enough if you're relying mostly on market research. People don't know what they want, and the market's only going to tell you what's already out there.

Steve Jobs knew this and continually created brand new products with features that people didn't know they wanted until they were available to them. How did he and others do this? By understanding problems and needs, or in other words, the *why*. I'd therefore highly recommend focusing primarily on problems and needs research. This presents a better path to true innovation and the creation of truly great products.

The *why* should be universally understood by everyone involved; in other words, by all stakeholders. In businesses, people and departments are usually incentivized through different goals and KPIs. True innovation requires a North Star *why* to be established and a shared vision and understanding among everyone regardless of the goals and incentives of specific people or departments.

The *why* should help develop a vision and strategy that can turn it into reality. Many existing frameworks are focused on creating bullet point lists or filling in canvases on paper or in digital form, including some canvas-based AI and machine learning frameworks.

Don't get me wrong—all of these frameworks can be amazingly helpful for guidance, but unfortunately they share some of the same characteristics that I'm proposing we should change. Specifically, they're not particularly focused on vision or strategy development.

PEOPLE AND BUSINESS FOCUSED

Most business frameworks focus mostly on the business side of things. AIPB focuses on both people and business at the same time. People are critical to the success of any business or product, which is something that I discuss in depth throughout this book.

Some frameworks and companies have begun to recognize this and use terms like customer centric and customer focused. Some even say that we're now in the age of the customer. This a great step in the right direction, but there are two things that AIPB improves upon here.

First, not every person that realizes value from a product is a customer. People can be users or benefactors, too. Also, the word "customer" sounds like a word attributing dollar signs to people. How about we just say people centric or people focused, which is exactly what AIPB aims to do.

People and business are not mutually exclusive and don't represent a zero-sum game. People and businesses have different goals, which can usually be achieved at the same time. A great product should be able to achieve goals for both people and businesses simultaneously, and AIPB shows us how to do that. AIPB doesn't trade focus from business to people, and vice versa. AIPB focuses on developing a vision and strategy for both.

UNIFIED AND HOLISTIC FOCUSED

Most business and innovation frameworks involve a limited group of people and therefore a limited breadth of expertise. They also tend to focus on a single process or subset of processes that are part of a larger whole. AIPB is unique and improves on that by creating a unified and holistic framework that drives a powerful and collaborative approach to innovation. Let's discuss both the unified and holistic aspects of AIPB now.

AIPB is unified in that it demands that people with appropriate expertise collaborate as needed for specific AIPB phases, and this *must not* only include senior executives and line-of-business owners. Great executives and managers have a lot to offer in terms of leadership, strategy, guidance, and decision making, for example, although they often become somewhat removed from the specific expertise required in certain subject matter areas, including knowing about and understanding many of the key considerations that should be taken into account. Given that, the right people should be involved regardless of job level. Note that I used the word collaboration and not consensus. There is a huge difference for me, and I discuss it later in the book.

Some of the frameworks listed earlier in the chapter assume a group of people with all required expertise will come together at the same time to implement the framework (e.g., to fill in a canvas). Others do make a point, however, to emphasize the need for cross-functional collaboration and suggest the type of people that should be involved, but the framework might focus on only a subset of the overall innovation process.

AIPB recognizes five groups of people in a business that should be represented when using the framework for innovation: managers, designers, builders, testers, and scientists. Figure 2-3 shows this.

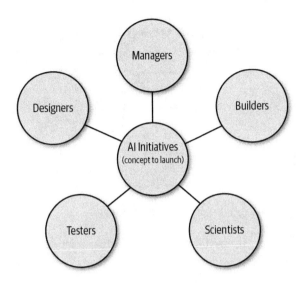

Figure 2-3. AIPB Experts

AIPB is also a holistic framework. Rather than focus on one phase or a subset of phases in the innovation process, AIPB aims to be holistic and end to end. AIPB additionally includes the following framework components, categories, and phases, with each phase of the methodology component having its own respective outputs. Figure 2-4 shows the three Assessment component categories, and Figure 2-5 shows the Methodology component phases and outputs per phase.

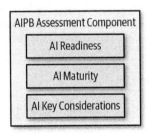

Figure 2-4. AIPB Assessment Component categories

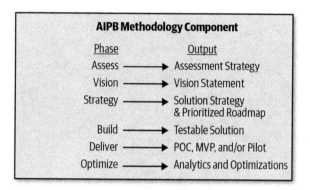

Figure 2-5. AIPB Methodology Component phases and outputs

In my opinion, an innovation framework must include all of these components and phases to be considered holistic. A good analogy for business is executive leadership in a company; for example, the C-suite. C-level executives are collectively tasked with having a big picture (holistic), end-to-end view of the company in terms of finances, operations, and both with respect to time; that is, developing a deep understanding of the company's history, current state, and future (e.g., goals, initiatives, investments, and strategy).

AIPB similarly has a holistic view of the entire innovation process end to end, including the direction it should take (vision and strategy) and overseeing the actual execution while also planning for the future. AIPB can also incorporate existing frameworks and models where appropriate and beneficial. It is meant to be modular and not overly prescriptive in that sense, in the same way that the CTO of a company does not necessarily dictate what continuous integration framework software developers must use.

EXPLAINABLE FOCUSED

Explainability is becoming very important when it comes to AI and machine learning, and rightly so. Both can be quite opaque in terms of how they work and what the results mean. Making AI more explainable is a great goal, and the outputs of AIPB should also be explainable.

One of the downsides of canvas-based frameworks is that the focus is on writing text in boxes and creating bullet point lists. Usually this content requires further explanation to those who were not involved in the process and/or to those less familiar. It is unlikely that you could hand a filled-out canvas to someone that did not participate in the process and have them fully understand what it contains, its value, and its implications just from a quick read. AIPB produces explainable output that should not require much further explanation.

I put a very high premium on the *why* of everything, as well as on generating a shared vision and understanding among all key stakeholders. I think that the output of an innovation framework should help facilitate this in a highly explainable way.

SCIENCE FOCUSED

AIPB is science focused given that innovative, emerging, and state-of-the-art technologies such as AI and machine learning are key ingredients and are by nature exploratory and experimental. This matters because these are fields based in statistics and probabilities, or put another way, in some form of uncertainty. This means that the entire process of planning around and using AI techniques is largely nondeterministic and therefore best represented by the concepts of science and processes such as the scientific method.

Why is this a benefit of AIPB? It's a benefit because of expectation management; that is, it helps set appropriate expectations. There are certain laws and theorems that essentially prove that things like the best algorithm, exact data, best data features, and best model performance can't be known in advance. AIPB recognizes this and helps set expectations accordingly.

Summary

In my opinion, the purpose of innovation is to benefit both people and business in new and powerful ways. This is accomplished by creating and executing a technology-based vision and strategy around real-world solutions that make these benefits a reality. In addition, generating a shared vision and understanding among key stakeholders along with proper expectation management is key. This can be difficult to accomplish with some of the existing frameworks due to the gaps outlined in this chapter.

The FPB and more general AIPB Frameworks represent a unique and powerful approach to innovation that is focused on benefiting people and businesses alike in order to create better human experiences and business success. AIPB fills the gaps of most existing business and innovation frameworks, and is unique in its guiding North Star (people and business), benefits pseudocomponent, and four core components, which we cover next.

3

AIPB Core Components

This chapter continues to develop our understanding of how to innovate using AIPB in order to create better human experiences and business success. You'll recall that the AIPB Framework consists of a North Star, benefits pseudocomponent, and four core components. Figure 3-1 provides a refresher of this.

We've already discussed the North Star and benefits pseudocomponent in the last chapter, so let's begin this chapter by discussing a relevant analogy and then look at the four AIPB core components in detail: experts, assessment, methodology, and outputs. We also discuss the concept of the *flipped classroom*, which is an important element in approaching the innovation process in new, more efficient and effective ways.

Before diving into the AIPB core components, let's first discuss Agile development as an analogy to certain characteristics of AIPB.

An Agile Analogy

You are probably familiar with the Agile software development movement and associated methodologies such as Scrum and Kanban. Agile was created to fill gaps and solve many problems previously experienced with the *waterfall approach* to building technology products. AIPB analogously intends to fill gaps and improve upon existing business and innovation frameworks.

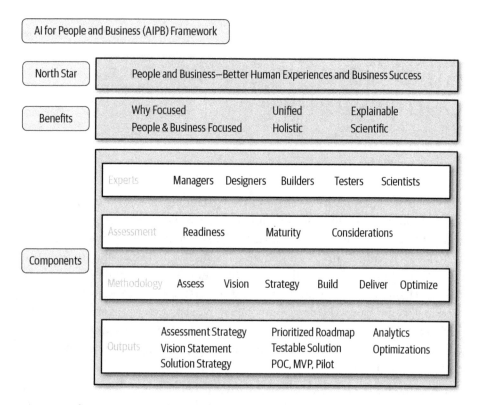

Figure 3-1. The AIPB Framework

Agile is based on the *Agile Manifesto* and the four Agile software development values that the manifesto defines (*https://agilemanifesto.org/*):

- Individuals and interactions over processes and tools
- Working software over comprehensive documentation
- Customer collaboration over contract negotiation
- Responding to change over following a plan

These four values are the basis for which all Agile principles and methodologies are built (interestingly, the values are phrased in terms of the *how* and *what* and not the *why*). That aside, the benefits pseudocomponent of AIPB is analogous to Agile's "four values," and it is meant to be the foundation on which everything else is built.

Continuing with our analogy, the experts component of AIPB is analogous to the roles defined in Scrum;[1] the Assessment Component is analogous to assessments conducted by scrum teams;[2] the Methodology Component, is analogous to recurring scrum meetings (aka ceremonies);[3] and, finally, the outputs component is analogous to the "product artifacts" defined by scrum.[4]

Both Agile and AIPB share a focus on people and process. One way that Agile differs from AIPB in that Agile does not necessarily involve all of the people required for innovation initiatives from concept to launch, nor does it represent the innovation process end to end.

Agile omits most of the vision and strategy aspects of innovation, for example, and focuses more on actual development, deployment, and maintenance based on an existing product roadmap. That said, Agile methods are very useful, and I'm a big fan, particularly of Kanban. I personally recommend Kanban for product development, which we can easily incorporate into the build methodology phase of AIPB (covered later in this chapter).

Now let's discuss each of AIPB's core components.

Experts Component

You must assemble the appropriate experts when pursuing AI initiatives. You should also bring them together during each AIPB methodology phase to collaborate and help ensure maximum success.

Often the people making critical product decisions (such as filling in canvases or SWOT lists) do not have all the requisite expertise. Or, they aren't able to properly empathize with the target market; that is, they're not the customer or user, and therefore view things more from the business perspective, even if they don't think that's the case.

The key takeaway, and a differentiator of the AIPB Framework, is that the right experts must collaborate in the appropriate AIPB Methodology phases. Con-

---

1 For example, scrum master, product owner, team member, and stakeholder. These roles are meant to bring together the voice of the business, voice of the customer (or user), domain expertise, and technical expertise when working collaboratively on a scrum team. This collaboration is used to determine the desirability, viability, and feasibility for any given product or product feature and to execute the Agile product development process itself.

2 For example, technical feasibility and sprint retrospectives.

3 For example, sprint planning (tasking and estimation), daily scrum (aka daily standup), sprint review (software demo and feedback gathering), and sprint retrospective.

4 For example, product roadmap, product and sprint backlogs, and a release plan.

sensus is not required, but expert ideas, opinions, and perspectives are. From there, the initiative owner must make the final decisions by taking all expertise into account, a responsibility usually best handled by a product manager for product initiatives, and likely will be handled more over time by data product managers, a new data and analytics-tailored product management role.

So who are these experts? AIPB establishes five groups of experts: managers, designers, builders, testers, and scientists. Certain people might fall into one or more categories based on a given assessment task or methodology phase of the framework. Figure 3-2 shows these categories with some example roles in each.

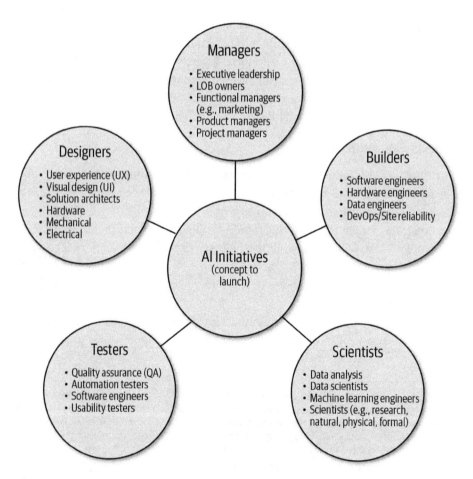

Figure 3-2. AIPB Experts

Let me first explain why I chose the categories builders and scientists, how they differ from each other, and how they differ from traditional functional designations.

You might have seen The LEGO Movie. I highly recommend watching it if you haven't. The movie is centered on a character named Emmet Brickowski who is a construction worker. Construction workers are builders who build objects with LEGO bricks by following instructions, just as one does after purchasing a LEGO kit. This is essentially the same as software engineers writing code based on product requirements and designs, or hardware assemblers who build physical objects based on specifications, materials, and designs. I refer to this group as *builders*—those that build from instructions that they've been given in one or more forms.

The movie also designates another group called *master builders*. Master builders are those people who are able to use their imagination to develop ideas and create instructions for building new innovative objects, without requiring explicit instructions themselves. These new ideas and objects can become building blocks upon which even more new ideas and objects are built, just as with real LEGO objects. Developing new ideas and outcomes as well as validating and optimizing them might require exploration, hypothesis development, and experimentation. Traditional scientists (and data scientists), mathematicians, and engineers fit perfectly in this category, for example. I refer to this group as *scientists*.

Scientists historically had no instructions for which to base their new ideas, hypothesis, and discoveries other than the laws, theorems, and empirically determined results established by previous scientists. These historic findings help scientists by providing guidance and a foundation on which to base new ideas and discoveries, but they do not provide explicit instructions to achieve a specific new discovery.

The scientist as the master builder must use their expertise and imagination for that. More specifically, new scientific discoveries come by way of one or more of the following: building on previous science, conducting experiments (thought, empirical, or both), and by making real-world or lab-based observations. In all cases, the scientists aren't sure what they will find in advance; rather, they are guided by a set of initial ideas and hypotheses.

Given the statistical, probabilistic, and scientific nature of AI and machine learning, the term scientists is the most apropos. Innovation means creating something new by definition, and therefore by default there are no instructions on how to achieve a certain outcome. Innovation requires expertise and imagination combined with strategies to validate key assumptions, mitigate risks, and achieve an intended result. Going a step further, scientific innovation—as compared to more deterministic innovation involving less uncertainty—is a key differentiator and very certainly can generate competitive advantage. The fact that visionaries and scientific innovators can and have created successful outcomes in the face of significant uncertainty is what makes them great.

So to recap, some questions simply do not have answers without exploration and experimentation. That's exactly the concept behind Lean and Agile product development, as well. Create an MVP of what you think best addresses a given need and has the highest chance of achieving product-market fit, and then iteratively experiment and test versions in order to reach the optimal solution—a solution that was not known in advance. This is how the scientific method works and thus why I use the term scientists.

One final note: data scientists, machine learning engineers, and AI researchers aren't the only scientists in this process. User experience (UX) designers and others can also be considered scientists in some cases, as well. The distinguishing factor is simply recognizing that some sort of hypothesis and test or experiment is required to make discoveries and find answers. For example, usability tests are conducted by UX researchers for product evaluation and to determine whether users understand how to use a certain product or product feature. This is experimental by nature and requires the test results in order to gain insights and drive actionable, data-driven changes to the product. There is no way to know the results in advance of the actual test. AI-based scientific innovation is no different and therefore requires a scientific mindset and one or more scientists to participate in the process. This requires a similar change in mindset as switching from waterfall to agile.

Designers and design in general are also critical components of any technology that people interact with in some way. Designers are thus also a very important category of experts recognized by AIPB. We discuss the importance of design, particularly in the context of AI solutions, in much greater detail later in this book.

Testers are another very important group of experts recognized by AIPB. Solution quality and minimization of liability and risk are paramount with any technology solution; I would argue more-so in most cases involving data and analytics-centric solutions such as those using AI. The importance of achieving maximum quality with minimal risk, and testers and other AIPB Experts that ensure it, will become abundantly clear in later chapters.

Finally, managers are also a very important group of experts recognized by AIPB, especially for leading and managing AI initiatives. Many managers, including executives, might not be domain-specific experts or technical subject matter experts (SMEs), but they should be experts in the following:

- assembling purpose-built teams
- setting goals
- creating strategies
- managing risks
- making key decisions
- delegating work
- providing direction and guidance
- providing autonomy
- facilitating collaboration and alignment
- properly setting expectations
- keeping initiatives on track
- providing needed resources (e.g., budgets)
- ensuring both initiative and business success

As with any of my former IndyCar racing teams, winning happens when everyone does their part and does it very well. Any one person can lose a race, but it takes everyone on the team working together at the highest level of performance possible and without mistakes to win.

Now let's turn our attention to the two process-related components of AIPB: assessment and methodology. Rather than discuss the outputs component separately, we look at the appropriate outputs as we go for each phase of the Methodology Component.

AIPB Process Categories and Recommended Methods

AIPB is meant to be modular, as mentioned previously. Certain methods and frameworks are time-tested and have proven to be both effective and efficient. This means that whatever collaborative (*not* consensus-based) process and methods gets you to the best answers and outputs is the right one.

Recall from Chapter 2 the AIPB process categories and some of my recommended methods, which I present again here for reference in this chapter.

- Assessment (e.g., gap analysis, competency analysis)
- Ideation and vision development (e.g., design thinking, brainstorming, Five *why's*)
- Business and product strategy (e.g., SWOT, Porter's five forces, cost-benefit analysis (CBA), the Product-Market Fit Pyramid)
- Roadmap prioritization (e.g., cost of delay, CD3, Kano model, importance versus satisfaction)
- Requirements elicitation (e.g., design thinking, interviews)
- Product design (e.g., design thinking, UX design, human-centered design)
- Product development (e.g., Agile, Kanban, GABDO, continuous delivery)
- Product evaluation, validation, and optimization (e.g., MVP/prototyping, success metrics, KPIs, usability testing)

I list my recommended process categories and methods where appropriate in this chapter, but I mostly omit the details of existing methods (e.g., SWOT) given the bigger picture focus of this book. You're encouraged to do further research as needed. Lastly, my recommendations are based on my experience and what I've found to be most effective. There might be perfectly valid alternatives that I haven't tried that can be applied to the Methodology Component phases, and the appropriate experts should choose what to use based on their experience and expertise. The end result being correct is what matters most. AIPB is modular and also expert driven!

Assessment Component

Pursuing AI initiatives and innovation in general requires that we identify and address certain gaps and key considerations, either partially or fully. This is the basis of the AIPB Assessment Component: to assess any gaps and key considerations and determine a strategy to address them. I break this into three categories, as follows:

- AI readiness

- AI maturity

- AI key considerations

The Assessment Component and its three categories are represented as the first AIPB Methodology Component phase (discussed shortly) and should be addressed very early by any company planning on undergoing an applied AI transformation. These assessments are so important that they are represented as a separate core component in AIPB. Making the appropriate assessments and developing strategies, collectively referred to by AIPB as an "assessment strategy," based on the findings will help ensure initiatives don't fail and, more importantly, that they're set up to win from the start.

Note that developing strategies and addressing gaps around readiness, maturity, and key considerations should not be considered a hard prerequisite for moving forward with AI, machine learning, or innovation in general. Rather, performing the assessment and developing your assessment strategy should be done first. In my opinion, it's necessary for most companies to begin with AI now rather than later and work on filling gaps and addressing key considerations along the way.

AI READINESS AND MATURITY

Readiness versus maturity? For me, readiness means being ready in certain ways before getting started with something. Figure 3-3 shows the AI Readiness Model that I created in which I organize AI readiness into four categories. I cover this model in depth in Chapter 12.

Maturity, on the other hand, represents one or more measures of progression. Although maturity in the context of technology is usually discussed in terms of levels of technical sophistication, I characterize maturity in different ways, as a few models that I have created illustrate, and that when combined specifically in terms of AI represent the way that I define AI maturity.

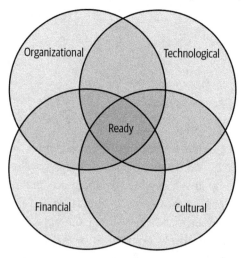

Figure 3-3. The AI Readiness Model

Two of these models are shown as a preview here. The first, shown in Figure 3-4, is a maturity model that represents analytics sophistication, and the second, shown in Figure 3-5, represents technical maturity, in general, as a collective measure (mixture) of the level of experience, technical sophistication, and technical competency around a given technical field or technology at a given point in time.

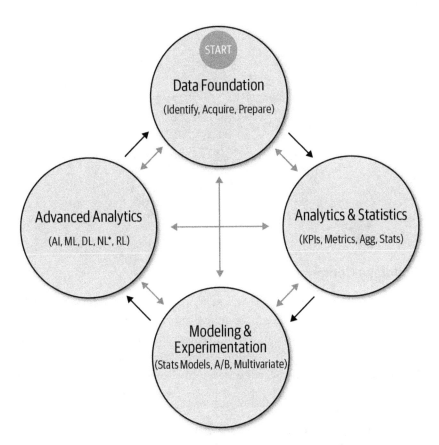

Figure 3-4. The AI Maturity Model

AI readiness and maturity, the basis to assess both, and all of these models are covered in much greater detail in Part III of this book, as are AI-related key considerations for which we must account. For now, the key takeaway is that readiness and maturity are both a process and a journey. You don't need to have a data warehouse or an extract, transform, and load (ETL) system built before pursuing an AI or machine learning task, but you definitely need to identify gaps, create appropriate strategies, and start getting more AI "ready" to begin advancing your AI maturity plan today.

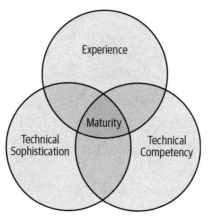

Figure 3-5. The Technical Maturity Mixture Model

Methodology Component

Let's move on to the *Methodology Component* of AIPB, which consists of six iterative phases: assess, vision, strategy, build, deliver, and optimize. Although represented as separate components in AIPB, I've logically combined the discussion of methodology and outputs in this section because each of the methodology phases has a specific output. Figure 3-6 shows each methodology phase, along with corresponding and recommended experts, process categories, and outputs, which we cover throughout this section.

Before diving into each phase, let's remember the North Star of AIPB, which is a focus on people and business, with the specific goals of creating better human experiences and business success. This is critical because this framework (and book) is about pursuing AI that benefits both people and business, not just business, and definitely not AI that will harm people in any way. This aspect of AIPB is critical and must guide everything else.

AIPB Methodology Component

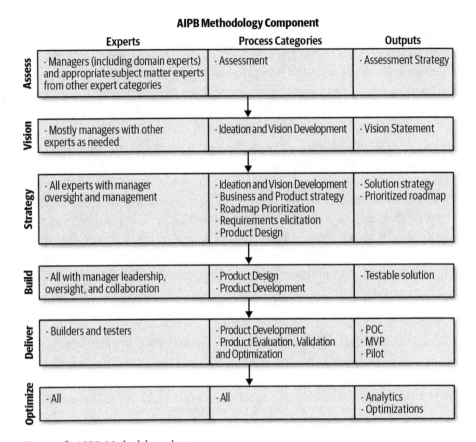

	Experts	Process Categories	Outputs
Assess	- Managers (including domain experts) and appropriate subject matter experts from other expert categories	- Assessment	- Assessment Strategy
Vision	- Mostly managers with other experts as needed	- Ideation and Vision Development	- Vision Statement
Strategy	- All experts with manager oversight and management	- Ideation and Vision Development - Business and Product strategy - Roadmap Prioritization - Requirements elicitation - Product Design	- Solution strategy - Prioritized roadmap
Build	- All with manager leadership, oversight, and collaboration	- Product Design - Product Development	- Testable solution
Deliver	- Builders and testers	- Product Development - Product Evaluation, Validation and Optimization	- POC - MVP - Pilot
Optimize	- All	- All	- Analytics - Optimizations

Figure 3-6. AIPB Methodology phases

We also talk about the experts that I think should be collaboratively involved in each phase. I use the high-level designation in most cases (e.g., designer, scientist) and leave it up to you to decide who in your company is the best suited "expert" in that discipline to participate in the given phase. I present some example roles, as well.

For all of the methodology phases and generating the appropriate output for each, the approach should be different than many existing frameworks usually suggest. This begins with using a flipped classroom, collaborative, interactive, and/or design thinking-style approach. It's not about creating paper sheets, bullet point lists, and filling in boxes; rather, it's about posing questions and answering them. It really doesn't matter how you arrive at the answers, just that you arrive at them and they're the right ones, or at least as right as possible. It is also paramount that these answers can be effectively communicated to any stakeholder as needed.

Depending on the phase, the questions might be about goals, benefits, outcomes, people, risks, costs, trade-offs, considerations, assumptions, strategies, techniques, or gaps. Regardless, the output of each phase should include explanations in plain English that are highly explainable to anyone, regardless of expertise and background. For many executives, this is a necessity.

For certain phases, the answers to the right questions in an easy-to-understand verbal form should be all that's needed to generate a shared understanding and also set expectations properly. From my experience, bullet point lists and other forms of documentation often fall woefully short in this respect.

So on that note, let's dive into the phases of the AIPB methodology and the outputs of each phase. Keep in mind that all phases can be iterative and participate in a feedback loop; in other words, the outputs of downstream phases might suggest iterations of previous phases to drive continuous improvements and maximize outcomes.

ASSESS

To recap, the Assessment Component includes assessments of the following:

- AI readiness
- AI maturity
- AI key considerations

Following are some questions around these categories that your assessments should answer:

- What are the gaps in my company's readiness for AI?
- Is my company able to pursue scientific innovation (i.e., be agile, exploratory, and experimental)?
- How would I characterize my company's data and analytics maturity? What about AI maturity? What gaps do I need to address?
- What are the AI-specific key considerations that we should understand and address?

- What are the critical assumptions and potential risks we need to understand and test?

From the AIPB process categories, the assessment category is applicable to answering these questions. Assessments should result in a plan—that is, a strategy. As such, the outputs of this component are defined by AIPB as an assessment strategy, which includes strategies for filling gaps related to AI readiness and maturity as well as strategies for addressing AI key considerations. Neither should be considered hard requirements to move forward as discussed, but they shouldn't just sit on a piece of paper as a bullet point list of gaps and considerations either. Turning assessments into an assessment strategy is critical; it helps planning and, most importantly, helps to avoid potential failure while ensuring maximum success.

Many AI initiatives fail, as already discussed. I would argue that most do so because of either lack of assessment strategy, as we've defined, or because of lack of vision, strategy, and the ability to execute, as we cover next. In either case, don't wait until it's too late to identify and address potential points of failure.

Lastly, given the business-level and strategic nature of these assessments, the experts involved should be mostly managers (including domain experts) and appropriate SMEs. This includes executive leadership, functionally appropriate executives and managers (e.g., CAIO, CDO, CAO, VP AI/Data Science, Director AI/Data Science), and appropriate individual contributor team leads brought in as needed for specific expertise and analysis.

VISION

In my opinion, a vision for a new business, product, service, or feature is the high-level *why*, *how*, and *what*. The why can be expressed in terms of goals, benefits, or outcomes. The *why* can be driven by solving a specific problem, meeting a certain need, or eliminating a given pain point, but it can also be driven by wanting to create better human experiences without requiring a problem, need, or pain point. The goal is to define the "right" *why's*, which can mean using a technique like the five *whys* to get there.

A great example are the swipe and pinch touch interactions that were introduced by products such as the first iPhone. I don't think many people would have considered it as being a solution to a problem per se, nor do I think many people ever thought that type of interaction was even a possibility at the time. That said, as soon as people experienced those touch interactions, it became a delighter for the masses. Further, many people viewed these new interaction possibilities as solutions to problems that they didn't even realize they had. Delighters can fuel a great vision in the same way that solving problems and eliminating pain points can.

Returning to AIPB's emphasis on people and business, the key is to define the *why* for both. For businesses, the *why* is most commonly framed as a business case: how will it help the business in terms of goals, KPIs, objectives, ROI, or some similar measure. This is where most frameworks or models stop.

AIPB must also define the *why* for the people that are benefactors of the solution, which can be a customer, end user, or internal employee. There are very few, if any, innovative technology applications that don't have an impact on a human in one way or another. Even full-blown automation affects people, although not always in a beneficial way if it is used to eliminate jobs without any job reassignment, retraining, or reskilling. We examine the topic of automation and job displacement in a later chapter, but for now keep in mind that this book is about how we can use AI to benefit people and businesses, and that includes beneficial augmented intelligence, job reassignment, retraining, and reskilling, as needed.

So, the key then is to define the business case and also the intended benefit for people who will experience the AI solution directly, regardless of whether the AI solution takes the form of insights, recommendations, predictions, augmented intelligence, optimization, or automation. All of these forms of AI can benefit stakeholders, so the goal is to identify who the stakeholders are and how they benefit.

So how do you formulate your AI vision and what is the final output? Let's begin by asking the right questions:

- In which of the following am I most interested? Achieving a company goal, reaching a specific KPI target, solving a problem, eliminating a pain point, creating better human experiences, saving lives, maximizing patient outcomes, or helping people with disabilities, for example?

- If I develop an AI-based solution based on the answer to the previous question, how will it benefit my business? How will it benefit people?

- What AI opportunities will help me make these benefits a reality (assuming more than one), and how do I choose and prioritize them?

- At a high level, what will the solution be?

- At a high level, how will I be able to make this solution a reality and a success?

- What is the potential ROI?

You'll notice I use the phrase "at a high level" for a couple of the questions. The reason is that we have not yet gone through the process of actually creating a strategy for making your vision a reality, and therefore we might not know many of the considerations, risks, details, designs, and so on that we'll discover along the way. We've also not yet gone through the exercise of determining the desirability, viability, and feasibility of a promising idea. Vision development is a starting point of an iterative process, and, as I mentioned earlier, it might need to be modified and improved based on downstream activities. This is perfectly fine and, if anything, will help ensure success.

In terms of answering these questions and producing the desired output of the vision phase, I recommend managers (which includes domain experts) as the primary experts to participate in the process; for example, executive leadership as well as functionally appropriate executives and managers. You also should bring in other experts as needed (particularly AI practitioners from the scientists category), and the process should be collaborative and interactive, involving high-level assessment, ideation, and prioritization because there might be multiple great opportunities.

For the AIPB methodology vision phase, and from the AIPB process categories, I recommend the ideation and vision development category. Many of the recommended methods in this category are commonly and successfully employed by product managers and UX folks.

The output of the vision phase should be a people *and* business-focused vision statement that specifies the answers to the questions posed in an easy-to-understand way that can be delivered as an elevator pitch. It should start with *why* and describe the purpose and goals of the AI application (for both people and business), *how* it will be built, and *what* the solution will be.

A great example of something similar is Amazon's "Working Backwards" customer-centric methodology.[5] It's an approach designed to work backwards from the customer in order to come up with product ideas, as opposed to the other way around.

The output of the process is a one-page internal press release written by a product manager that announces the not-yet-existent finished product. The idea is that the press release must indicate who the target customer is, what benefits the product will provide to them, how existing products fail, and how the new product will be better than the existing alternatives.

Ian McAllister from Amazon notes:

> "If the benefits listed don't sound very interesting or exciting to customers, then perhaps they're not (and shouldn't be built). Instead, the product manager should keep iterating on the press release until they've come up with benefits that actually sound like benefits. Iterating on a press release is a lot less expensive than iterating on the product itself (and quicker!)."

> **—IAN MCALLISTER, DIRECTOR**

McAllister suggests writing these press releases in what he calls "Oprah-speak." In other words, write it in the way you would imagine Oprah Winfrey explaining it to her audience (*http://bit.ly/2XeKbLo*).

Although not exactly phrased in terms of the type of vision statement that I'm recommending for AIPB, it's certainly a great example. I especially like his term "Oprah-speak"; that is, if Oprah can deliver the vision to an audience and have everyone understand it, it's probably well built. I provide an example of developing an AIPB vision at the end of Part II.

STRATEGY

With an AI vision in the form of a vision statement in place, the next step is to develop an AI strategy. Developing an AI strategy (or data and analytics strategy in general) is something with which I find many companies, executives, and managers struggle with.

AI applied in the real world is relatively new, not generally well understood, engrossed in excessive marketing hype, needs a certain amount of technical

---

5 *http://bit.ly/2XeKbLo* and *http://bit.ly/2Wl5t4B*

expertise that is in short supply, and requires acceptance of uncomfortable concepts such as nondeterminism and uncertainty to truly understand and develop a strategy based on it. These are some of the many reasons why AI leadership is critical to successfully developing a vision and strategy around AI.

So, what exactly do I mean by AI strategy? In the context of AIPB, an AI strategy is the plan for execution of your AI vision in order to make it a successful reality. It also represents a plan for executing the end-to-end process of taking an idea through to becoming a continually optimized solution in production. An AI strategy guided by AIPB should take the form of a solution strategy and prioritized roadmap.

The solution strategy (i.e., the plan) should define the people, processes, and resources (e.g., tools) required to do the following:

- Make your AI vision a successful reality
- Execute your assessment strategy initiatives while executing your AI strategy
- Iteratively execute the Five Ds (discussed shortly)

The purpose of the AIPB solution strategy is to successfully execute your AI vision by helping to develop an AIPB prioritized roadmap. It's also to ensure successful downstream AIPB Methodology phases, outputs, and resulting AI-initiative benefits and outcomes. Having the ability to create and execute a successful AI vision and strategy is a critical part of pursuing AI initiatives.

The actual format of the solution strategy is less important than the strategy itself. We can materialize it as one or more documents, diagrams, whiteboards, or any other format as long as it serves its purpose and gets the job done. A prioritized roadmap, on the other hand, should have a well-defined format, as we'll later discuss.

From a product strategy, design, and development methodology perspective, I use my own version of a model that some refer to as the *Five Ds* for describing the iterative and end-to-end process of building successful AI products and product features. Figure 3-7 shows the stages of the Five Ds.

Note that actually performing some of the work outlined by the Five Ds (e.g., design, develop, deliver) is covered by certain downstream methodology phases of AIPB, so the purpose of the Five Ds during the strategy phase of AIPB is to develop a plan for successfully executing these downstream phases.

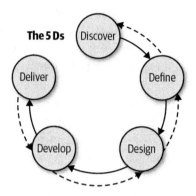

Figure 3-7. The Five Ds

To create a solution strategy as part of your AI strategy, answer the following questions for each stage of the Five Ds. They are posed in the context of the AI solution defined by your vision.

Discover:

- What are the *why's*, goals, needs, and/or pain points?

- How does the solution create better human experiences and business success?

- Who are the stakeholders and benefactors of the solution around which your vision is based?

- What are the solution's business and individual use cases?

- What does the potential market look like (market analysis) and how is your solution differentiated from your competitors (competitor analysis)?

- How can you ensure that your solution will achieve the intended benefits for both people and business?

- When applicable, how can you ensure that the solution is highly delightful, usable, and sticky (see Chapters 7 and 8)?

- How complete will the solution be—design prototype, PoC/pilot/MVP, full solution?

Define:

- What data will be used? Does the data already exist? Do you need to generate any new data? If yes, by what mechanism (e.g., augmentation methods, IoT)? Are there any external data sources that would be beneficial (through purchase or that are publicly available)?

- Who owns each of the data sources and what steps are necessary to get access?

- What data pipeline (access, ingestion, ETL, processing, integration, storage), if any, is required?

- How will the data be prepared (cleaned, validated, transformed, labeled) for your solution?

- What platform or tools (e.g., Amazon Web Services [AWS] or Google Cloud Platform [GCP] cloud) will be used to train, validate, and optimize models or perform any other AI and machine learning tasks?

- What software programming languages, architecture, and technologies are required for your solution (tech stack)? This includes firmware and embedded software such as those involved in IoT, and edge and fog computing.

- What hardware, materials, and manufacturing are required for your solution?

- What are the software and hardware requirements for your solution (both functional and nonfunctional) on which all designs and working software/hardware will be based? Note that this should be in the context of Agile requirements for software and more waterfall-esque for hardware because, as they say: measure twice, cut once.

Design:

- What software and hardware designs are required for your solution? This includes visual designs, mechanical designs, and any other assets associated with designing a UX (e.g., information architecture, interaction and flow design, user journey, use cases) or physical object.

- What technical diagrams, charts, graphics, or schematics are needed?

Develop:

- What hypotheses do you have, and with what AI and machine learning software, algorithms, and techniques will you explore and experiment? Remember, this is scientific innovation.

- How will you turn all requirements and designs into a high-quality, successful reality?

- How will you ensure that you follow software and hardware development best practices?

- What Agile software development methodology will you use (e.g., Lean, Kanban, Scrum)?

- What Continuous Integration/Continuous Delivery (CI/CD), and general release mechanisms will you use?

- What version control technology (e.g., Git) and branching strategy will you use?

- How will you test everything to ensure maximum quality?

- How will you test usability and gauge other aspects of the UX?

- How will you measure success, what metrics will you use, and what tracking mechanisms must you build into the solution?

Deliver:

- How will you deploy your solution to a production environment so that it is being used by actual benefactors in the real world?

- How will you monitor the health of the solution and address any issues?

- How will you continue to learn from new data and make data-driven improvements to the solution over time?

- How will you ensure that the intended benefits of the solution are being realized by both people and your business (efficacy)?

- How will you monitor the efficacy of the solution and address any issues (e.g., stale models; aka model drift)?

- How will you scale the solution as needed, and ensure that all other non-functional requirements are being met?

Your solution strategy is all about making your AI vision a successful reality. This begins by performing discovery in order to guide the prioritization and definition of the best solution (prioritized roadmap), which then guides how you design, build, deliver, monitor, and improve the solution.

Note that some of the discovery questions given here were also included in our discussion of developing your AI vision. There is some overlap. The initial discovery and understanding from the higher-level vision phase will guide your strategy development and increase granularity in terms of discovery and definition.

From a product management perspective, a product vision and strategy is manifested as a prioritized product roadmap that consists of a plan to deliver a working solution either through continuous delivery (CD), product releases, or both. The product roadmap can be either time constrained based on product development team estimates or rough and not necessarily based on fixed time and effort estimates.

The latter is more appropriate with increasing levels of pioneering, innovation, and uncertainty (i.e., scientific innovation) and depends on your company's degree of AI readiness and maturity. Statistics- and probability-based technologies are scientific, empirical, and nondeterministic by nature, and this certainly applies to using state-of-the-art and emerging AI techniques.

Developing an end-to-end, AI-based innovation strategy in the forms of a solution strategy and prioritized roadmap requires expertise across most functional areas of a business. This means that all AIPB expert categories are applicable as needed, with oversight and management as the responsibility of the manager group of experts (especially product managers given the prioritized roadmap output).

For the AIPB methodology strategy phase, and from the AIPB process categories, I recommend the following:

- Ideation and vision development
- Business and product strategy
- Roadmap prioritization

- Requirements elicitation

- Product design

I provide an example of creating an AIPB strategy in Chapter 14.

Now let's move on to discussing the final three phases of the AIPB methodology, beginning with executing the strategy and actually building the solution. Given the target audience of the book, and that these three phases are more tactical in nature, we cover them at an overview level here, but the remainder of the book focuses on developing an AI vision and strategy, subjects that are better suited to the target audience.

The build phase centers on software, hardware, and analytics product development, and includes design, development, and testing at a high level. It assumes all discovery and definition work has been completed and a prioritized roadmap is available to guide the build phase process.

In reality, all phases discussed so far tend to be iterative, and as much as people try, some requirements, use cases, and other defining aspects are usually missed or not fully understood at the outset (Agile, not waterfall). This means that some amount of discovery and definition might continue during the build process. Also, and most important, I recommend an Agile approach where the Five Ds process is carried out on a more granular (feature-level), as-you-go basis, as opposed to performing discovery and definition for an entire roadmap at once (which is more waterfall). A competent product manager and product development team can facilitate this process, and Kanban is my recommended development methodology for this phase.

After you have developed a prioritized roadmap and Agile requirements, design, development, and testing work should follow. Requirements should include both functional and nonfunctional requirements. Functional requirements specify how the solution should work, look, and feel, whereas nonfunctional requirements specify solution requirements around scalability, reliability, and maintainability, for example.

Testing includes software, quality assurance (QA), and user acceptance testing (UAT). Note that any development not requiring designs can begin while design work is happening in parallel with other features (e.g., data preparation, exploratory analytics, predictive modeling).

All experts are involved in the build phase of AIPB—managers, designers, builders, testers, and scientists—with manager involvement centered mostly on leadership, oversight, and collaboration. Product-related roles such as product manager represent the primary management roles from the managers group of experts for the build phase, although other stakeholders in management will continue to participate in the build process through demos, feedback gathering, and status updates.

For the AIPB methodology build phase, and from the AIPB process categories, I recommend the product design and product development categories. Methods, techniques, and best practices associated with these two tend to evolve or change relatively often over time, so the experts involved should make decisions and provide guidance accordingly.

The output of the build phase is a testable solution, and that either represents a part or the entire solution. The output can be from one or multiple categories such as designs, software, hardware, models, and algorithms. The key point is that the output is in a testable state.

Testable design outputs include all relevant design assets such as wireframes, mockups, interactive prototypes, and flow diagrams. Software and hardware outputs include working functionality that can be executed and demonstrated to stakeholders. Analytics outputs can include insights, data visualizations, reports, descriptive analytics, predictive models, or other AI-powered software, models, and engines (e.g., recommendations, natural language processing).

As soon as each roadmap item is built in accordance with the requirements and is successfully tested for maximum quality, it is delivered, either continuously (continuous delivery) or as a release, which we discuss next.

DELIVER

The AIPB deliver phase is about delivering high-quality, working solutions to a production environment; that is, an environment in which actual benefactors (business, users, customers) will take advantage of it. In the case of automation, the solution is deployed to automate a real process involving real-world data.

Deploying working solutions to production environments involves specialized experts and processes. Like the build phase, the result of the deployment process has both functional and nonfunctional requirements as well. Functionally, the solution must look and work as expected after it's deployed. This is usually verified with certain production tests (e.g., smoke tests, QA, UAT). Nonfunctionally, the solution must successfully operate under the real-world conditions to which it will be subjected; for example, the solution must be able to scale as needed and be always available.

The experts involved in the deliver phase of AIPB include mostly builders and testers. For the AIPB methodology deliver phase, and from the AIPB process categories, I recommend the product development and product evaluation, validation, and optimization categories. As in the build phase, experts should employ the latest methods, techniques, and best practices.

The output of the deliver phase is a working solution. It will likely be minimalistic for new innovations, and represent an MVP, PoC, or pilot. I would recommend an Agile and Lean approach as a key strategy in order to ensure iterative validation, pivots, and success as quickly as possible. This means building an MVP first to test the riskiest assumptions, validate product-market fit, ensure that the solution actually accomplishes its goals, and better understand aspects of the UX such as usability and delight (concepts we discuss later in the book). You can continue to build on and improve the MVP with subsequent updates.

The deployed solution should have active health monitoring, logging, and tracking (e.g., tagging, event capture) in which to detect issues and perform analytics. Monitoring and analytics should provide data-driven insights around the health of the solution, whether the solution is providing the intended benefits (to both people and business!) and whether the solution is achieving intended KPIs and to what extent (e.g., success metrics, ROI), and ensuring that all nonfunctional needs are being met (e.g., scalability).

One specific and AI-related item to closely monitor is stale models and model drift. Markets, trends, fads, environments (e.g., economic), competitors, interests, and people change constantly. Data changes constantly as a result, which means that models trained and optimized to a certain performance level on yesterday's data might not perform well on tomorrow's data. AI-based solutions typically require ongoing retraining and improvement; or, put another way, continued data gathering, knowledge development, and ongoing learning. This is best facilitated by developing a data feedback loop in which new data generated by the solution is regularly fed back into the system for updated learning and performance improvement.

After you deploy a solution to a real-world environment and are continuously monitoring and analyzing it, as discussed, you need to direct your attention to optimization, the topic of the next section.

OPTIMIZE

The optimize phase is the final phase of the AIPB Methodology Component. After you have delivered an AI-based solution with appropriate monitoring and tracking, and you have determined that the solution is worth developing further (e.g., to achieve product-market fit), you should optimize it for better performance and user delight.

Health monitoring and logging should indicate whether any functional or nonfunctional issues need to be fixed or optimized. You should regularly address any signs of stale models and model drift with ongoing learning and performance optimization using a prebuilt data feedback loop. You should regularly analyze KPIs and metrics to determine the efficacy of the solution based on the intended vision and goals and also for discovering any patterns and insights indicating areas of further improvement and lift. You should regularly solicit, capture, and analyze user, customer, and stakeholder feedback in order to further improve and optimize the solution, as well.

Experimentation and testing are also powerful optimization tools that carry the added benefit of helping to determine cause and effect. Correlation does not imply causation, and predictive models are usually unable to uncover all causes leading to specific effects or outcomes. Experimentation techniques such as A/B and multivariate testing are very well suited to continued optimization through strategic experiments and gaining a deeper causal understanding as well. These techniques can also be used to compare the efficacy of different AI models, and generally using AI solutions as compared to the status quo.

Finally, AI and machine learning are rapidly evolving and advancing fields. This is true in all aspects, including research, software, algorithms, and hardware (e.g., deep learning optimized processors such as Graphics Processing Units [GPUs] and Tensor Processing Units [TPUs]). Optimization of AI and machine learning deployments is not only related to better model performance (e.g., predictive accuracy), but also to hardware and training cost reductions, increases in training speeds, reduced computational complexity and resources required, and faster and automated analytics.

The experts involved in the optimize phase of AIPB include everyone. The optimize phase is based on literally everything upstream of it, and any and all aspects can likely be optimized or at least improved. This includes potential involvement of all of the process categories and associated methods from the AIPB process categories. In fact, I'm a huge proponent of kaizen. It's a Japanese word for improvement with a focus on continuous improvement that was made famous by the Lean manufacturing movement and Toyota's renowned Toyota Production System (TPS).

The output of the optimize phase is a solution whose intended benefit and outcome performance is well understood and continuously improved in all possible ways; for example, goals, KPIs, lift, user delight, benefits, and performance. Put another way, the outputs are effective analytics and data-driven continuous optimizations.

The Flipped Classroom

Recall that I said that the unique value of AIPB was its North Star, benefits, structure, and approach. We've already discussed the North Star, benefits, and structure, so now let's discuss the recommended approach.

There are many collaborative and interactive techniques (e.g., brainstorming, prioritization) that are employed by skilled educators and practitioners of various disciplines, particularly very good product managers. One method I especially recommend when executing AIPB, and in general, is the concept of a *flipped classroom*.

The flipped classroom "flips" the traditional in-class versus out-of-class work, and has students review instructional material (e.g., lectures, readings) outside of class (i.e., the time traditionally used for doing homework, research, and project work) and often online. This allows class time to be much more productive and effective through discussions, collaboration, projects, and other forms of actual "doing" as opposed to just listening and being lectured at. At the risk of sounding obvious, actually doing gets things done, and provides better learning, experience, and understanding.

With the proper approach, this is easily translated to work environments, as well. Rather than schedule a meeting and spend a good part explaining methods, techniques, and subject matter details, have attendees review all of that beforehand so that the meeting is purely focused on getting things done. For example, if the goal is to create a prioritized roadmap of goal-aligned initiatives, have attendees and participants review the prioritization concepts and techniques to be used ahead of time. You can answer any questions people have up front, but the majority of collaboration time should be actual selection and prioritization, with the output being a prioritized roadmap that will drive next steps.

Additionally, people regularly send meeting invites to colleagues with absolutely zero description, agenda, or any other information that would otherwise assist them in understanding the purpose and goals of the meeting. Part of the flipped classroom approach here is to never do that. There's a great TED talk by David Grady that goes over this called "How to save the world (or at least yourself) from bad meetings." (*http://bit.ly/31wjQba*) Always let people know exactly what the purpose of the meeting is, what you'll be covering, the agenda, what the outcomes should be, and anything else that's relevant. This matters.

Lastly, people might argue that they're busy and don't have enough time outside of the meeting to review suggested materials, or might simply not do their part beforehand. Those who have not reviewed the materials in advance are usually obvious based on their questions or lack of understanding of what is to be done and the goals of the session. In the end, you can't force people and maybe they are truly too busy, but the end result is what is too often seen in the real world: unproductive and ineffective meetings, time wasted, slow progress, and sometimes failure. This might require a cultural shift, but it's worth it.

Summary

AIPB is a unique AI-based innovation framework that emphasizes the benefits of innovation for both people and business. It has many benefits as discussed, and these benefits combined with the framework's unique North Star (better human experiences and business success), structure, and approach are its key differentiators. AIPB is meant to be a one-stop-shop for AI vision, strategy, execution, and optimization for maximum success.

AIPB requires that the appropriate experts are included and collaborate effectively throughout all phases of end-to-end AI-based innovation. Each phase is modular in that the process categories and associated methods employed should be either those recommended by me or by the experts involved based on their experience, expertise, and current best practices. The outputs of each phase should drive innovation toward the end goal, which is AI-powered better human experiences and business success. For the latest AIPB information and resources, visit *https://aipbbook.com*.

Now let's turn our focus to understanding AI and machine learning at a high and nontechnical level, followed by a close look at the ways that AI is being used in the real world today and the vast potential it presents for tomorrow.

4

AI and Machine Learning: A Nontechnical Overview

Although it is not necessary to be an expert or practitioner of AI in order to develop an AI vision and strategy, having a high-level understanding of AI and related subject matter areas is critical to making highly informed decisions. Helping you to develop this understanding is the goal of this chapter.

This chapter defines and discusses AI-related concepts and techniques, including machine learning, deep learning, data science, and big data. We also discuss how both humans and machines learn and how that is related to the current and future state of AI. We finish the chapter by covering how data powers AI and data characteristics and considerations necessary for AI success.

This chapter helps develop a level-appropriate context for understanding the next chapter on real-world opportunities and applications of AI. Let's begin by discussing the field of data science.

What Is Data Science, and What Does a Data Scientist Do?

Let's kick off the discussion by defining data science and the role and responsibilities of a data scientist, both of which describe the field and skills required to carry out AI and machine learning initiatives (note that more specialized roles are becoming more common, such as machine learning engineer). Even though data scientists often come from many different educational and work experience backgrounds, most should be strong (or, ideally, experts) in four fundamental areas that I call the four pillars of data science expertise (*http://bit.ly/2WDEbaL*).

In no particular order, these are the areas in which data scientists should have expertise:

- Business in general or in the relevant business domain
- Mathematics (including statistics and probability)
- Computer science (including software programming)
- Written and verbal communication

There are other skills and expertise that are highly desirable, as well, but these are the primary four in my opinion. In reality, people are usually strong in one or two of these pillars, but not equally strong in all four. If you happen to meet a data scientist who is truly an expert in all, you've found a person often referred to as a unicorn. People with an appreciable degree of expertise and competency in all four pillars are very difficult to find, and there's a significant shortage of talent.

As a result, many companies have begun to create specialized roles around specific pillars of data science, which when combined, are the equivalent of having a data scientist. An example could be creating a team of three people, of which one person has an MBA-type background, another is a statistician, and another is a machine learning or software engineer. The team could also include a data engineer, as well, for example. This team then could work on multiple initiatives at once, with each person focusing on a specific aspect of an initiative at any given time.

Based on these pillars, a data scientist is a person who should be able to use existing data sources and create new ones as needed in order to extract meaningful information, generate deep actionable insights, support data-driven decision making, and build AI solutions. This is done with business domain expertise, effective communication and results interpretation, and utilization of any and all relevant statistical techniques, programming languages, software packages and libraries, and data infrastructure. This, in a nutshell, is what data science is all about.

Machine Learning Definition and Key Characteristics

Machine learning is often considered a subset of AI. We discuss machine learning first in order to develop a foundation for our discussion of AI and its limitations later in this chapter.

Remember our simple definition of AI as intelligence exhibited by machines. This basically describes the ability of machines to learn from information and apply this knowledge to do things as well as continue learning from experience. In many AI applications, machine learning is set of techniques used for the learning part of the AI application process. Specific techniques that we discuss later can be considered subsets of AI and machine learning, and commonly include neural networks and deep learning, as shown in Figure 4-1.

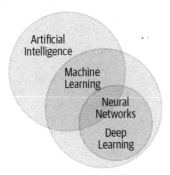

Figure 4-1. AI, machine learning, neural networks, and deep learning relationships

I really like this short and succinct definition of machine learning that I came across in a Google Design blog article: "Machine learning is the science of making predictions based on patterns and relationships that've been automatically discovered in data." (*http://bit.ly/2IFZWlp*)

A nontechnical definition of machine learning that I usually give is that machine learning is the process of automatically learning from data without requiring explicit programming, with the ability to expand the knowledge learned with experience. A key differentiator of machine learning relative to rules-based techniques is the lack of explicit programming, particularly around specific domains, industries, and business functions. In advanced techniques such as deep learning, domain expertise might not be required at all, whereas in other cases, domain expertise is provided in the form of the features (in nonmachine learning applications referred to as variables, data fields, or data attributes) selected or engineered to train models. In either case, the part about not requiring explicit programming is absolutely critical, and is really the most important aspect of machine learning to understand. Let's put this in the context of an example.

Suppose that you were a programmer before machine learning was a thing, and you were tasked with creating a predictive model capable of predicting whether a person applying for a certain type of loan would default on that loan and therefore should be approved or not approved for it. You would have written a long software program that was very specific to the financial industry with inputs such as a person's FICO score, credit history, and type of loan being applied for. The code would contain lots of very explicit programming statements (e.g., conditionals, loops). The pseudo code (programming code written in plain English) might look something like this:

```
If the persons FICO score is above 800, then they will likely not default
   and should be approved
Else if the persons FICO score is between 700 and 800
   If the person has never defaulted on any loan, they will likely not
   default and should be approved
   Else the will likely default and should not be approved
Else if the persons FICO score is less than 700
   ...
```

This is an example of very explicit programming (a rules-based predictive model) that contains specific domain expertise around the loan industry that is expressed as code. This program is hard-coded to accomplish only one thing. It requires domain/industry expertise to determine the rules (aka scenarios). It is very rigid and not necessarily representative of all factors contributing to potential loan default. The program must also be manually updated for any changes to the inputs or the loan industry in general.

As you can see, this is not particularly efficient or optimal and also will not result in the best predictive model possible. Machine learning using the right data, on the other hand, is able to do this without any explicitly written code, particularly code expressing loan industry expertise. Giving a slightly oversimplified explanation here, machine learning is able to take a dataset as input without knowing anything about the data or domain involved, pass it through a machine learning algorithm that also knows nothing about the data or domain involved, and produce a predictive model that has expert knowledge of how the inputs map to the output in order to make the most accurate predictions possible. If you understand this, you pretty much understand the purpose of machine learning at a high level.

It's worth mentioning that while machine learning algorithms themselves are able to learn without requiring explicit programming, humans are still very much needed and involved in the entire process of ideation, building, and testing machine learning–based AI solutions.

Ways Machines Learn

Machines learn from data through a variety of different techniques, with the most predominant being *supervised, unsupervised, semisupervised, reinforcement,* and *transfer learning.* The data used to train and optimize machine learning models is usually categorized as either labeled or unlabeled, as shown in Figure 4-2.

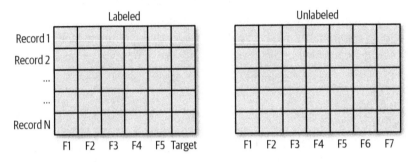

Figure 4-2. *Labeled versus unlabeled data*

Labeled data has a target variable, or value, that is intended to be predicted for a given combination of feature values (aka variables, attributes, fields). In predictive modeling, a type of machine learning application, a model is trained on a labeled dataset in order to predict the target value for new combinations of feature values. The presence of target data in the dataset is why the data is referred to as labeled. Unlabeled data, on the other hand, has feature values, but no particular target data or labels. This makes unlabeled data particularly well suited for grouping (aka clustering and segmentation) and anomaly detection.

One thing worth noting is that, unfortunately, labeled data in enough quantity can be very difficult to come by and can cost a lot of money and time to produce. Labels can be added to data records automatically or might require being added manually by people (think of a data record, aka sample, as a row in a spreadsheet or table).

Supervised learning refers to machine learning using labeled data, and unsupervised learning with unlabeled data. Semisupervised learning uses both labeled and unlabeled data.

Let's briefly discuss the different learning types at a high level. Supervised learning has many potential applications such as prediction, personalization, recommender systems, and pattern recognition. It is further subdivided into two applications: *regression* and *classification*. Both techniques are used to make predictions. Regression is used primarily to predict single discrete or real number values, whereas classification is used to assign one or more classes or categories to a given set of input data (e.g., spam or not-spam for emails).

The most common applications of unsupervised learning are clustering and anomaly detection, whereas in general, unsupervised learning is largely focused on pattern recognition. Other applications include dimensionality reduction (simplifying the number of data variables and also simplifying model complexity) using principal component analysis (PCA) and singular value decomposition (SVD).

Although the underlying data is unlabeled, unsupervised techniques can be employed in useful predictive applications when labels, characterizations, or profiles are applied to discovered clusters (groupings) through another process outside of the unsupervised learning process itself. One of the challenges with unsupervised learning is that there is no particularly good way to determine how well an unsupervised learning–generated model performs. The output is what you make of it, and there is nothing correct or incorrect about it. This is because there is no label or target variable in the data and therefore nothing against which to compare model results. Despite this limitation, unsupervised learning is very powerful and has many real-world applications.

Semi-supervised learning can be a very useful approach when unlabeled data is plentiful and labeled data is not. Other popular types of learning that we cover more in the next chapter include reinforcement learning, transfer learning, and recommender systems.

In machine learning tasks involving labeled and unlabeled data, the process takes data input and maps it to an output of some sort. Most machine learning model outputs are surprisingly simple, and are either a number (continuous or discrete, e.g., 3.1415), one or more categories (aka classes; e.g., "spam," "hot dog"), or a probability (e.g., 35% likelihood). In more advanced AI cases, the output might be a structured prediction (i.e., a set of predicted values as opposed to single value), a predicted sequence of characters and words (e.g., phrases, sentences), or artificially generated summary of the most recent Chicago Cubs game (GO CUBS!).

AI Definition and Concepts

Earlier we gave a simple definition of AI as intelligence exhibited by machines, which includes machine learning and specific techniques such as deep learning as subsets. Before further developing a definition of AI, let's define the concept of intelligence in general. A rough definition for intelligence is:

Learning, understanding, and the application of the knowledge learned to achieve one or more goals

So, basically intelligence is the process of using knowledge learned to achieve goals and carry out tasks (for humans, examples include making a decision, having a conversation, and performing work tasks). Having now defined intelligence in general, it's easy to see that AI is simply intelligence as exhibited by machines. More specifically, AI describes when a machine is able to learn from information (data), generate some degree of understanding, and then use the knowledge learned to do something.

The field of AI is related to and draws from aspects of neuroscience, psychology, philosophy, mathematics, statistics, computer science, computer programming, and more. AI is also sometimes referred to as machine intelligence or cognitive computing given its foundational basis and relationship to cognition; that is, the mental processes associated with developing knowledge and comprehension.

More specifically, cognition and the broader field of cognitive science are terms used to describe the brain's processes, functions, and other mechanisms that make it possible to gather, process, store, and use information to generate intelligence and drive behavior. Cognitive processes include attention, perception, memory, reasoning, comprehension, thinking, language, remembering, and more. Other related and somewhat deeper and philosophical concepts include mind, sentience, awareness, and consciousness.

So what powers intelligence? For AI applications, the answer is information in the form of data. In the case of humans and animals, new information is constantly collected from experience and the surrounding environment through the five senses. This information is then passed through the cognitive processes and functions of the brain.

Amazingly, humans can also learn from existing information and knowledge already stored in the brain by applying it to understand and develop knowledge about something else as well as to develop one's thoughts and opinions about a new topic, for example. How many times have you thought through something given information you already understood and then had an "aha!" moment that resulted in a new understanding of something else?

Experience factors heavily into AI, as well. AI is made possible by a training and optimization process that uses relevant data for a given task. AI applications can be updated and improved over time as new data becomes available, and this is the learning-from-experience aspect of AI.

Continually learning from new data is important for many reasons. First, the world and its human inhabitants are always changing around us. Trends and fads come and go; new technologies are introduced, and old technologies become obsolete; industries are disrupted; and new innovations are continuously introduced. As a result, data today related to online shopping, for example, might be very different than the data you receive tomorrow, or years from now. Automotive manufacturers might begin asking what factors contribute most to people purchasing flying vehicles, as opposed to the electric vehicles that are gaining popularity and wider use today.

Ultimately, data and the models trained from it can become stale, a phenomena referred to as *model drift*. It is therefore critical that any applications of AI are refreshed and continue to gain experience and knowledge through continued learning from new data.

AI Types

Often AI is referred to with a qualifier like strong or narrow. These qualifiers, which we cover next, are meant to describe the nature of the AI being discussed. The aspect of AI being described by the qualifier can be related to the number of simultaneous tasks that an AI can carry out; the architecture of a given algorithm, in the case of neural networks; the actual use of the AI; or the relative difficulty of solving a given problem using AI.

Although this might differ depending on the reference or researcher, AI can be grouped into categories and relationships, as shown in Figure 4-3.

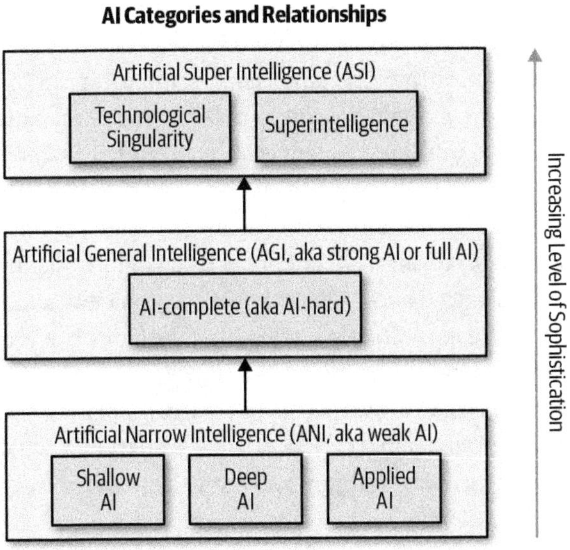

AI Categories and Relationships

Figure 4-3. AI categories and relationships

Starting with *artificial narrow intelligence* (ANI), the terms "weak" and "narrow" are both used interchangeably to indicate that an AI is specialized and able to carry out only a single, narrow task; it is not able to demonstrate cognition. This means that weak AI, although often considerably impressive, is not sentient, aware, or conscious in any way. As of this writing, almost all AI is considered weak AI.

"Shallow" and "deep" are qualifiers used to describe the number of hidden layers in a neural network architecture (discussed in detail in Appendix A). Shallow AI usually refers to a neural network with a single hidden layer, whereas deep AI (synonymous with deep learning) refers to a neural network with more than one hidden layer.

Applied AI is as it sounds. It is the application of AI to real-world problems such as prediction, recommendation, natural language, and recognition. These days you often hear the term *smart* used to describe AI-powered software and hardware solutions (e.g., smart homes). That is, some form of AI is being used as part of the solution, although companies often exaggerate their use of AI. Given that all AI today is considered narrow, applied AI is shown as being related to narrow AI. That might change in the future, which brings us to the next category.

Artificial general intelligence (AGI) is also called "strong" or "full" AI. AGI sets the bar in that it represents machine intelligence able to demonstrate cognition and carry out cognitive processes to the same degree as a human. Or, in other words, it has cognitive abilities that are functionally equivalent to a human. This means that a machine can perform any task a human can and is not limited to applying intelligence to a single specific problem. This is an extremely high bar to set. We discuss AGI and the challenges of achieving it in more detail later in this chapter.

It's worth noting that certain AI problems are referred to as *AI-complete* or *AI-hard* (e.g., AGI, natural language understanding), which just means that these problems are very advanced and difficult to solve completely and in general. Creating machines that are equivalently intelligent to humans is a very difficult problem to solve, and is not the AI that we have today.

Artificial super intelligence (ASI), and related concepts such as technological singularity and superintelligence, describe the scenario in which AI becomes self-improving in a runaway fashion and ultimately surpasses human intelligence and technological advancement. Even though the possibility of a singularity and superintelligence is largely debated (*http://bit.ly/2IVn1Av*), it is highly unlikely anytime in the near future, if at all. Also, although it's not anything to worry about right now, it's worth noting that certain techniques such as deep reinforcement learning are being used in AI applications for self-directed learning that improves over time.

Learning Like Humans

Consider that babies and very young children are able to recognize an object such as a particular animal in almost any context (e.g., location, position, pose, lighting) despite having seen a picture or illustration of a particular animal only once, for example. This is a remarkable feat of the human brain, which involves initial learning followed by the application of that learning to different contexts.

There is a great article that was published in the *MIT Technology Review* called "The Missing Link of AI," written by Tom Simonite (*http://bit.ly/2MVfLdr*). The article is about the way that humans learn and how AI techniques must evolve in order to be able to learn in a similar way and ultimately exhibit human-like intelligence. Jeff Dean from Google is quoted there as saying, "Ultimately, unsupervised learning is going to be a really important component in building really intelligent systems—if you look at how humans learn, it's almost entirely unsupervised." Yann LeCun expands on this: "We all know that unsupervised learning is the ultimate answer."

The article points out that infants learn by themselves that objects are supported by other objects (e.g., book on a coffee table) and therefore supported objects do not fall to the ground despite the force of gravity. Children also learn that inanimate objects will remain in a room in the same place after they leave the room, and they can expect them to still be there when they return. They do this without being explicitly taught, or in other words, this learning is unsupervised and does not involve labeled data, where the label could be a parent teaching a child something.

Children also learn by trying different things over time, such as through experimentation and trial and error. They do this even when they're not supposed to, or even when knowing that some outcomes might be negative, but they do so in order to learn about cause and effect and to learn about the world around them in general. This method of learning is highly analogous to reinforcement learning, which is a very active area of research and development in AI and can potentially help make significant progress toward human-like intelligence.

In the context of human learning in general, humans are able to sense the world around them and put meaning to things on their own. These things can be recognizing patterns, objects, people, and places. It can be figuring out how something works. Humans also know how to use natural language to communicate. Much of how humans learn happens in an unsupervised, self-learning, and trial-and-error way. These are all remarkable feats of the human brain; feats that are very difficult to emulate with algorithms and machines, as we discuss next.

AGI, Killer Robots, and the One-Trick Pony

AGI—producing an AI that is able to do and understand anything a human can at least as well—is still a long way off. This means that we don't need to worry about killer robots for now, or maybe ever. Pedro Domingos, in his book *The Master Algorithm*[1] states, "People worry that computers will get too smart and take over the world, but the real problem is that they're too stupid and they've already taken over the world." He goes on to say that the chances of AI taking over the world are zero given the way in which machines learn and, most important, because computers don't have a will of their own.

AGI is a very difficult problem to solve. Think about it—to truly replicate all human intelligence in a machine, the AI would need to be able to observe the

---

1 Domingos, Pedro. *The Master Algorithm: How the Quest for the Ultimate Learning Machine Will Remake Our World*. New York: Basic Books, 2015.

world around it, self-learn on an ongoing and self-directed basis (i.e., demonstrate true autonomy) in order to continuously make sense of everything, and potentially self-improve like humans. It would need to understand everything humans do, possibly more, and be able to generalize and transfer knowledge to any context. This is largely what children and adults do. But how do you do that when unsupervised learning has no correct answers as we discussed earlier? How do you train a machine to learn something without teaching it—that is, make it self-learning?

These are great questions, and the answer is that you don't, at least not with today's state-of-the-art AI and machine learning methods. Currently, the most advanced techniques in AI include neural networks, deep learning, transfer learning, and reinforcement learning. These techniques are not particularly suited for unsupervised learning applications. They are also very focused on a single, highly specialized task.

A deep learning neural network that is trained to recognize cats in an image is not able to also predict your home price three years from now; it's capable of nothing more than recognizing cats in an image. If you want a predictive model to predict your home price, you must create and train a separate model. AI is therefore not good at multitasking, and each instance is pretty much a one-trick pony for now.

Although the human brain remains a mystery to neuroscientists as to how it works exactly, one thing appears to be clear: The brain is not a pure calculating machine in the same sense as a computer. The brain is thought to process sensory information with a complex, algorithmically based biological neural network mechanism that can store memories based on patterns, solve problems, and drive motor actions (behavior) based on information recall and prediction.

This is a process that begins at birth and continues throughout our lifetimes, and often in a highly unsupervised, trial-and-error-based way as mentioned. The brain's incredible memory storage and recall mechanism is what differentiates it from a pure calculating machine, and is what makes human unsupervised learning possible. A single human brain is able to continuously learn and store all information learned and memories developed in an entire human lifetime. How would a machine emulate that? It wouldn't—at least not anytime soon.

Unlike the unsupervised and self-learning of humans, computing machines are completely dependent on extremely detailed instructions. This is what we call software code. Even automatically learned and nonexplicity programmed predictive models (the magic of AI and machine learning) are incorporated into software-based programs written by computer programmers. Given the current state-of-the-art of AI, AGI is impossible if a machine isn't trained on or programmed exactly for every possible sensory scenario that it will encounter in any environment and under any condition.

One implication of this is that intelligent machines cannot have free will like humans; that is, the ability to make any decision or take any action within reason in the way that humans do, given a limited or even unlimited set of possibilities. With the exception of techniques like reinforcement learning, intelligent machines are constrained to only mapping inputs to certain outputs.

Human brains, on the other hand, can react to scenarios that they have or have not previously encountered. They can integrate sensory information from the five senses naturally in real time, with seemless ease, and with great relative speed. Humans are able to continuously adapt to unplanned changes in their environment, such as having unexpected conversations with people (e.g., a phone call, running into a friend), figuring out why the TV suddenly won't turn on, dealing with sudden changes in weather, reacting to accidents (e.g., car, spills, broken glass), missing a bus, determining that an elevator is out of service (humans immediately know to locate the stairway instead), a credit card not working, a grocery bag breaking, avoiding a child that suddenly runs across their path—the number of real-world examples are almost infinite.

Humans are also able to think, a process that does not require sensory input data. You could be sitting on a beach staring out at the ocean waves while thinking about many things totally unrelated to the beach and ocean, but today's AI algorithms are like meat grinders: you need to put beef into the grinder in order to get ground beef. Aside from techniques such as reinforcement learning, AI algorithms do not produce an output without related inputs, especially not anything close to human thoughts.

In *The Book of Why*[2] the authors discuss that humans are also able to reason, make decisions, take actions, and come to conclusions based on having a causal understanding (cause and effect) of the world and the ability to reflect. Reflection means that we're able to retrospectively look at our decisions or actions, analyze the results, and decide whether we would have done things differently, or will do something different in a similar situation next time. This is a form of natural human learning where the inputs are previous actions taken or decisions made.

---

2 Pearl, Judea and Dana Mackenzie. *The Book of Why: The New Science of Cause and Effect.* New York: Basic Books, 2018.

We also have a causal understanding of the world that we continue to develop throughout our lifetimes. We know that correlation does not imply causation, and yet most AI and machine learning algorithms are based on correlations (e.g., predictive analytics) and have absolutely no concept of causation. A well-known example is the fact that increases in ice cream sales are accompanied by increased drowning deaths, therefore a predictive algorithm might learn that increased ice cream consumption causes drowning. With a little thought, humans can easily figure out that the missing factors, *called confounding variables*, are time of year and temperature, which are the true causes of the increases in both. AI would be unable to figure this out.

Lastly, there is a significant difference between automation and autonomy, both of which are highly relevant in the context of the progression of robotics and AI toward AGI. Automation is the result of writing software programs that automatically perform a task on a one-off or repeating basis that previously required some human assistance. Autonomy, on the other hand, is all about independence, self-direction, and the ability to respond to interactions and changes in the environment. There are varying degrees of both automation and autonomy in existing robotics and AI applications, with the majority of applications being more on the automation side at this time.

True autonomy is very difficult for reasons already mentioned in the context of AGI but also because of limitations with sensing techniques such as computer vision. Computer vision and image recognition have come a long way in terms of object detection and identification in controlled and consistent circumstances, but the technology is not very good at understanding in ever-changing, inconsistent, and surprise-filled environments that better reflect reality.

The Data Powering AI

There is one thing that AI, machine learning, big data, IoT, and any other form of analytics-driven solutions have in common: data. In fact, data powers every aspect of digital technology.

This chapter covers the power of data, including using data to make decisions, common data structures and formats used in AI applications, data storage and common data sources, and the concept of data readiness.

BIG DATA

The world has never collected or stored as much data as it does today. In addition, the variety, volume, and generation rate of data is growing at an alarming rate. Rio Tinto, for example, a leading mining company that generates more than $40 billion in revenue, has embraced big data and AI to make data-driven decisions from 2.4 terabytes of sensor data generated per minute (*http://bit.ly/2x2ChpK*)!

The field of big data is all about efficiently acquiring, integrating, preparing, and analyzing information from these enormous, diverse, and fast-moving datasets. However, handling and extracting value from these datasets might not be feasible or achievable due to hardware and/or computational constraints. To deal with these challenges, new and innovative hardware, software tools, and analytics techniques are required. Big data is the term that is used to describe this combination of datasets, techniques, and customized tools.

Also, data of any kind is basically useless without some form of accompanying analytics (unless the data is being monetized). In addition to the description given, big data is also used by people to describe performing analytics on very large datasets, which can include advanced analytics techniques such as AI and machine learning.

DATA STRUCTURE AND FORMAT FOR AI APPLICATIONS

At a high level, we can classify data as *structured*, *unstructured*, or *semistructured* as illustrated in Figure 4-4.

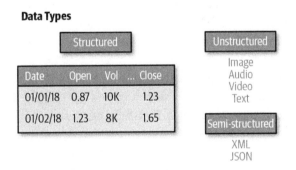

Figure 4-4. Data types

Let's begin with structured data. We can think of structured data as, well, as data having structure. Although shown in Figure 4-4 in tabular form, structured data is data that is generally organized and can easily fit into a table, spreadsheet, or relational database, for example. Structured data is typically characterized as having features, also called *attributes* or *fields*. When structured this way, it is commonly referred to as a data model, and it becomes relatively easy to query, join, aggregate, filter, and sort the data.

Figure 4-4 shows an example of structured data in table format. In this case, the data is organized into columns and rows, where rows represent individual data examples (aka records, samples, or data points). The columns represent the data features for each example. Figure 4-4 also shows examples of labeled and unlabeled data, concepts we discussed earlier.

Unstructured data is the opposite of structured data and is therefore not organized or structured in any way, nor characterized by a data model. Common examples include images, videos, audio, and text such as that found in comments, the body of emails, and speech translated to text.

Note that unstructured data can be labeled, as is often the case with images. Images can be labeled based on the primary subject of the image; for example, images labeled as either cat or dog depending on which animal type is depicted.

Semistructured data has some structure, but is not easily organized into tables like structured data. Examples include XML and JSON formats, both of which are often used in software applications for data transfer, payloads, and representation in flat files.

The final type and format of data that is relevant to AI applications is *sequence data*, with *language* and *time series* as two common examples. Sequence data is characterized by data ordered in a sequence for which the ordering mechanism is some sort of index. Time is the index in time-series data, and sensors in an IoT or data acquisition system are a great example of a source of time-series data.

Another example of sequence data is language. Language is characterized not only by grammar and use in communication, but also by the sequences of letters and words. A sentence is a sequence of words, and when the word sequence is rearranged it can easily take on a different meeting, or in the worst case, make no sense whatsoever. Words are arranged in a way that has a very specific meaning and makes the most sense to those that speak a given language.

DATA STORAGE AND SOURCING

Companies and people in general generate a ton of data, and often through disparate and nonunified software and hardware applications, each built on a unique "backend," or database. Databases are used for both permanent and temporary data storage. Databases come in many different types, which includes the way they physically store data on disk, the type of data they store (e.g., structured, unstructured, and semistructured), the data models and schemas they support, the query language they use, and the way they handle governance and management tasks such as scalability and security. In this section, we focus on some of the most commonly used databases for AI applications: *relational databases* and *NoSQL databases.*

Relational database management systems (RDBMS) are very well suited for storing and querying structured relational data, although some support storing unstructured data and multiple storage types, as well. Relational data means that data stored in different parts (i.e., tables) of the database are often related to one another according to predefined types of relationships (e.g., one to many). Each table (or relation) consists of rows (records) and columns (fields or attributes), with a unique identifier (key) per row. Relational databases typically offer data integrity and transactional guarantees that other databases do not.

NoSQL database systems were created for, and have gained widespread popularity primarily due to benefits relating to, scalability and high availability. These systems are also characterized as being modern web-scale databases that are typically schema-free, provide easy replication, and have simple application programming interfaces (APIs). They are best suited for unstructured data and applications involving huge volumes of data—for example, big data. In fact, many of these systems are designed for extraordinary request and data volumes that can take advantage of massive horizontal scaling (e.g., thousands of servers) in order to meet demand.

There are multiple types of NoSQL databases, with document, key–value, graph, and wide-column being the most prevalent. The different types refer mainly to how the data is stored and the characteristics of the database system itself. It's worth noting another type of database system that's been getting some attention in recent years. *NewSQL* database systems are relational database systems that combine RDBMS-like guarantees with NoSQL-like scalability and performance.

SPECIFIC DATA SOURCES

There are a lot of specific types of data sources, and many are used simultaneously at any given large company. Certain types of data can be used to automate and optimize customer-facing products and services, whereas others are better suited for optimizing internal applications. Here is a list of potential data sources, which we will look at individually:

- Customers
- Sales and marketing
- Operational
- Event and transactional
- IoT
- Unstructured
- Third party
- Public

Most companies use a customer relationship management tool, or CRM. These tools manage interactions and relationships with existing and potential customers, suppliers, and service providers. Additionally, many CRM tools are able to manage multichannel customer marketing, communications, targeting, and personalization either natively and/or through integrations. As a result, CRM tools can be a very significant source of data for customer-centric AI applications.

Although many companies use CRM tools as their primary customer database, customer data platform (CDP) tools such as AgilOne are used to create a single, unified customer database by combining data sources around customer behavior, engagement, and sales. CDP tools are intended to be used by nontechnical people, and are similar to data warehouses in that they're used to drive efficient analytics, insights gathering, and targeted marketing.

Sales data is some of the most, if not the most, important data that a company has. Typical data sources include point-of-sale data for companies with brick-and-mortar locations, ecommerce data for online shopping applications, and accounts receivable for sales of services. Many companies that sell products at physical locations also sell products online and therefore are able to use both sources of data.

Marketing departments communicate and provide offers to customers through multiple channels and generate channel-specific data accordingly. Common marketing data sources can include email, social, paid search, programmatic advertising, digital media engagement (e.g., blogs, whitepapers, webinars, infographics), and push notifications for mobile apps.

Operational data is centered around business functions and processes. Examples include data associated with customer service, supply chain, inventory, ordering, IT (e.g., network, logs, servers), manufacturing, logistics, and accounting. Operational data is often best harnessed to gain deep insights into internal company operations in order to improve and potentially automate processes to achieve goals such as increasing operational efficiency and reducing costs.

For companies built primarily around digital products such as Software as a Service (SaaS) applications and mobile apps, there is usually a lot of event and transactional-based data generated and collected. It's worth noting that even though individual sales can certainly be considered transactional, not all transactional data is associated with sales. Event and transaction data can include bank transfers, submitting an application, abandoning an online shopping cart, and user interaction and engagement data such as clickstream and data collected by applications like Google Analytics.

With the IoT revolution in full swing, research indicates that it will generate up to $11 trillion dollars in economic value (*https://mck.co/2In3SbP*) through more than 75 billion connected devices worldwide by 2025 (*http://bit.ly/2WOtMcz*). Needless to say, a huge and increasing amount of data is generated by connected devices and sensors. This data can be very useful for AI applications.

Companies also have a lot of highly valuable unstructured data that often goes largely unused. Unstructured data as previously discussed can include images, videos, audio, and text. Text data can be particularly useful for natural language processing applications when stemming from product or service customer reviews, feedback, and survey results.

Lastly, companies usually employ multiple third-party software tools that might not have been mentioned in this section. Many software tools allow data to be integrated with other tools and also exported for analysis and portability. Third-party data can be purchased in many cases, as well. Lastly, with the internet explosion and open source movement, there is also a tremendous amount of freely available and highly useful publicly available data that we can use.

The keys to using data to help generate deep actionable insights and power AI solutions are data availability and access, whether to centralize the data or not, and all of the data readiness and quality considerations, which I cover in the next section.

DATA READINESS AND QUALITY (THE "RIGHT" DATA)

Let's close this chapter with a critical concept that is a major consideration in AIPB—the concept of data readiness and quality. High quality and ready data (as we'll define) that can successfully power a certain AI solution is what I call the "right" data. This is paramount to solution success.

I use the term data readiness to collectively refer to the following:

- Adequate data amount
- Adequate data depth
- Well-balanced data
- Highly representative and unbiased data
- Complete data
- Clean data

Let's discuss the concept of *feature space* before going over each of these data readiness points in turn. The term "feature space" refers to the number of possible feature value combinations across all features included in a dataset being used for a specific problem. In many cases, adding more features results in an exponential increase in the amount of data required for a given problem due to a phenomenon known as the *curse of dimensionality*, which we discuss further in the sidebar that follows in a few moments.

Adequate Data Amount

Let's begin with the need for an adequate amount of data. Enough data is required to ensure that the relationships discovered during the learning process are representative and statistically significant. Also, the more data you have, the more accurate the model is likely to be. More data also allows for simpler models and a reduced need to create new features from existing ones, which is a process known as *feature engineering*. Feature engineering can be as simple as converting units; other times, it involves creating entirely new metrics from combinations of other features.

Adequate Data Depth

It's not enough to have adequate amounts of data in general: AI applications also require enough varied data. This is where adequate data depth comes into play. Depth means that there's enough varied data that adequately fills out the feature space—a good enough set of combinations of different feature values that a model is able to properly learn the underlying relationships between data features themselves as well as between data features and the target variable when present in labeled data.

In addition, imagine having a data table consisting of thousands of rows of data. Suppose that the vast majority of the rows consists of the exact same feature values repeated. In this case, having a lot of data doesn't really do us any good if the model is able to learn only whatever relationships are represented between the repeated feature data and the target. One thing to note is that it is highly unlikely that any given dataset will have every combination of all feature values and therefore completely fill the given feature space. That's okay and is usually expected. You often can get adequate results with enough variation in the data.

The Curse of Dimensionality

Let's discuss a concept known as the "curse of dimensionality," in which the terms dimensionality or dimensions can be used interchangeably with features. The curse of dimensionality, in simple terms, essentially means that adding additional features to a given dataset will cause a nonlinear, exponential growth of the number of possible feature value combinations across all features, collectively referred to as the *feature space*, for a given problem. This increase in the set of possible feature value combinations across all features can have many potentially challenging consequences, which we discuss more in a moment.

In supervised learning, we could likewise call the range of all possible values of the target variable the "target space." For binary classification tasks, this might consist of only two possible values, but for multilabel or regression tasks, this could span a much larger amount of possible values. As a side note, we discuss parametric learning in Appendix A, where parametric machine learning algorithms have the goal of finding the optimal parameter values for the best possible model. All potential values for all model parameters represent what's known as the *parameter space*.

Features-wise, each feature of a dataset can take on different value types and ranges. For example, some features might be binary and take on only one of two possible values; others might be text labels for a given category or class (e.g., cat or dog), and some values might be numeric from a continuous range of possible values (e.g., stock price).

The first problem is that for each feature added, an exponentially increasing amount of additional data is needed in order to fill in an adequate amount of values from the newly enlarged feature space. This is so the model can better learn all of the possible combinations of feature values and underlying relationships and correlations. Without additional data to fill in the additional areas of the feature space needed, the model will lose predictive power; that is, the ability to accurately predict a given target value for a given combination of feature values.

The other consequence of adding additional features and the curse of dimensionality is that the computational speed and memory required for model training increases exponentially, as well, which can also increase model training cost. Certain machine learning algorithms in particular are not well suited to handle high-dimensional data, whereas others are better. There are techniques like *dimensionality reduction* and *feature selection* that we can use to help with this issue, but more rather than fewer features might be needed, depending on performance and accuracy requirements. This means that balancing the curse of dimensionality with performance needs is a trade-off that requires decisions to be made.

In his book, *The Master Algorithm*, Pedro Domingos states that no machine-based learning algorithm is immune to the curse of dimensionality and that it's the second worst problem in machine learning after overfitting (as discussed in Appendixes A and B).

Well-Balanced Data

A related concept is that of having balanced data, which applies to labeled datasets. How balanced a dataset is refers to the proportion of target values in the dataset. Suppose that you have a spam versus not-spam dataset with which you want to train an email spam classifier. If 98% of the data is not-spam emails and only 2% are spam emails, the classifier might not have nearly enough spam examples to learn what real-world spam emails might contain in order to effectively classify all new and not-yet-seen future emails as either spam or not-spam. Having equal proportions of target values is ideal, but that can be difficult to achieve. Often, certain values or classes are simply more rare and therefore unequally represented. There are some data modeling preparation techniques that you can use to try to compensate for this, but they are out of the scope of this discussion.

Highly Representative and Unbiased Data

Another related concept is having representative data. This is similar to having enough data depth to adequately fill the feature space. Having representative data means not only filling the feature space as much as possible, but also representing the range and variety of feature values that a given model will likely see in the real world under all circumstances, present and future. From this perspective, it's important to make sure that not only does the data have enough variety and combinations of feature values, but also that it covers the real-world ranges and combinations likely to be seen after it's put in production.

If you're working with data that is a sample or selection from a much larger dataset, it is important to avoid sample selection bias, or simply sampling bias (a type of selection bias). Avoiding skewed or biased data samples results in highly representative data, as discussed. Randomization is an effective technique to help mitigate sampling bias. Another and much more serious form of bias that should be avoided is known as algorithmic bias, a topic we cover further in Chapter 13.

Complete Data

Data completeness means having all data available that includes leading factors, contributors, indicators, or other ways to describe having the data that has the biggest relationship and influence on the target variable in supervised learning applications. It can be very difficult to create a model to predict something when the data available doesn't include the factors that contribute to that something's value the most.

Sometimes, simply adding additional data features can do the trick, whereas other times, new features must be created from existing features and raw data; in other words, the feature engineering process, as previously mentioned. Part of ensuring that your data is complete also includes making sure to deal with any missing values. There are many ways to deal with missing values, such as imputation and interpolation, but further discussion is out of scope here.

Clean Data

Finally, data cleanliness is a critical part of data readiness. Combined with feature engineering and feature selection, data cleaning and preparation are two of the the most critical tasks in AI and machine learning development. Data cleaning and preparation—often also referred to as *data munging, wrangling, processing, transformation,* and *cleaning*—are usually handled as part of the actual data-science and modeling process, which I cover in-depth in Appendix B. Data is rarely clean and well suited for machine learning and AI tasks. It usually requires a lot of work to clean and process, and practitioners often say that 80% of AI and machine learning work is cleaning data, and the other 20% is the cool stuff; for example, predictive analytics and natural language processing (NLP). This is the classic Pareto Principle example at work.

We can consider data "dirty" for many different reasons. Often data consists of outright errors. For example, a mistake might have been made when preparing the dataset, and the header doesn't match the actual data values. Another example would be an email address data feature labeled as "Email" but all values consisting of a phone number. Sometimes values are incomplete, corrupted, or incorrectly formatted. An example could be phone numbers that are all missing a digit for some reason. Maybe you have text strings in the data that should be numbers. Datasets often consist of strange values such as NA or NaN (not a number), as well. Data that is reliable and error free is a measure of data veracity and is highly sought after.

A Note on Cause and Effect

One very important concept worth mentioning is the difference between cause and effect and how this relates to AI, machine learning, and data science. Even though measuring effects as captured in data can be relatively easy, finding the underlying causes that result in the observed effects is usually much more difficult.

In predictive analytics, there are ways to use the parameters of certain model types (which I cover in Appendix A) as an estimate of the effect a certain feature or factor has on a particular outcome, and thus the relative and quantitative impact a predictor has on the target variable that we are interested in and are trying to predict. Likewise, we can use statistical techniques to measure correlations between features, such as how strongly tied to one another they are. Both of these are very useful techniques and provide useful information, but that information can be misleading.

As a completely contrived example to illustrate the point, perhaps we determine that increased marshmallow sales is directly related to rising home prices, and the correlation between the two seems very strong. We could conclude that marshmallow sale causes the effect of increased home prices, but we are smart and know that this is highly unlikely and there must be something else going on. Usually there are other factors at play that we don't measure or know about (i.e., the aforementioned confounding variables).

In this example, perhaps s'mores have become a super-trendy dessert at restaurants in an area that is experiencing a huge increase in real estate demand and growth due to the influx of large corporations. The true underlying cause of increased home prices here is the influx of corporations, and the increased marshmallow sales is simply a trend in the area, but both are happening at the same time.

Understanding the true underlying causes of a particular effect is ideal because it allows us to gain the deepest understanding and insight, and also make the most appropriate and optimal changes (i.e., pull the right levers by the right amount), to achieve a certain outcome. Various methods of testing and experimentation (e.g., A/B and multivariate) have been devised to determine causal relationships, but these techniques can be difficult or impossible to perform in practice for certain scenarios (e.g., trying to determine the causes of lung cancer). As a result, other techniques have been devised such as *observational causal inference*, which attempts to gain the same insights from observed data.

Summary

Hopefully, this chapter helped you to better understand the definitions, types, and differences between AI and its related fields. We discussed how humans and machines learn, and that AI and machine learning represent the techniques used by machines to learn from data without requiring explicit programming, and then use the knowledge gained to carry out certain tasks. This is what makes machines exhibit intelligence; it is the secret sauce. It allows humans to use analytics in ways they would otherwise not be able to on their own.

Data science, on the other hand, represents what I call the four pillars of data science expertise (business/domain, math/stats, programming, and effective communication) along with a scientific processes in order to cultivate adequate data and iteratively generate deep actionable insights and develop AI solutions.

We also discussed how data powers AI solutions and the important data characteristics and considerations necessary for AI success. Most important, this includes the concepts of data readiness and quality. Both of these are required for AI success.

With the knowledge gained from this chapter, let's next discuss real-world opportunities and applications of AI. This should help spark ideas and provide the needed context for developing an AI vision, which is the subject of Part II of this book.

5

Real-World Applications and Opportunities

One of the questions that I am asked most often is how AI can be used in real-world applications. This chapter is a high-level overview of real-world applications and examples of AI. In particular, the goal of this chapter is to show how AI can create real-world value and help inspire visions for AI innovation.

It's worth noting that this topic could be an entire book in and of itself, so the goal here is for you to understand how the application types work at a high level and to provide one or more examples of how we can apply each one. Before getting into specific real-world applications and examples, let's review the current state of AI and the opportunities available.

AI Opportunities

A 2018 McKinsey AI adoption report (*https://mck.co/2YNGNVb*) noted that AI has gained the most traction in business areas that generate the most value within a given industry, which in order of greatest to lowest adoption includes service operations, product and/or service development, marketing and sales, supply-chain management, manufacturing, risk, human resources, strategy, and corporate finance. Further, it showed that industries adopting AI in the greatest numbers (*https://mck.co/2YNGNVb*) from highest to lowest include telecom, high tech, financial services, professional services, electric power and natural gas, health care systems and services, automotive and assembly, travel/transport/ logistics, retail, and pharma/medical products.

PWC estimates that AI may contribute up to $15.7 trillion to the global economy by 2030 (*https://pwc.to/2DOYhpd*), and McKinsey estimates that certain AI techniques "have the potential to create between $3.5 trillion and $5.8 trillion in value annually across nine business functions in 19 industries." (*https://mck.co/2Hv22VP*)

Teradata estimates that 80% of enterprise companies worldwide have already incorporated some form of production AI into their organization (*http://bit.ly/2HQMwCS*), and Forrester estimates that "truly insights-driven businesses will steal $1.2 trillion per annum from their less-informed peers by 2020." (*http://bit.ly/2HyJNzz*)

As these industries and figures indicate, AI represents huge opportunities and is starting to be widely adopted across industries and business functions. These numbers are likely to increase significantly given the current rise of IoT. IDC predicts global spending on IoT will total nearly $1.4 trillion by 2021, and the global IoT market will grow to $457 billion by 2020 (*http://bit.ly/2VW2Iwk*).

How Can I Apply AI to Real-World Applications?

Another question that I am often asked (usually by executives and managers) is: "How can I apply AI to make decisions and solve problems?" Few people truly understand what AI is, what it can do, or specifically how they can apply it in real-world applications. Ideally a business executive, manager, or practitioner with AI expertise and business acumen can help answer this, but I've included this section for those who either do not have the luxury of AI expertise at the executive level or who would like to be able to figure this out on their own.

Everything involved with AI, machine learning, and data science, including potential applications, can be far from obvious. In fact, it can be downright daunting and overwhelming. How do you know which techniques apply to what use cases? How do you know what AI applications and outcomes are most common for your industry or business function? How do you know what level of granularity you should be thinking at? As an executive or manager, the key is to simply understand the top-level approaches and let the data scientists and machine learning engineers figure out what specific techniques to try. The key word being "try"—it's an experimental and scientific process!

Translation between the business and technical sides of AI is one of the primary challenges in my experience. This is partly because AI is very technical and difficult for many people to understand in general. It's also because the sky is almost the limit with AI and harnessing data to create value.

Let me explain further. Most AI and machine learning techniques can be applied to all industries and business functions in one way or another. Every company has data regardless of whether it is an early-stage startup or enterprise company, or whether it's a health care, manufacturing, or retail company. Likewise, every business function (i.e., department) has data regardless of whether it's marketing, sales, or operations.

Insurance companies want to predict customer churn just like retail companies do, and both can use the same techniques. We can use image recognition to replace key cards for getting into office buildings just like we can use it to diagnose cancer in radiographic images. In this case, the technique used and goals of recognizing or identifying certain objects in images is more or less the same. The only real difference is the data being used and the industry application. This can often be a difficult thing for those who are less familiar with AI to understand, and also for those more familiar to explain.

A combination of business folks, domain experts, and AI practitioners must work collaboratively to determine what opportunities are available, select and prioritize the ones to pursue, and determine which approaches, as outlined in this chapter, will work best. Most of the following approaches aren't specific to an industry; rather, they're customizable to specific data and goals. Also, you should strategically identify and prioritize AI opportunities and applications based on the potential value (and/or ROI) to the industry or business function being considered.

Table 5-1 should answer some of your questions, particularly around ways that you can apply AI. These techniques are applicable in one way or another to mostly every type of industry and business function. Because there are far too many different industries and business functions for it to be practical to include in this discussion, I've taken the approach of providing a specific type of goal and then listing one or more techniques to help accomplish it. This list and the contents of this chapter in general are not exhaustive.

Table 5-1. Examples of AI techniques by goal

Goal	Technique
Predict a continuous numeric value (e.g., stock price)	Supervised learning (regression)
Predict (or assign) a class, category, or label (e.g., spam or not-spam)	Supervised learning (classification)
Create groupings of similar data (to understand each group's profile; e.g., market segments)	Unsupervised learning (clustering)

Goal	Technique
Identify highly unusual and/or dangerous outliers (e.g., network security, fraud)	Unsupervised learning (anomaly detection)
Personalize your product, services, features, and/or content to customers	Recommendations (e.g., media, products, services); Ranking/ scoring; Personalization (e.g., content, offers, messaging, interactions, layout)
Detect, classify, and/or identify specific spatial (space), temporal (time), or spatiotemporal (both; e.g., audio, video) patterns; Detect and classify human sentiment (from voice, text, images, and video)	Recognition (image, audio, speech, video, handwriting, text); Computer vision (e.g., detection: motion, gesture, expression, sentiment); Natural language processing (NLP)
Have AI self-learn to optimize a process over time (e.g., game playing, automation)	Reinforcement learning
Allow people and processes to find highly relevant information quickly and easily (e.g., articles, images, videos, documents)	Search (text, speech, visual); Ranking/scoring
Turning unstructured text/speech (e.g., subjective feedback, comments, documents) into quantifiable, objective, and actionable analytics, insights, and predictions	Natural language processing (NLP)
Create a personal or virtual assistant, chatbot, or language-driven agent (e.g., Amazon Alexa, Apple Siri)	Natural language processing (NLP); Natural language understanding (NLU); Examples: question answering and conversations
Create better forecasts	Time–series methods
Generate data from one kind to another (e.g., text, audio, image, video, speech)	Generative AI (including natural language generation [NLG])
Automate aspects of the data science and machine learning process	AutoML
Build hybrid applications involving software, hardware, and firmware (e.g., autonomous vehicles, robots, IoT)	All techniques may be applicable either individually or in combination

Goal	Technique
Predict or translate a sequence (e.g., language translation; predict characters, words, or sentences)	Deep learning; Sequence-to-sequence learning
Augmented intelligence or automate processes (e.g., repetitive tedious tasks, decision making, insights)	All techniques might be applicable either individually or in combination

It's worth mentioning that you can combine many of these techniques into a single AI application—an application that leverages multiple approaches. Remember that pretty much all AI today is narrow and a bit of a one-trick pony. This means that we don't yet have algorithms that can do more than one of these at the same time. Again, the trick is to have business folks, domain experts, and AI practitioners working together to choose the best approaches and combinations as needed.

Real-World Applications and Examples

Now let's dive into an overview of real-world AI applications by approach category and with examples. The examples given are far from exhaustive and are predominantly business-focused (we will go over people-focused examples in Chapter 9). Also, I could have grouped applications by industry or business function, but instead I've chosen to group by type of approach given what we talked about earlier regarding how each approach can most likely be applied in some way across any industry or business function.

The idea is that you gain a solid understanding of the different types of techniques and applications without becoming bogged down in the technical details, thus the focus on explainability. We'll use the word "algorithm" in an oversimplified way to describe either a single algorithm, model, or software program that uses multiple algorithms. In each category, I discuss the types of data inputs, the algorithm as a black box (for simplicity purposes, and even when the real algorithms aren't black boxes), and the output(s).

Because this is meant to be a high-level overview, you are encouraged to further research any specific applications of interest, and how they are being applied in your industry or business function of choice. There are also many resources available to learn more about the technical details and specific algorithms used, as well.

PREDICTIVE ANALYTICS

Prediction, aka *predictive analytics* or *predictive modeling*, is the process of predicting an output based on labeled, and sometimes unlabeled, input data. Predictive analytics in the context of machine learning and AI can be further categorized as either regression or classification.

The following two subsections on prediction cover making predictions from labeled (supervised) data. Predictive analytics involving time–series and sequential data is covered in a later section.

Regression

Figure 5-1 demonstrates how regression is the process of taking labeled input data, passing the data through a predictive model (we assume black boxes throughout for simplicity), and generating a numeric value from a continuous number range (e.g., a stock closing price).

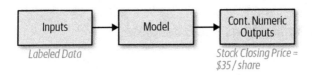

Figure 5-1. Regression

Applications include customer lifetime value and net profit (*http://bit.ly/ 30DDpxB*), revenue and growth forecasting (*http://bit.ly/2YKUl3H*), dynamic pricing (*http://bit.ly/2Hv4VG9*), credit (*http://bit.ly/30DNwCM*) and loan default risk (*http://www.underwrite.ai*), and algorithmic stock trading (*http://bit.ly/2Qgg4xk*).

Classification

Classification is the process of taking labeled input data, passing the data through a model (classifier), and assigning one or more classes (categories/ labels) to the input, as depicted in Figure 5-2.

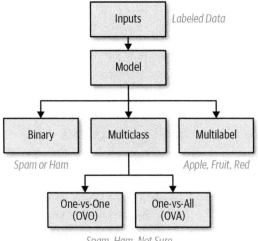

Figure 5-2. Classification

A standard example of a binary classifier is an email spam filter. An email represents the input data that is passed through a classifier model, which then determines whether the email is spam or not-spam, not-spam being a phrase used in this case to refer to a good, non-spam email. Spam emails are sent to the spam folder, and not-spam emails are sent to the inbox.

Suppose a third class was included and labeled as "unsure." Now the classifier can assign three possible classes to a given email input: spam, not-spam, and unsure. This is an example of multiclass classification because there are more than two possible classes. In this case, the email client could have a "Possibly Spam" folder for the user to review and verify each email, thus teaching the classifier how to better distinguish between spam and not-spam.

When there are three or more possible classes to assign to an input, the algorithm can either select a single class to assign to the input or it can assign probabilities for each of the possible classes for the given input. In the latter case, the class with the highest probability can be used as the assigned class, or the probabilities for all classes can be used in whatever customized way you want. In this example, suppose that a new incoming email is determined to be 85% likely to be spam, 10% likely to be not-spam, and 5% likely to be unsure. You could either just say the email is spam since the probability is highest or use the different probabilities in another way.

Lastly, certain algorithms can assign multiple labels to the same input. An example related to image recognition could be an image of a red apple as input data, with multiple classes assigned to the image such as red, apple, and fruit. Assigning all three classes to the image would be appropriate in this example.

Applications include credit risk and loan approval (*http://bit.ly/30BRI68*) and customer churn (*https://amzn.to/2WYyNQv*). Classification can be combined with recognition applications as discussed in a later section of this chapter.

PERSONALIZATION AND RECOMMENDER SYSTEMS

Recommender systems are a form of personalization that use existing information to make suggestions and results that are more relevant to individual users. You can use this to increase customer conversions and sales, delight, and retention], for example. In fact, Amazon increased its revenue by 35% with the addition of these engines, and 75% of the content watched on Netflix is generated by its recommendations (*http://bit.ly/2CjeoM5*).

Recommender systems are a specific type of information filtering system. You can also use search, ranking, and scoring techniques for personalization, which we discuss later in the chapter. Recommender systems make recommendations by taking inputs such as items (e.g., products, articles, music, movies) or user data and passing the data through a recommender model, or engine, as shown in Figure 5-3.

Figure 5-3. Recommender systems

It's worth mentioning the "cold-start problem" associated with recommender systems. The cold-start problem refers to situations in which an intelligent application does not yet have enough information to make highly personalized and relevant recommendations to a specific user or group. An example includes users who have not yet generated information about their preferences, interests, or purchase history. Another example is when items (e.g., clothes, products, videos, songs) are first introduced to the public. There are multiple techniques that you can use to help address this problem, but because of space restrictions, we won't discuss those here.

Recommender system applications include generating recommendations for products, movies, music and playlists (*http://bit.ly/2VN5AH6*), books, and TV shows (e.g., Amazon, Netflix, Spotify). In addition to recommendations, personalized content can also include news, feeds, emails, and targeted advertising (e.g., Twitter). Other examples include personalized medicine and medical treatment plans (*http://bit.ly/2XoeRN6*), personalized images and thumbnails (e.g., YouTube (*http://bit.ly/2YJ6TbU*), Netflix (*http://bit.ly/2EkPQ8f*), Yelp (*http://bit.ly/2wgh5fy*)), wine recommendations (*https://cnb.cx/2HJmRf1*), personalized shopping such as perfect jacket matching (*https://www.thenorthface.com/xps*), fashion matching (e.g., StitchFix (*http://bit.ly/2Ep11ws*)), and automated complete outfit recommendations (*https://www.findmine.com*).

COMPUTER VISION

Computer vision is a broad field that includes pattern recognition (another approach discussed in the next section) when it involves visual information such as images and video. Computer vision represents the process of taking inputs such as photo images, video still images, and a sequence of images (video), passing the data through a model, and producing an output, as illustrated in Figure 5-4.

The output can be recognition, detection, and identification of specific objects, features, or activities. Vision-related applications imply a degree of automation, particularly when automating vision, typically requiring a human in applications (e.g., inspection). Machine vision is a term used to describe similar and somewhat overlapping techniques used in industrial applications such as inspection, process control, measurement, and robotics.

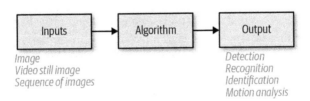

Figure 5-4. Computer vision

There are many very interesting and powerful applications of computer vision, and the use cases are growing rapidly. For example, we can use computer vision for:

- Video analytics and content screening (*http://bit.ly/2ErGuHJ*)

- Lipreading (*http://bit.ly/2JAY1kP*)

- Giving "sight" to autonomous vehicles (e.g., cars, drones)

- Video recognition and description (*http://bit.ly/2WZ9xJX*)

- Video captioning (*http://bit.ly/2LZrKGe*)

- Human interaction prediction (*http://bit.ly/2WqBFZG*) such as hugs and handshakes

- Robotics and control systems (*https://www.bostondynamics.com*)

- Crowd density estimation (*http://bit.ly/2Hu6hRs*)

- People counting (*http://bit.ly/2VKhstc*) (e.g., lines (*http://bit.ly/2WVedAI*), infrastructure planning, retail)

- Inspection and quality control (*http://bit.ly/2QiKIGh*)

- Retail customer foot traffic path and engagement analytics (*http://bit.ly/2WjiSze*)

Unmanned aerial vehicles (UAVs) are vehicles usually referred to as drones. By applying computer vision, drones are able to perform inspections (e.g., oil pipelines, cell towers), explore areas and buildings, help with mapping tasks, and deliver purchased goods (*https://amzn.to/2wgiRNK*). Computer vision is also becoming widely used for public safety, security, and surveillance. Of course, care should be taken so that applications are ethical and for the benefit of people.

One final thing to note about computer vision. I used the term "sight" earlier. Humans are able to sense the environment and world around them through the five common senses, which are sight, smell, hearing, touch, and taste. Information is "sensed" through sensing organs and then passed to our nervous system to translate the information and also decide what action or reaction should occur, if any. Computer vision is the analogous mechanism for giving AI applications the sense of sight.

PATTERN RECOGNITION

Pattern recognition involves taking unstructured input data, passing the data through a model, and detecting the presence of a particular pattern (detection), assigning a class to a recognized pattern (classification), or actually identifying the subject of the recognized pattern (identification), as illustrated in Figure 5-5.

Inputs in these applications can include images (including video—a sequence of still images), audio (e.g., speech, music, sounds), and text. Text can be further characterized as digital, handwritten, or printed (e.g., paper, checks, license plates).

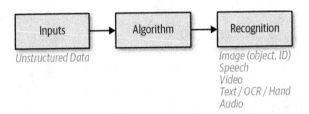

Figure 5-5. Pattern recognition

For cases in which images are the inputs, the goal might be object detection, recognition, identification, or all three. A good example is facial recognition. Training a model to detect a face in an image and classify the detected object as a face is an example of object recognition where the object is an unidentified face. "Detection" is a term used to indicate that something is detected that differs from the background. It can also include object location measurements and specification of a bounding box around the object detected. Recognition is the process of actually assigning a class or label (face in this example) to the detected object, and identification takes this a step further and assigns an identity to the face detected (e.g., Alex's face). Figure 5-6 presents some image recognition examples.

Figure 5-6. Image recognition and detection

Biometric identification such as facial recognition can be used to automatically tag people in images. Recognizing specific people by their fingerprints is another form of biometric identification (*http://bit.ly/2YHta9W*).

Other applications include:

- Reading text from images and video (*http://bit.ly/2wfHPNi*)
- Image tagging and categorization (*http://bit.ly/2HLprBu*)
- Image-based automobile damage-level assessment for automotive insurance (*https://cnb.cx/2VKFapc*)
- Information extraction from images and videos (*http://bit.ly/2Es1orF*)
- Face and voice-based emotion recognition (*http://bit.ly/2JBiw11*)
- Facial expression recognition (*https://thght.works/2X7dyfH*)

Audio recognition applications include:

- Speech recognition (*http://bit.ly/2I33b43*)

- Converting speech to text (*http://bit.ly/2Wi8tUl*)

- Speaker isolation and identification (*https://zd.net/2M2uzGH*)

- Sentiment analysis from voice, real-time customer service and sales phone call emotional intelligence analysis (*http://bit.ly/2X8HLus*)

- Logging and deforestation sound detection (*http://bit.ly/2wkqq61*)

- Flaw detection (e.g., due to manufacturing defects or part failure)

Lastly, handwritten or printed text can be converted to digital text through the process of optical character recognition (OCR) and handwriting recognition. Text can also be converted to speech, but that can be considered more of a generative application as opposed to a recognition application. We discuss generative applications later in this chapter.

CLUSTERING AND ANOMALY DETECTION

Clustering and anomaly detection, shown in Figure 5-7 are the two most common unsupervised machine learning techniques. They are also considered pattern recognition techniques.

Both processes take input data, which is unlabeled, pass it through the appropriate algorithm (clustering or anomaly detection), and then produces groups in the clustering case, or a determination if something is anomalous in the case of anomaly detection. Let's discuss clustering first.

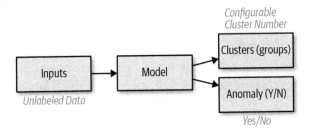

Figure 5-7. Clustering and anomaly detection (different models)

Clustering turns unlabeled data into groupings of similar data. The number of groups is determined by the person performing the clustering task, usually a data scientist. There isn't really a right or wrong number of clusters, but often a number is selected through trial and error and/or is considered an ideal number for a given application.

Because the data is unlabeled, the practitioner must assign some sort of meaning or label to each group that best describes it (e.g., sports enthusiasts). The model then can be used to assign new data to one of the groups and thus assume the label or description of that group. This can be thought of as a form of predictive classification; that is, assigning a class (via a labeled group) to a new data point. Assigning new data points (e.g., customers) to clusters (aka segments) provides a way to better target, personalize, and strategically position products and sell to each group in an appropriate way.

Clustering applications include market/customer segmentation and targeting (*http://bit.ly/2JAyNmE*), 3D medical image segmentation (*http://bit.ly/2HMohFJ*), product groupings for shopping (*http://bit.ly/2VHm2IL*), and social network analysis.[1]

Anomaly detection is a technique used to detect data patterns that are anomalous; that is, highly unusual, outside the norm, or abnormal. Anomaly detection applications include audio-based flaw and crack detection (*http://bit.ly/30F3cpd*), cybersecurity, network security, quality control (e.g., manufacturing defect detection), and computer and network system health (e.g., NASA (*https://go.nasa.gov/2Qglwiv*), fault and error detection (*http://bit.ly/2M33GCi*)).

In the case of anomaly detection applications in cybersecurity and network security, common threats include malware, ransomware, computer viruses, system and memory attacks, denial of service (DoS) attacks, phishing, unwanted program execution, credential theft, data transfer and theft, and more. Needless to say that there's no shortage of use cases for anomaly detection.

NATURAL LANGUAGE

Natural language is a very interesting and exciting area of AI development and use. It is usually broken into three subcategories: natural language processing

---

1 Hu, H. (2015). Graph-Based Models for Unsupervised High Dimensional Data Clustering and Network Analysis. UCLA. ProQuest ID: Hu_ucla_0031D_13496. Merritt ID: ark:/13030/m50z9b68. Retrieved from eScholarship (*http://bit.ly/2Wimlhl*).

(NLP), natural language generation (NLG), and natural language understanding (NLU). Let's cover each of these individually.

NLP

NLP is the process of taking language input in the form of text, speech, or handwriting, passing it through an NLP algorithm, and then generating structured data as output, as shown in Figure 5-8. There are many potential NLP use cases and outputs.

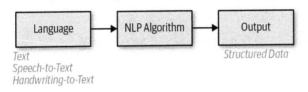

Figure 5-8. NLP

It's worth mentioning that NLP is sometimes considered a superset of NLG and NLU, and therefore natural language applications in AI can be considered a form of NLP in general. Others think of it as a specific set of natural language applications, some of which we discuss now.

Specific tasks and techniques associated with NLP include quantified and objective text analytics, speech recognition (speech to text), topic modeling (e.g., topics and the prominence of each discovered in a document), text classification (e.g., Game of Thrones), sentiment analysis (e.g., positive, negative, neutral), entity detection (e.g., person, place), named recognition (e.g., Grand Canyon, Miles Davis), semantic similarity (e.g., similarity in meaning between individual words and text in general), part-of-speech tagging (e.g., noun, verb) and machine translation (e.g., English-to-French translation).

One specific NLP application involves recording business meetings, transcribing them, and then providing a meeting summary (*https://reason8.ai*) with analytics around topics discussed and meeting performance (*https:// www.chorus.ai*). Another application (*https://textio.co*) uses NLP to analyze job descriptions and assign an overall score based on factors such as gender neutrality, tone, wording, phrasing, and more. It also provides recommendations for changes that would improve the score and overall job description.

Other applications include:

- Sentiment-based news aggregation (*http://bit.ly/2Qf8p2q*)
- Social media sentiment-driven investments (*http://bit.ly/30E8hOv*) and brand monitoring (*http://bit.ly/2M35gEe*)
- Message board-based parental vaccine concern insights (*http://bit.ly/ 2YGi1Gn*)
- Sentiment analysis of movie reviews (*http://bit.ly/2M5BxuB*) and product reviews (*http://bit.ly/2WfiQIN*)
- Animal sound translation (*http://bit.ly/2JZGIJU*)

Many cloud-based service providers are now offering NLP services and APIs that provide some of this functionality.

NLG

NLG is the process of taking language in the form of structured data as input, passing it through an NLG algorithm, and then generating language as output, as depicted in Figure 5-9. The language output can be in the form of text or text-to-speech, for example. Examples of structured input data are sports statistics from a game, advertising performance data, or company financial data.

Figure 5-9. NLG

Applications include:

- Automatically generating text summaries based on sentences and documents (*http://bit.ly/30F6JUO*) (*https://arxiv.org/abs/1602.06023*, *https://arxiv.org/abs/1603.07252*)

- Recaps (e.g., news and sports)

- Stories about images (*http://bit.ly/30C2lpf*)

- Business intelligence narratives (*http://bit.ly/2JVWQvW*)

- Recruiting people for hospital research studies (*http://bit.ly/2Y4LLgg*)

- Patient hospital bills in natural language format (*http://bit.ly/2QjBvNZ*)

- Fantasy football draft summaries and weekly matchup recaps (*http://bit.ly/2WLzNeV*)

- Property descriptions and real estate market reports (*http://bit.ly/2WLzNeV*)

- Associated Press corporate earnings stories (*http://bit.ly/31I6WqP*)

Andrej Karpathy (*http://bit.ly/2WPniKm*) created models that automatically generate Wikipedia articles, baby names, math papers, computer code, and Shakespeare. Other applications include generating handwritten text (*http://bit.ly/2WL2kMN*) and even jokes (*https://arxiv.org/pdf/1703.09902.pdf*).

NLU

Lastly, NLU is the process of taking language input (text, speech, or handwriting), passing the input through an NLU algorithm, and then generating "understanding" of the language as an output, as shown in Figure 5-10. The understanding generated can be used to take an action, generate a response, answer a question, have a conversation, and more.

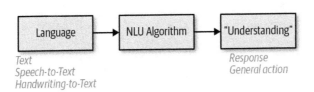

Figure 5-10. NLU

It's very important to note that the term understanding can be very deep and philosophical and also involves concepts like comprehension. Comprehension loosely refers to the ability to not only understand information (as opposed to just rote memorization), but also to incorporate that understanding into existing knowledge and use it as part of one's ever-growing knowledge base. Lack of human-like language understanding and comprehension is one of the major shortcomings of natural language–based AI applications today, and the shortcoming stems from the extraordinary difficulty associated with machines achieving human-like language understanding. Remember our discussion of AI-complete/AI-hard problems? This is definitely one example.

Without getting into a full-blown philosophical discussion, let's just use the term understanding to mean that the algorithm (again, hugely oversimplified) is able to do more with the input language than just parse it and perform simpler tasks like text analytics. NLU is a significantly more difficult problem to solve than NLP and NLG (and for AI problems in general) and is a major foundational component to achieving artificial general intelligence (AGI).

Given the current state-of-the-art for NLU, applications include personal and virtual assistants (*http://bit.ly/2Roo8cN*), chatbots (*http://bit.ly/2x4aSnm*), customer success (support and service) agents (*https://www.answeriq.com*), and sales agents. These applications usually include some form of written or spoken conversation, often centered around information gathering (*http://bit.ly/31DMoiX*), question answering (*https://arxiv.org/abs/1412.1632*) or some sort of assistance.

Specific examples include personal assistants such as Amazon's Alexa, Apple Siri, Google's Assistant, and Nuance's Nina (*http://bit.ly/2WVaGGJ*). Chatbot examples include an oil and lube expert (*http://bit.ly/2KWppKb*), job interviews (*https://www.apli.jobs/*), student loan money mentorship (*https://www.nextgenvest.com*), and a business insurance expert agent (*http://bit.ly/2J2ak7p*). This is a very active area of research and potential advancement in AI, so it's definitely worth keeping an eye on it.

TIME-SERIES AND SEQUENCE-BASED DATA

In many cases, data is captured in sequences in which the data order is important and is determined by a specific index. One of the most common data sequence indexes is time, and data sequenced by time is called time–series data. Daily stock price fluctuation during market hours, DNA sequences, IoT sensor data, and scientific phenomena such as wind patterns are good examples of time–series data. Time–series analysis and modeling can be used for learning, predicting, and forecasting time dependencies, including those due to trends, seasonality, cycles, and noise.

Sequences of letters and words are also valid types of sequential data for certain applications, and these sequences are given labels such as n-grams, skip-grams, sentences, paragraphs, and even language itself, where language is either spoken, written, or digitally represented. Audio and video data is sequential, as well.

Applications include:

- Prediction (regression and classification)
- anomaly detection (*http://bit.ly/2WNz8Vh*)
- forecasting future currency exchange rates (*http://bit.ly/2Ilikku*)
- real-time health trend tracking (*http://bit.ly/31DKRcN*)
- marketplace forecasting (*https://ubr.to/2ITkIOn*)
- weather forecasting (*http://bit.ly/2KVoEOt*)
- sequence-based recommendations (*http://bit.ly/31FOZsT*)
- sentiment analysis (*https://arxiv.org/pdf/1801.07883.pdf*)
- DNA sequence classification (*http://bit.ly/2WUGw6s*)
- text sequence generation (*https://stanford.io/2WPh5Tt*)
- sequence-to-sequence prediction (*http://bit.ly/2RmWobJ*), such as machine translation (*http://bit.ly/2XUGQOH*)

SEARCH, INFORMATION EXTRACTION, RANKING, AND SCORING

Many powerful AI applications are centered around finding, extracting, and ranking (or scoring) information. This applies mainly to unstructured and semi-structured data in particular, with examples including text documents, web pages, images, and videos. We can use this type of data, along with structured data in some cases, for information extraction, providing search results or prioritized recommendations, and ranking or scoring items in terms of relevance, importance, or priority. This group of techniques is associated with personalization in many cases because search results and other items can be ordered or ranked by most-to-least relevant to the particular user or group.

Currently, many search tasks are conducted by typing or speaking into a search engine such as Google, which is powered by Google's proprietary AI-based search algorithm. Ecommerce applications also have their own search engines to search for products. Search can be driven by text, sound (voice), and visual inputs. Text-based search applications include Google Search (I bet you saw that one coming!), Microsoft Bing, and a decentralized, transparent, and community-driven search (*https://www.presearch.io*).

Sound- and image-based search applications include:

- Clothes (*https://markable.ai*) and fashion search (*https://www.syte.ai/retailers*)
- Song and artist search (*http://bit.ly/2RhGRd2*)
- Pinterest Lens search (*http://bit.ly/2Zt8WRB*)
- Image and video search (*http://bit.ly/2XT1IpR*)
- Font search (*http://bit.ly/2WPhjKj*)

Visual search is conducted based on the contents of the image. There are already shopping applications that work this way. The user takes a picture and submits it to the visual search engine. The image is then used to generate relevant results such as clothing. Some of these image-based engines can also present visually similar items and recommendations, as well.

Ranking and scoring methods are alternatives to classification techniques, and applications include:

- Sales (*http://bit.ly/2MOEUGn*) lead (*http://bit.ly/31B1CVY*) scoring
- Information and document retrieval (*https://arxiv.org/pdf/1710.05649.pdf*) (e.g., webpage search)
- Machine translation (*http://bit.ly/2KX5aMi*)
- Disease-causing gene search and identification (*http://bit.ly/2ZqcFiO*)
- Sequence-based protein structure prediction (*http://bit.ly/2KX5aMi*)

REINFORCEMENT LEARNING

Reinforcement learning (RL) is a completely different AI technique than those described thus far (recall that we mentioned it briefly when discussing the ways that humans learn). The general idea is that there is a virtual agent taking actions in a virtual environment with the goal of getting positive rewards. Each action can cause a change in the state of the environment, and each action taken is determined by a model called a *policy*. The policy tries to determine the optimal action to take when in a given state. Don't worry if this doesn't make much sense; I give an example that will hopefully make this more clear. Figure 5-11 shows a visual representation of RL.

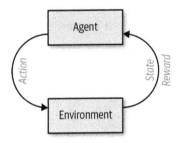

Figure 5-11. Reinforcement learning

You can consider Ms. Pac-Man (why not call her Ms. Pac-Woman?) as an example. On any given screen, Ms. Pac-Man has the goal of eating all the dots, but in a bigger picture sense has the goal of scoring the maximum amount of points possible. Why is scoring the maximum amount of points the true goal, or *why* of the game? First, the more points you score, the more free lives you get and therefore the longer you're able to play and continue to accrue more points. Second, you get serious bragging rights if you can complete the game or set the world record, and who doesn't want that?

In this case, the points are the reward, Ms. Pac-Man is the agent, the environment is the screen, and the human in the loop (the player) is the policy that determines the actions to take through a joystick. The environment has states, as well. There's the regular noninvincible Ms. Pac-Man that has to dodge ghosts that are chasing her while eating dots and fruit, and then there's the invincible Ms. Pac-Man that ate the pill of invincibility (I have no clue what it's actually called) and can eat ghosts for a lot of extra points. The change between invincible and not invincible is a change of state of the environment, and also of the agent's abilities within the environment.

It's worth noting that people playing Ms. Pac-Man are sometimes driven by the goal of finishing screens and getting as far as possible rather than maximizing points. In that case, people will just use the invincible state to hurry up and eat as many dots as possible unimpeded and might not maximize points by eating ghosts. Suppose that you have an RL application for which the goals is to maximize points, though. In this case the application will try to learn how to do that and that will involve eating as many ghosts and fruits as possible.

There is one more thing to mention here. Scoring points is a positive reward. Touching a ghost and losing a life is a negative reward. Over time, the RL application should try to maximize getting points and minimize losing lives. Although this example is framed in the context of a game, we can use RL in many other ways.

Applications include:

- Beating the world champion of Go (*http://bit.ly/2FgrMEo*)
- Finding the optimal configuration for a neural network (*http://bit.ly/2FnMDFd*)
- Robotics (*http://bit.ly/2WWyIBb*)
- Optimizing medication dosing (*http://bit.ly/2RjLdk7*)
- Traffic signal control optimization (*http://bit.ly/2x3bcmA*)
- Chemical reaction optimization (*http://bit.ly/31FY84A*)
- Autonomous driving (*http://bit.ly/2Zxr25a*)

HYBRID, AUTOMATION, AND MISCELLANEOUS

In this last section on real-world applications, I point out some applications that I have categorized as hybrid or miscellaneous because they involve multiple, combined approaches or do not fit into any of the categories already discussed.

Example applications include:

- Autonomous self-driving cars and fleets (*https://www.nutonomy.com*) and Self-driving shuttles (*http://bit.ly/2KnkFO6*)

- Real-time flight route prediction and air traffic flow optimization (*http://bit.ly/2IoIGSY*)

- Driverless racing (*https://roborace.com*)

- Warehouse logistics and picking automation (*http://bit.ly/2MWHHgQ*)

- Dog (*http://bit.ly/31OzcIi*) and human-like robotics (*http://bit.ly/2KnZJqq*)

- Robotic human-like hand dexterity (*http://bit.ly/2WMajJh*)

- Coral reef monitoring jellyfish robots (*https://bbc.in/2XT64xd*)

- Hospital patient–care workflow automation (*http://bit.ly/2XmuoMf*)

- Disease outbreak prediction (*http://aime.life*)

- Reduction in cooling bills (*http://bit.ly/2Zrz8w3*)

- Space weather prediction (*https://www.swpc.noaa.gov*)

- Meeting scheduling automation (*https://x.ai*)

- Predictive maintenance (*http://bit.ly/2ZtJAmG*)

- Intelligent systems such as those associated with the IoT

Another really interesting field of AI development is generative applications, which basically refers to AI that is able to generate something from an input of a certain type for a given application. Some examples include:

- Generating images from text (*http://bit.ly/2FeXscQ*)

- Generating image and image region descriptions (*http://bit.ly/2XkaPTl*)

- Generating images of galaxies and volcanoes (*https://go.nature.com/2XVfXdu*)

- Generating images from sketches (*http://www.k4ai.com/cgan*)

- Generating music from song characteristics (*https://www.jukedeck.com*)

- Diverse speech (*http://bit.ly/2IUpifk*) and voice generation (*http://bit.ly/2XWAjDo*)

- Synthesized singing (*http://bit.ly/2L4LdDB*)

- Software code generation from design mockups (*http://bit.ly/2XVg6h2*)

- Generating video from text (*https://www.wibbitz.com*)

Other applications include transformations such as style transfer (e.g., transforming a normal image to a "fine art" rendition (*https://deepart.io*) in the style of Van Gough or Picasso). Another technique is called super-resolution imaging (*http://bit.ly/2WP86So*), where a 2D image is converted to a 3D image by generating the missing 3D image data (*http://bit.ly/2KlWJuv*). Finally, automatic colorization of images (*http://bit.ly/2MRa543*) is another interesting AI application.

Summary

Hopefully this chapter has helped answer questions, or at least given you ideas about how you can take advantage of different AI approaches to solve problems and achieve goals. As we've discussed, there's no shortage of different techniques. The key is to understand the available options at an appropriate level and then choose and prioritize high-value use cases and applications as part of your overall AI vision and strategy. This is an important part of AIPB, and we now turn our attention to developing an AI vision.

Developing an AI Vision

So far, we've covered AI for People and Business (AIPB), and how it can help guide end-to-end, goal-driven innovation and value creation with AI. We've also provided the AI and machine learning context and understanding required to create a high-level AI vision and strategy.

Now let's turn our discussion to developing an AI vision. A great vision for a business, product, or service based on AI will help produce a great strategy for AI success. As one of the main topics of this book, an AI vision should also be aligned to goals for both people and businesses alike. This is to ensure maximum and long-lasting success. The vision should be materialized as a vision statement as covered in Part I.

To help you develop an AI vision, Part II begins with an in-depth discussion of *why* to pursue AI, followed by how to define AI vision–aligned goals for different stakeholders such as businesses, customers, and users. We then go over what people need and want, and how to turn that into great AI-based products and better human experiences.

6

The Importance of Why

Why is AI valuable for people and businesses? Why can AI improve human experiences and business success? Why should AI be pursued with caution? Why do some AI initiatives succeed and others fail? And lastly, why do we need a new framework to help plan for and maximize AI initiative success.

It all begins with *why*. This chapter centers on the importance of defining the *why* for any AI vision and strategy, as well as the ability to generate a shared vision and understanding among key stakeholders using the *why* and great leadership.

Start with Why

It is critical to understand and be able to explain the *why* of things before focusing on the *how* and *what*. Nobody illustrated that better for me than Simon Sinek in his seminal book, *Start With Why*,[1] and his related TED talk, "How Great Leaders Inspire Action" (*http://bit.ly/2Qi7DSg*).

He argues that every business knows "what" they do and, sometimes, "how" they do it. But rarely do businesses and people know "why" they do what they do. This is a deep concept, and as Mr. Sinek points out, the *why* isn't a result or outcome like increasing revenue (which is more of a goal or objective). The *why* is the belief, the grand vision, the true meaning.

Think about it. It can take companies a very long time, even with a lot of people involved, to come up with messaging around a company's vision, mission,

---

1 Sinek, Simon. *Start with Why: How Great Leaders Inspire Everyone to Take Action*. New York: Portfolio/ Penguin, 2009.

and value proposition. I've been through the process of developing all of this multiple times with different companies (including my own!), and it always amazes me how much complexity, volume of words, opinions, and back-and-forth dialog are required before finally getting to simple and effective messaging that actually speaks to the true *why*. A very apropos quote attributed to Mark Twain (*http://bit.ly/2Eta93e*), is "If I had more time, I would have written you a shorter letter."

Sinek argues that great leaders and businesses are great because they think, act, and communicate from the inside out; or in other words, they start with *why*. He goes on to say that people don't buy what you do, they buy why you do it. It's all about people understanding and buying what you believe, not what you do. Adopting this mindset and being driven by this concept is easier said than done.

Some people refer to the *why* with terms like "goal driven," "outcomes driven," or "benefits driven." All of these are perfectly fine, but in my opinion only when viewed through the lens of start with *why*. I have extended this concept to everything I do on a daily basis. I try to start with *why* when speaking to colleagues, employees, family, and friends. With enough practice, it becomes quite natural, and people's reactions, apparent interest, and understanding are more than noticeable. It pays dividends.

So why does starting with *why* matter in the context of AI and how can we use this concept to improve human experiences and business success? The reason is that the *why*, when fully defined and understood upfront, serves as the North Star or guiding light for everything else. It helps those creating an AI vision and strategy better and more easily explain the potential value and outcomes of AI initiatives. This hopefully then inspires, motivates, and excites everyone involved.

Product Leadership and Perspective

As a person who has held executive leadership roles in both advanced analytics (AI, machine learning, data science) and product management, I view many things through the lens of making great products. To make great products, a product leader must understand (nonexhaustive):

- What makes products great
- What constitutes great product design and UX

- How to best map people's problems to solutions that take advantage of technology
- How to create a product vision and strategy
- How to execute a product strategy to build and deliver great products
- How to communicate a product vision to all stakeholders including the product development team
- How to determine the ROI of products
- How to properly assess markets and competition
- How to measure product success

For the remainder of this book, I discuss AI-based innovation along with developing an AI vision and strategy through the lens of making great products as outlined. An innovation framework known as "Jobs to Be Done" presents an interesting perspective in that people hire businesses, products, and services in order to get a "job" done; or, put another way, to accomplish something. Similarly, we can think of AI as something that can be hired to get a job done.

Leadership and Generating a Shared Vision and Understanding

We have established that the *why* is critical, but now what? How do you use it, what is it used for, and how do you turn *why* into a successful business, product, or human experience?

For me it begins with what I refer to as *generating a shared vision and understanding*. I use this phrase regularly, and this capability is critical. A shared vision and understanding sounds simple and high level, but this is a very deep concept for me. Let's discuss why, and set some relevant context for the remainder of this book.

There are two distinct parts to this: shared vision and shared understanding. A shared vision for me is where all stakeholders completely understand *why* a solution is being proposed and built and what the solution will be exactly. This includes outlining all intended benefits and outcomes.

A shared understanding is critical to properly setting expectations and is where everyone completely understands the following:

- What the prioritized product roadmap looks like
- Why the roadmap is prioritized in a particular way
- How the solution will be defined and built
- Development progress at any time (including potential blockers and risks)
- The existence and status of any upcoming important milestones and deliverables

Issues, unmet expectations, misalignment, and failure can happen when stakeholders do not have a shared vision and understanding. The same is true when target users or customers do not properly understand many of these things, as well; most important among them the purpose, benefits, and how to use the solution.

A very important concept for me here is consensus versus collaboration. Seth Godin is quoted as saying, "Nothing is what happens when everyone has to agree." (*http://bit.ly/2X2n9nE*) That's a great quote, and I couldn't agree more. I'm a huge fan of collaboration—the appropriate people working together toward a common goal while soliciting, listening, and accounting for collaborator feedback.

But collaboration is not the same thing as consensus. In many cases, I have seen the mandate of consensus heavily derail or effectively destroy initiatives and products. This is because it's very unlikely that everyone will agree about everything, and most stakeholders usually approach initiatives and products with different incentives and agendas. The typical result when consensus is required is that either nothing gets done or the final outcome is a far cry from optimal or originally intended. It is usually a highly compromised version of what it could have been with properly executed collaboration.

Summary

Tying everything together, the art of creating a successful AI vision and delivering successfully on it comes from the *why*, leadership, a shared vision and understanding among all stakeholders, and with collaboration over consensus. This is the formula to which I attribute many great successes.

Accomplishing all of this is much easier said than done and is difficult to teach. It's more an art based on emotional intelligence, soft skills, and leadership than a rigorous set of rules. The skills that are most important here are visionary and strategic thinking, start-with-why thinking, effective communication and listening, emotional intelligence, empathy, expectation setting and management, and general leadership skills such as cultivating excitement, motivation, and meaning.

Now that we understand the importance of why, let's turn our attention to how that relates to specific goals for both people and businesses and, particularly, how AI can help achieve them.

7

Defining Goals for People and Business

As discussed, the *why* should be the driving force and North Star for an AI vision, which in the case of AIPB is better human experiences and business success at the highest level. We also can state the *why* more granularly and simply refer to it as a goal. All initiatives should align to one or more goals.

This chapter gives you an overview of different AI solution stakeholder types and the potential goals associated with each. These goals highlight why AI can be beneficial to both people and businesses alike.

Defining Stakeholders and Introducing Their Goals

AI is a technique by which value is created by machines exhibiting intelligence. We can express the value created as benefits or goals. The goals that people and businesses have for pursuing AI initiatives depend on who the stakeholder is; in other words, the person receiving the benefits that the goals are intended to produce.

There are three potential stakeholders for AI applications, with a single solution sometimes involving all three. These are business stakeholders (e.g., P&L owners, board members, shareholders), customers, and users. We examine the characteristics and differences between each next; for the rest of this book, I refer to business stakeholders simply as the "business."

An example of a product that has all three stakeholders is social media platforms that sell advertising like Twitter. In this case, the business has certain goals, whereas the customers (advertisers) have other goals, and the users yet other goals. Let's use Twitter as an example.

As most people know, Twitter is a social media tech company that has a created a platform that allows people to read and write *tweets*. A single tweet can include text, URLs, and hashtags. The stakeholders in this case are Twitter (the business), the advertisers (the customers), and the users of Twitter's platform. Each have different goals.

For most publicly traded companies, the primary goals are to increase profitability and grow revenue over time. Social responsibility and stability are also common goals for public companies. In reality, companies usually have a large number of goals (aka objectives), both primary and secondary, along with Key Performance Indicators (KPIs) to measure them. These goals often change or are reprioritized over time.

If the goal is growing revenue, the most common ways to do this are customer acquisition, retention, and growth. If the goal is increasing profits, obviously increasing revenue should help, but this can also be achieved by decreasing costs. Decreasing costs can be achieved in many different ways, including automation, improving efficiency, and eliminating sunk costs.

An often overlooked and yet critical way of increasing revenue and competitive advantage is to create great products that are superbly designed and that provide the best possible UX. I cannot state this enough. Most people will stop using products that are cumbersome, unintuitive, or generally dysfunctional. Remember that we're using the term product to include services, as well, so the UX of working with a services company is just as critical. Also, most people would prefer to use a product with fewer features if it has much better UX and is more delightful as compared to the competition. Ultimately, UX and delight are critical elements to achieving customer retention and growth, and will be discussed further in Chapter 8.

It's worth noting that the ISO 9241-11 standard (*https://www.iso.org/obp/ui*) defines usability as the extent to which a product can be used by specified users to achieve specified goals with effectiveness, efficiency, and satisfaction in a specified context of use. This leads us to the concept of stickiness. There are a lot of ways we can define stickiness. Generally speaking, we can think of it as a measure of user retention and engagement. Products and services are sticky if users not only continue to use them, but use them a lot, and use them in place of alternatives and competitors. Twitter has achieved that for its specific type of application.

Let's return to the business goals of increasing profits and revenue growth. We actually haven't gone deep enough though. As discussed earlier in this book, there is a technique called the five whys (*http://bit.ly/2VVmGY2*), developed by Sakichi Toyoda of the Toyota Motor Corporation. The general idea is that there are usually many deeper levels of explanation, which in the case of the original technique was used to determine the root cause of a problem. The person using this technique should ask why the problem occurred and then ask why again relative to the answer from the previous question five or more times (although five tends to be enough) until the root cause is discovered.

Adapting this technique to some of Twitter's goals[1], the question becomes "Why does Twitter want to increase revenue and profits?" Twitter executives could answer by saying that increased profits would allow the company to hire more and better talent, or to make shareholders or customers happy, for example. The next question could be why does Twitter want to hire better talent? This could continue and become somewhat of a rabbit hole. Given that, there's a bit of a subjective art to choosing the appropriate level of the goals, and in reality, AI initiatives usually also require defining application-specific goals that are quite a bit more granular than increasing revenue, for example. Defining more granular, application-specific goals must be assisted collaboratively by business folks, domain experts, and AI practitioners.

In either case, we've established the business goals in this example, so what are the customer goals? The customer is the advertiser in our example (note that sometimes the user and customer are the same), so why do businesses want to advertise? Because it allows them to acquire new customers, maintain market visibility, enhance brand recognition, and stand out from competitors.

These customers also likely want to achieve optimal advertising success and enjoy a great UX when working with their vendors and advertising platforms. Perhaps in the case of massive tech companies like Twitter, the UX isn't as critical, because the advertiser doesn't have much choice if it wants to access and reach the companies massive user bases. Fortunately, many vendors and suppliers aren't massive tech companies and the UX definitely does matter.

Finally, in our Twitter example, the users are people who use a product, service, or solution that a business offers. Unless the user is a person who uses a Twitter account to primarily pay to promote a business, product, or service, the user has goals around keeping up with news, people, information, and events. The user also wants to share their own thoughts and opinions and interact with others. These are collectively some of the user's primary goals.

Other user goals are great UX, design, ease of use, great features, and API access (for developers), and so on. Given two products with equal feature sets, the

---

1 See the following financial reports: *http://bit.ly/2L92fAo* and *http://bit.ly/2FsFgfP*

user will almost always choose the option that is better designed, has better usability, and is generally more delightful and pleasurable to use. Many users will give up extra features in exchange for these things.

Goals by Stakeholder

To simplify things moving forward, I refer to the two primary stakeholders as people and business (hence the meaning behind this book's title and framework!). People stakeholders have human interests, needs, and wants that are not business related. This includes users and human customers in the B2C case.

Business stakeholders, on the other hand, are concerned with the interests, needs, and wants of a business (e.g., executives, directors, shareholders), and can include companies that are customers in the B2B case.

In this section, we discuss the idea of stakeholder-specific goals in more depth, and talk about how AI can help improve human experiences. Goals and benefits are critical, foundational elements of AIPB—ultimately, they drive everything else.

Some of the goals discussed for each stakeholder overlap, and rightfully so. They might be the same or similar, but can be viewed and experienced from each stakeholder's perspective differently. Keep that in mind as we move forward.

GOALS AND THE PURPOSE OF AI FOR BUSINESS

Businesses usually have goals at varying levels and across disciplines of the organization. An organization's top-level goals are those that C-level executives, board members, and shareholders are most interested in. Examples include increasing revenue, increasing profits, decreasing costs, generating a certain percentage company growth over a given time period, increasing operational efficiency, and capturing new markets while expanding current ones.

Line-of-business (LoB) managers often have different goals that should be aligned to one or more top-level goals (although that's not always the case). Common goals for the VP/head of marketing might be to increase brand exposure and awareness, increase inbound sales and leads, optimize company and product positioning and messaging, and increase user engagement with the brand. Many of the goals could be aligned to a top-level goal like increasing revenue, for example.

Alignment of goals at various levels of an organization allows for a given initiative to achieve multiple goals at the same time (e.g., increasing inbound leads to increase revenue). Aligned goals are the *why* that initiatives try to achieve. In fact, initiatives are the tactical part of a strategy, where the strategy is the plan to achieve the vision as defined by a given set of goals.

In addition to achieving business goals, the following is a nonexhaustive list of outcomes that business stakeholders might use AI to produce:

- Generate deep actionable insights and make better decisions
- Augment human intelligence
- Create new and innovative business models, products, and services
- Capture new markets or expand total addressable markets (TAMs)
- Influence new and optimized processes
- Drive differentiation and competitive advantage
- Transform business and disrupt industries

Let's examine each of these, beginning with deep actionable insights and the ability to make better decisions.

Deep Actionable Insights

I draw a difference between actionable insights and "deep" actionable insights, which I base on varying levels of analytics sophistication. Let's discuss these varying analytics sophistication levels and how I define the difference between regular and deep insights in more detail.

You might be familiar with the field of business intelligence (BI). BI is best described as the process of gaining a data-based understanding of different aspects and performance of a business, in the past and the present, and also making comparisons over comparable time periods. We do this using specialized tools that access and query specific data sources to harness the data to generate metrics, descriptive statistics, and data visualizations in order to better understand patterns, trends, and general insights. In this case, I would call this gaining "shallow" insights, and the insights are usually largely dependent on the interpretation of the data by a BI specialist or analyst, and which may differ from person to person.

BI tools can provide different ways of looking at data, but usually they aren't able to tell you what the data means and how best to take action to achieve optimal outcomes. Knowing that sales increased 5% last month is interesting, but it's not particularly useful if you don't know exactly why it happened, or how to maintain or grow the sales increase. In fact, there are often many reasons why a certain KPI/metric change isn't obvious or even discoverable by humans if not assisted by advanced analytics techniques.

Analytics in general can be broken down into more specific categories, which include *descriptive, predictive,* and *prescriptive* analytics. Descriptive analytics look at the data from the past to gain insights as we described for BI. BI is therefore related to descriptive analytics.

Predictive analytics use existing historic data to understand what might happen in the future if certain actions or changes are made; or, put another way, if levers are pulled. Finely tuned predictive models are created for this purpose.

Prescriptive analytics takes this a step further to not only predict what will happen for certain actions and changes, but also provide optimal actions or decisions for a given outcome (via automation or recommendations, for example). Predictive and prescriptive analytics generate what I refer to as "deep" actionable insights. These two fields of analytics give you insight into what outcome to expect and which actions are optimal for a given outcome; as a result, they provide much deeper insights than those gathered by analysts simply making their own interpretations of historical data.

We can consider predictive analytics and prescriptive analytics as subfields of the larger category of advanced analytics, which also includes other machine learning and AI techniques. Advanced analytics techniques can generate deep actionable insights and allow people and businesses to make better decisions. In fact, AI can help generate better, faster, and more efficient decisions, actions, and outcomes in general.

Deep actionable insights can be generated in an automated, ad hoc, or self-service way, and should be used to better inform strategic business and product decisions, as well as to create better human experiences. You should think of advanced analytics techniques as a complement to BI rather than a replacement.

Augment Human Intelligence

Augmenting human intelligence (augmented intelligence) appears to be one of, if not the, biggest reasons that large organizations are pursuing AI solutions at this time.

Augmented intelligence refers to the idea that AI should be used to automate and assist with many routine, rote, boring, and/or tedious tasks that people perform regularly while carrying out their job. This allows workers to focus on the aspects of their job that provide the most value to the company, as well as to themselves—tasks that are the most enjoyable and therefore increase job satisfaction. In addition, augmented intelligence allows the worker to be more creative, productive, and efficient.

Ensuring worker happiness and enjoyment should be at the very top of any company's priority list. This is especially true when you consider that most people spend more time every day at work than at home and thus how important it is to retain great work talent.

There are many potential applications for augmented intelligence across most professions and industries. One example of this is in customer service. A lot of questions people call customer service centers for do not require a human to answer. In fact, routing every call to a human when not needed often causes very valuable customers, who might be calling for reasons or assistance that does require human intelligence, to wait a long time and have a bad customer experience. Using advanced analytics and AI techniques such as those involving NLP allow these call centers to use augmented intelligence to determine whether a call can be addressed via AI or whether it requires a human and can route the call accordingly. This allows representatives to focus entirely on the highest value work and provide the best possible experience if the automation part is executed really well.

Another really interesting example is automated science, and Carnegie Mellon University has created a master's degree program (*http://bit.ly/2WZr4S9*) based on just that. The idea is that scientists will be able to simplify and solve more complex problems and do more overall (increase productivity) in a shorter period of time by utilizing machines that are able to help them identify and select experiments through automation. This also helps maximize the outcomes and cost effectiveness of the AI-driven experimentation strategy given that machines have been found to be much better than humans (*http://bit.ly/2Hz75ER*) at this.

Create New and Innovative Business Models, Products, and Services

Another reason to use AI is to discover and develop new and innovative business models, products, and services. We can use AI to create new offerings that can be presented as standalone products, or as products in larger suites of products. AI can also be used to separate functionality by level of intelligence and resulting value. Meaning, you can use AI to generate a new business model around tiered fixed or subscription prices based on the amount of value provided through increasing use of advanced AI functionality. This makes sense from an R&D perspective because AI resources are not typically low cost, and this therefore provides a model to better justify recouping the costs of development.

A good example of this in the financial investment industry is the introduction and proliferation of robo-advisors (i.e., algorithmically driven automated investing). Even though robo-advisors originated from innovative startup companies, bigger incumbent companies have introduced their own robo-advisor products (*https://whr.tn/2QkKi26*) as well.

In addition to introducing new business models and products centered on low-cost, low-maintenance, and highly accessible investment tools, robo-advisors have also allowed companies to capture new markets and expand their existing TAMs. We discuss that next.

Capture new markets or expand TAMs

As already discussed, AI can power new products that address a new market for which existing products are not meant. A product also might have captured a certain proportion of its TAM, but has not been able to expand its TAM shares due to limited or peaked functionality, or there could be many users that would adopt a given product if there were slight improvements either in functionality or delight. AI can potentially introduce very exciting and high-value improvements into existing products and therefore help acquire new customers in a market who were on the fence previously, or, even better, acquire new customers all together.

For example, the robo-advisor market is expected to reach $16 trillion dollars by 2025, and the growth is largely due to "investment strategies based on Harry Markowitz's Nobel Prize-winning modern portfolio theory and investment management priced at a fraction of typical financial advisory fees" according to a June 2018 article in *U.S. News & World Report* (*http://bit.ly/2YDe6Km*). This represents a significant expansion of the total addressable market for certain established companies, and also identifying and capturing a new market of individuals and companies looking for low-cost alternatives to traditional financial advisement and fee structures.

Influence new and optimized processes

We can also use AI to optimize existing processes and create innovative new ones. We can use automation for both purposes and reduce inefficiencies and lower costs. In the customer service example, the introduction of AI for call routing and low-level support introduced a new AI-based process into a previously largely human-based process. It also helps with optimization of the existing process given the increased utilization of representatives to perform value-added work, and also improves their enjoyment while performing their daily job. There could be many similar applications in manufacturing, fleet management, and other industries.

A good example involves drug discovery, which is the process of finding new drugs to treat diseases, disorders, syndromes, and conditions. The AI division of Insilico Medicine (*https://insilico.com*) is taking advantage of AI techniques such as deep learning to innovate and optimize the drug discovery process and maximize process outcomes, particularly when applied to diseases related to cancer and aging. The company uses these techniques in combination with data sources that include multiomics, drug, and clinical data. According to its mission statement, they use AI to extend healthy longevity through AI solutions.

Drive differentiation and competitive advantage

Innovation, differentiation, and generating competitive advantage go hand in hand. We examine each at a high level here because these topics could easily warrant an entire book (and do).

Innovation is both a process and result. There are many different definitions of innovation, but, loosely, we can consider it the process of generating new ideas that lead to the creation of new products, services, and processes.

I think of innovation in two ways: innovation that improves something that already exists, and innovation that results in something never done before. Before discussing each and to provide context, let's look at Figure 7-1, which shows a diagram that I created to show the evolution of data. The terms data and information are interrelated and somewhat synonymous in that data simply refers to the digital version of information (i.e., ones and zeros, bits and bytes).

As Figure 7-1 shows, data and information first took the form of oral tradition and memory. The next step was symbolic and written information followed by organized groupings of information. The explosion of capitalism and the industrial revolution saw businesses form large, highly formalized, and specialized business functions (e.g., engineering, sales, marketing) with a lot of expertise within their departments (tribal knowledge), but that was not centralized or readily available to other groups.

Oral tradition and memory

Early symbols

Writing

Tribal knowledge

Information Age

Big Data and Advanced Analytics

Figure 7-1. The evolution of data

The twenty-first century brought about the *information age*, also called the *digital age*. This is the age of data (digital information) and technology, largely characterized until recently by data storage and centralization, the internet and cloud computing, SaaS platforms, mobile apps, and traditional data analytics (e.g., BI). Due to massive advancements in high-powered, inexpensive compute and data storage resources, along with a proliferation of data sources, I say that we are now in the age of *big data and advanced analytics*.

Returning to innovation that improves something that already exists, traditional data analytics and BI are good examples. Although data centralization, the internet and cloud computing, software and BI has definitely helped generate insights spanning multiple data sources and in a way that provided greater accessibility across business functions, generating historical insights (descriptive analytics) and taking action accordingly is not really innovation in the latter sense. Further, BI requires analysis and interpretation by people (e.g., data analysts, managers) to derive insights, as does preceding methods such as historical precedent and gut feel, where experience is the data that insights on which these methods are based.

Innovation in the latter sense is building things that have never been built or done before, especially for the end consumer (e.g., people, business, process). I would consider advanced analytics such as AI and machine learning as definitely qualifying under this category of innovation. Advanced analytics has made automatic predictive and prescriptive analytics (and without requiring explicit programming) possible as well as many other things covered in this book. More important, advanced analytics have enabled people to generate deep insights that humans *cannot* discover on their own and thus led to outcomes not possible before, as well.

AI and the innovation it inspires is a great way to achieve differentiation for a company and its offerings. Differentiation can be a result of multiple things. It can result simply because a company had a head start and therefore has differentiation due to timing (e.g., first mover), although many companies will likely catch on and eventually catch up. Another possibility is that the company has developed very specific intellectual property (IP) that is either legally protected and/or very difficult to replicate. Another can be simply due to outstanding processes, services, approaches, and UX. Whatever the case, differentiation is key to developing a company's unique value proposition.

Continued innovation around emerging and state-of-the-art advanced analytics techniques (e.g., AI and machine learning), for example, are excellent ways to generate differentiation and competitive advantage while also helping to avoid commoditization and downward price pressure. As long as you have competitive advantage, including a great UX, there's a good chance your product will enjoy success and large market share.

One truly remarkable example is Amazon's recent introduction of its Amazon Go stores (*https://amzn.to/3oGeI3S*). Think of these as convenience-type stores that a person can walk into, grab items to purchase, and then leave without any human assistance or physical payment transaction. According to the Go website, the implementation of this relies on many different AI and machine learning techniques, including computer vision, sensor fusion (combining and evaluating different sensor type data for improved accuracy), and deep learning. Although this might be commonplace in the future, as is what happens with commoditization, at the moment this is absolutely mind-blowing stuff, with major disruptive and competitive advantage potential.

Other examples include companies such as nuTonomy and Zoox, both of which are helping power autonomous cars. nuTomomy in particular is creating software to power driverless fleets of cars, and make these fleets available to people living in cities.

Transform business and disrupt industries

Finally, AI as a tool of innovation can and has transformed businesses and disrupted industries. Google is a great example of a transformed business. The company originally started out focused on their search engine and algorithms. In the process of trying to optimize the search product, Google hired some of the smartest and most well-educated technical people out there in order to develop extremely advanced, complex, and state-of-the-art technologies and advanced analytics–based products and algorithms. Now, Google is basically an AI-driven company (*https://ai.google/about*) that incorporates AI and machine learning in many of its offerings.

This has resulted in huge differentiation and competitive advantage, and now Google controls the vast majority of search and the results that a large proportion of the human population sees. As a result, other AI-first companies have surfaced that are trying to create open, community-driven, and decentralized search as an alternative. It will be very interesting to see whether this gains momentum and captures market share, and whether there is any way to truly disrupt the search industry. Google has held onto it for a long time.

As of this writing AI is gaining huge momentum and popularity, and new real-world applications are popping up every day, but AI is also in its infancy. Companies that began by using AI aren't necessarily transformed businesses, but they certainly have industry disruption potential.

Ride-sharing platforms like Uber and Lyft are great examples of this. These platforms have completely disrupted the taxi industry. Ultimately, it's up to the incumbents to either adapt to and adopt the disruption or go out of business in many cases.

GOALS AND THE PURPOSE OF AI FOR PEOPLE

What about people? As previously mentioned, people have different interests, needs, and wants (and therefore goals) than businesses, and usually people have a lot of underlying psychological, experiential, emotional, social, and other factors that determine whether a solution accomplishes a certain goal adequately and will continue to be used.

As indicated by the title and subtitle of this book, AI can produce many benefits for people, including creating better human experiences. This is true where a business is the entity creating the solutions that make peoples lives and experiences better in ways that we'll look at soon. With proper empathy and perspective, businesses should prioritize these goals for the people that buy or use their products. The point here is the focus and perspective of AI for people specifically, not business. This is one of the key premises of this book and this section specifically.

Here is a nonexhaustive list of outcome categories that people stakeholders might experience as the result of AI-based innovations:

- Better health and health-related outcomes

- Better personal safety and security

- Better financial performance, savings, and insights

- Better UX, convenience, and delight

- Better and easier planning and decisions

- Better productivity and enjoyment

- Better learning and entertainment

Let's now go over each of these categories at a very brief and high level. Keep in mind as we progress that although some of this is very obvious, AI is able to help generate benefits and outcomes in all of these categories, which is less obvious and not widely understood. I go into much greater detail about that and related topics and concepts in the next two chapters, and I give AI-specific examples for each category in Chapter 9, which focuses specifically on AI for better human experiences.

Better health and health-related outcomes

Humans obviously are very concerned with having good health and also experiencing the best outcomes possible whenever they have any health-related issues. Both this category and the next are closely related to fundamental human needs for survival—physical and mental.

Better personal safety and security

As with the health category and its relationship to survival needs, humans are obviously very concerned with personal safety and security, as well. This is the case in public, at work, and at home.

Better financial performance, savings, and insights

Humans want to improve their financial performance (income and investments, for example), reduce costs, save more money, and get better insights about their current financial well-being and impact of investments on future wealth.

Better UX, convenience, and delight

Humans interact with technology in many ways and for many purposes every day, and most often it's through a UI of some sort. Examples of these interfaces include websites, web apps, mobile apps, desktop apps, and connected devices (e.g., personal assistants). These interfaces aren't limited to only the more obvious software interfaces noted here, they also include televisions, transportation vehicles (e.g., cars and airplanes), work-related equipment, theaters, and audio systems, for example.

Humans naturally want these interactions and experiences to be easy to understand, simple to use and experience, and ideally be delightful, as well. Humans are also often very interested in increasing convenience and reducing the time required to carry out tasks due to busy schedules and other reasons.

Better and easier planning and decisions

Humans need to plan and make decisions in many areas of their lives every day, often in areas outside of their expertise (e.g., retirement planning and portfolio management) and with far too many options to choose from. As a result, humans are highly motivated to find ways to simplify, automate, and improve planning and decision making where possible and beneficial. The ability to create easier and better plans and decisions is key.

Better productivity, efficiency, and enjoyment

Humans are very interested in improving their productivity, efficiency, and overall enjoyment of carrying out tasks both at work and outside of work. We covered this already in the work context when discussing augmented intelligence for business use, although here the perspective is flipped to the human side.

People use technology and carry out tasks in their everyday, nonprofessional lives, as well. Most of us create lists, write documents and emails, buy groceries, and perform other administrative-type tasks outside of work. Augmented intelligence is applicable to these situations, too.

Better learning and entertainment

Humans want to learn and be entertained as well as find new, better, and more fun ways to do both. This helps increase knowledge and happiness as well as decrease boredom. Additionally, humans love it when things are made to be fun that are not always considered to be fun (e.g., learning.

Summary

Overall, when all of these benefits to people are combined, the key takeaway is that AI can help people get "jobs" done in better ways and also have better experiences. An AI vision guided by AIPB should be viewed as a tool for accomplishing that—for people and businesses alike. Businesses should take advantage of AI through that lens and with the understanding that if they are able to help people get jobs done in better ways while also creating better human experiences, then revenues, profits, and everything else will follow.

Identifying goals and the stakeholders with whom they're associated is a critical first step of developing your AI vision and strategy, and any vision and strategy that's innovation-driven for that matter. Not coincidentally, goal identification and prioritization is a critical element of AIPB. The key is to start by asking what it is that you want to accomplish exactly, and most importantly, *why*.

Also, business goals differ from human goals. AI is able to help achieve goals for both, some at the same time, in fact, and many that are mutually beneficial. Lastly, and as Chip Heath wrote in his book *Made to Stick*, "You can't have five North Stars, you can't have five most important goals." This is indeed true, so make sure to prioritize and choose the most important one or two goals to begin and then add more as needed later.

Lastly, it's worth restating that the goals discussed in this chapter were presented at a relatively high level. In reality, AI initiatives usually also require defining application-specific goals that are much more granular than those covered in this chapter. Defining more granular, application-specific goals must be assisted collaboratively by business folks, domain experts, and AI practitioners.

Now that we have developed the importance of the *why* and having goals, let's shift our focus to what makes products great and how AI is able to create better human experiences. A better understanding of these topics will help you to create an AI vision.

8

What Makes a Product Great

Now that we've covered goals and the purpose of AI for both people and business, let's turn our attention to how can we create an AI vision around building great products that are able to achieve these goals.

This chapter is meant to give you an overview of the concept of importance versus satisfaction, the four components that I think make products great, and also Lean and Agile development concepts that we can use when building AI solutions.

Importance versus Satisfaction

Let's begin by discussing the concept of importance versus satisfaction. This provides helpful context to keep in mind as we cover the four components that make products great in the next section.

We introduced the "Jobs to Be Done" Framework previously, which is part of a larger strategy and process called outcome-driven innovation (ODI). As discussed people hire businesses, products, and services to get a "job" done. The reasons behind people hiring a product to get a job done are often not obvious, or immediately understood by the people doing the "hiring," nor are they easily explainable.

Sometimes, the reasons are because one product makes them "feel" a certain way, which is a bit intangible but can be certainly real. Examples include hiring a bowl of ice cream to make you feel better, a toothbrush to get your teeth cleaning job done, an accountant's services to get your annual tax filing job done, and finally, an email client such as Gmail to get your emailing jobs done.

Well-known author and Harvard professor Clayton M. Christensen, along with his coauthors, points out that there can be powerful social and emotional factors (*http://bit.ly/2BCoG8t*) beyond just the functional that influence people's perception of whether a solution does a job well or not, and the experiential aspect can be very important as well. Ultimately, people tend to continue working with companies, products, and services that they've "hired" if they do the job very well, otherwise, they might get "fired" if they do not.

Further, all jobs consist of steps, and the Jobs to Be Done framework is an organized way to brainstorm and unlock innovative ideas (*http://bit.ly/2YGHX4E*) around how to make the steps easier, faster, or unnecessary. This represents a very big change in the way people normally create products. It shifts the focus from business metrics to customer metrics, and from making the product better to making the jobs and outcomes better for people.

In other words, the focus is on the jobs to be done and not the product itself. It's also on the voice of the customer instead of assuming to know what the customer needs or wants. Product ideas should follow naturally, and this approach enables both innovation and greater business success. A happy customer means a more successful business. In a few moments, we examine in detail additional concepts and approaches to human-centered product design and development.

Jobs to Be Done also heavily emphasizes the concept of opportunity and outcomes as a function of importance to customers and their satisfaction with existing alternatives. Figure 8-1 shows this relationship.

Figure 8-1 shows three different market segments, particularly those where the outcomes are underserved or overserved. This provides a graphical way to segment customers based on understanding a job that they're trying to get done and determining the degree of opportunity that the customer's desired outcome represents. The biggest opportunity is where the customer's needs are largely unmet, which in this context means that the importance of getting the job done and achieving the desired outcome is high, whereas the customer's satisfaction with alternative ways of getting the job done is low (lower-right quadrant).

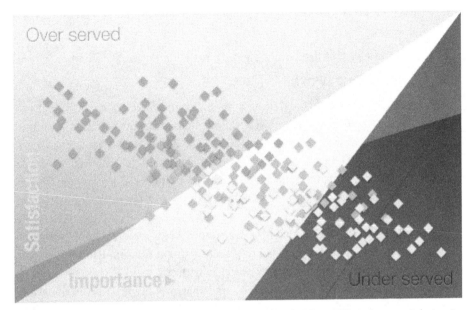

Figure 8-1. Importance versus satisfaction (from Anthony Ulwick, "A Three-Segment Solution," The Marketing Journal, http://bit.ly/2HS4IvT, accessed February 23, 2019)

It's worth noting that we can apply the importance versus satisfaction relationship to individual features as well as entire products. This is one way to help prioritize and order which features to build in benefit-driven product development. With our understanding of why people "hire" businesses, products, and services in order to get a "job" done, let's now discuss what makes products great, which ultimately prevents them from being "fired."

The Four Ingredients of a Great Product

What makes a product great? What causes people to use one product over another? What causes people to use a product daily as opposed to once a month? What causes people to engage and interact with a product more over time, and for longer durations with each use?

It boils down to four primary ingredients:

- Products that just work

- Ability to meet human needs, wants, and likes

- Design and usability

- Delight and stickiness

Let's discuss each of these ingredients in turn.

PRODUCTS THAT JUST WORK

Nothing makes me want to stop using a product more than it not working or not working well. Quality matters, and you should spend time and effort ensuring it, and yet this isn't always the case. Products that don't work might have bugs, crash regularly, or need workarounds. Conversely, products that "just work" do exactly what they are meant to do, in the exact way that they're meant to do it, and without error. Or at least that's the case for products that are not error-based. Let me explain further.

Not all but most AI and machine learning models are error based in some way, which means that the models are trained using a training dataset until the chosen performance metric (e.g., accuracy) is within acceptable range when the model is tested against a test dataset. AI and machine learning solutions aren't perfect and aren't able to be correct 100% of the time. Acceptable range is another way of saying that the performance metric (and subsequent error-level reduction) is "good enough."

Unfortunately, good enough is not a very quantitative measure. Also, sometimes reaching a target performance level, or even an acceptable performance level, can be very difficult depending on many factors, and certain errors can have life or death consequences, all topics that we discuss later in this book.

That said, often the benefits of "good enough" far outweigh any potential downsides, which makes it a reasonable goal. Also, some applications can get pretty close to perfect. Business folks, domain experts, and AI practitioners must work collaboratively to determine what errors are acceptable (good enough) for a specific application. When all of the criteria in this section are met, including "good enough," an AI application should "just work," and that's an important goal.

ABILITY TO MEET HUMAN NEEDS, WANTS, AND LIKES

A product's ability to actually meet human needs, wants, or likes is critical and should be somewhat obvious, but it's definitely worth discussing. There is a lot of nuance here that will be considered throughout this section, including the difference between the three.

To begin, the more that human needs, wants, or likes are prioritized and understood when developing technology solutions, including those built with AI, the more successful the product and better the human experience will be for users. Humans don't necessarily care what technologies or underlying nuts and bolts are being used as long as they solve a problem or meet certain needs, wants, or likes in a delightful way. The best applications of AI are those for which the use of AI is abstracted away and the user knows only that a product meets one or more of these things and is better than the alternatives.

To better understand concepts around human needs, let's briefly go over Maslow's hierarchy of needs.

Maslow's Hierarchy of Needs

Many of us are familiar with, or at least have heard of, Maslow's hierarchy of needs. These needs are significant drivers of human motivation, and are largely geared toward physical and mental survival and health, as well as self-actualization. The point of bringing it up here is to provide a brief recap and discuss these needs in the context of technology and AI specifically.

Figure 8-2 shows Maslow's hierarchy of needs as a five-level hierarchy, with the need categories in order of importance, from bottom to top: physiological, safety, belongingness and love, esteem, and self-actualization.

Figure 8-2. Maslow's hierarchy of needs

The bottom four layers of the hierarchy are referred to as *deficiency needs*. Humans are most motivated to fill needs lower in the deficiency part of the hierarchy because they are required for fundamental physical survival, and humans become more motivated to fill these needs the more that they are deprived. As those needs are met, motivation shifts to fill needs that are more social and mental. Interestingly, the framework suggests that motivation again increases, potentially significantly, after deficiency needs are met in order to meet self-actualization needs (top of the hierarchy). Unlike deficiency needs, which are based on lacking fulfillment in certain areas, self-actualization needs are driven by desire for personal growth and fulfillment. Examples include professional growth, becoming an SME, climbing Mount Everest, or learning to play a musical instrument.

Originally Maslow stated (*http://bit.ly/2JzpuUj*) that the needs must be met in order, but later clarified that motivation decreases for a specific need once it's "more or less" met, and focus will shift to the next unmet set of needs (salient needs). Although people naturally try to fulfill needs from the bottom to the top of the hierarchy, life events and other circumstances (e.g., disease diagnosis, divorce, getting laid off) often make that an iterative and ever-changing dynamic.

Maslow also thought that due to fundamental differences between people and what motivates them, certain needs higher up the hierarchy can become more important than even basic physiological or other lower needs (anorexia, as an example). Additionally, people can be motivated by multiple needs simultaneously. Social media is a great example. People often use social media because it provides a sense of love and belonging while also helping with their personal self-esteem.

It's also worth noting that there are certain criticisms of Maslow's hierarchy (*http://bit.ly/2wfJCSx*). Some include the lack of spiritual, altruistic (putting others needs ahead of ones own), and societal (self-centered versus society-centered cultures) needs in his framework, all of which can obviously be very powerful.

The difference between needs, wants, and likes

An important distinction to make is between human needs, wants, and likes. They are all similar and related, but not the same.

Needs such as those included in Maslow's hierarchy represent things humans need for survival, strong mental health, and self growth in the case of self-actualization. Wants on the other hand represent things that humans want to have, but don't necessarily need to survive mentally and physically.

The farther from a need a certain want is, the more people's focus is placed on concepts like utility, usability, and delight (discussed further shortly). Also, humans might want (desire) something because they think it will meet one of their noncritical needs, or they think they'll like it after they have it, but that's not always the case. Think of all the toys that kids want at first, but that never see the light of day after the first use or so.

Likes are the end result—the degree to which someone likes something (e.g., product, food, trip destination) whether they wanted it or not. We're often presented with opportunities to try things we didn't know about or want (e.g., grocery store samples) but then realize how much we like or dislike it.

Human needs, wants, and likes are powerful forces that drive human decisions, technological innovation, and the difference between great products and not great products. With all of this in mind, let's turn our discussion to actually meeting needs, wants, and likes and the factors that we must consider in order to do so.

Human-centered over business-centered products and features

Actually meeting human needs and wants with technology products is often much easier said than done. There are many reasons why, with the most important arguably being the difference between designing and building human-centered versus business-centered products and features. Products are all too often made in a business-centered as opposed to a human-centered way, which usually results in products that don't properly address the user's needs, wants, and likes.

Businesses owners and workers aren't the customer or users of their products despite how often many create product ideas and make product decisions as if they were. This results in business-centered as opposed to human-centered products and features, and quite simply, the less human-centered any user-facing product or feature is, the less successful it will be.

A related and contributing factor is the so-called *highest-paid person's opinion* problem (aka the HiPPO problem, which usually refers to company owners and senior executives). The HiPPO problem occurs when product decisions become disproportionately weighted based on a HiPPO over actual customers or users. Another manifestation of this problem is when the HiPPO overrides those with greater expertise in making great products (e.g., UX designers, product managers).

Lastly, business stakeholders typically have differing goals and incentives related to their business function, and therefore tend to compete with one another for product features that can benefit them directly. If not managed carefully or left unchecked, this can become a runaway scenario in which a product winds up including everything but the kitchen sink. This will ultimately result in a bad UX and diminish the ability of a product to meet human needs, wants, and likes as well because the desired functionality can become buried in a sea of non-essential features and UI elements.

Products should always be benefit-driven, not feature-driven, and, most important, have the user's needs, wants, and likes as the driver of everything else. There are many ways to ensure this and avoid the issues discussed; for example through UX research and design, human-centered design, user-centered design, and design thinking in particular.

An example is empathetic research and design as baked into the empathy stage of the Design Thinking process (discussed in Chapter 9). Empathetic design centers on observing consumers and understanding their needs, as opposed to relying solely on market research or nonconsumer perspectives.

Also, Google started an effort it calls human-centered machine learning (HCML) (*http://bit.ly/2YIn88T*) to handle some of these considerations, along with a focus on how to leverage AI and machine learning in inclusive ways. The effort emphasizes the importance of the UX axiom that says "you are not the user," and provides a lens (*http://bit.ly/2HP4qGo*) that allows them to "look across products to see how ML can stay grounded in human needs while solving them in unique ways only possible through ML."

As a final note to this section, there are many ways to measure whether a product meets human needs, wants, and likes. They include product performance analysis (e.g., sales, customer acquisition), customer engagement and retention analysis, and analyzing user feedback for example.

DESIGN AND USABILITY

Design is an often-underestimated area when creating a product vision and strategy, and yet it is critical to product success. Design is a very broad term, though, so a little bit of specificity is in order. This book is about harnessing emerging technologies such as AI to innovate; therefore, we focus on design as it relates to innovation and technology.

Dan Olsen (*https://dan-olsen.com*), a product management consultant and author of *The Lean Product Playbook*,[1] created two frameworks that we discuss in this chapter. The first is called *The UX Design Iceberg* and the second is called *The*

---

1 Olsen, Dan. *The Lean Product Playbook: How to Innovate with Minimum Viable Products and Rapid Customer Feedback*. New Jersey: Wiley, 2015. *https://dan-olsen.com*

Product-Market Fit Pyramid (covered later in this chapter). Let's cover The UX Design Iceberg first, shown in Figure 8-3.

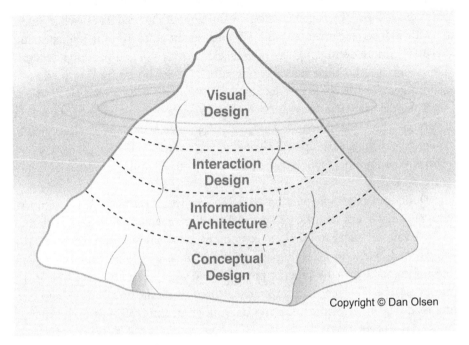

Figure 8-3. The UX Design Iceberg

The part of the iceberg that is above the water surface is what users see and interact with; or, in other words, is the visual and interactive part of the UX. The layers of the iceberg below the water is what the UX is based on—it's the design foundation. Let's briefly discuss each of these foundational pieces, starting from the bottom.

Conceptual design represents the earliest stage of the design process. It is where a high-level understanding of user needs is generated, and subsequently turned into initial concepts of what the solution or product will look and feel like. This is the beginning from the design perspective of mapping the problem space to the solution space.

Information architecture is the part of the design process during which the designer determines how the information is logically organized in the product and what the path or flow of information retrieval is like for the user. The logical organization includes the structure and layout of information across the entire product. Product navigation and subnavigation order and options, along with content layout in a feed, for example, are all aspects of information architecture.

Interaction design is the design of user interactions with the product. This can take the form of navigation and flow throughout the product as well as interact with individual elements of the UI, such as inputing information, speaking (becoming more dominant), selection, clicking, swiping, and pinching. Interaction design also includes interaction feedback design in the form of messages, notifications, and errors (e.g., validation), for example.

The final user-facing design layer is visual design. This is the aesthetic aspect of design—how the product's UI looks. This includes colors, contrast, fonts, typography, logotypes, graphical elements, positioning, and sizing. This is not a complete list, but hopefully this helps establish many of the key areas of visual design.

Designing and implementing everything as described by the UX design iceberg does not mean that the design or UX will be good or effective. This is true even if you have met the first two criteria of great products: the product "just works" and is able to meet human needs or wants. People need to understand the information that the product presents, and also how to interact with it. In most cases, people experience a technology product for the first time without having read a user manual or receiving training on it (think of most of the mobile apps you've tried).

This is where the very important concept of *usability* comes in. This is an entire field consisting of important research, concepts, and testing methodologies, an in-depth discussion of which is out of scope here. That said, let's discuss the most important concept and key takeaway for usability.

In the book *Don't Make Me Think*,[2] author Steve Krug talks about how, as much as is possible, the purpose and functionality of a web page or app should require almost zero mental effort for the user to understand and use; the user should just "get it." He uses terms like self-evident, obvious, and self-explanatory interchangeably to describe this.

Although he explains usability using the terms self-evident and self-explanatory as being the same, I think of it slightly differently. I usually explain usability to people using three categories of degree of usability, from suboptimal to optimal. These categories are "Explanation Required" (suboptimal), "Self-

---

2 Krug, Steve. *Don't Make Me Think, Revisited: A Common Sense Approach to Web Usability*. 3rd ed., New Riders, 2014.

Explanatory," and "Self-Evident" (optimal). We can apply these categories to any technology that provides an interface for a user to interact with directly (e.g., web app, mobile app, smart home). Note that the categories represent more of a spectrum than hard divisions.

The "Explanation Required" category means that the UX is not particularly "usable." This means that for a user to understand and use a technology interface, some degree of explanation is required. This explanation can be in the form of training or documentation, for example. This is suboptimal and you should avoid it if at all possible.

The next level is "Self-explanatory," which is pretty good, and where most good (not great) products are in terms of usability. "Self-explanatory" means that although not immediately obvious, a little careful observation, text reading, and context studying in the UI should shed the necessary light on what everything means and how to use it.

"Self-evident" is the optimal case. It means that zero explanation is required because everything about the UX is completely and immediately obvious. This is a very high bar to achieve and obviously won't be the case for every user, but hopefully it will be for most. This is also a distinguishing characteristic of truly great products.

DELIGHT AND STICKINESS

Delight and stickiness are two extremely important concepts when it comes to great products, and both lead to successful products that enjoy highly engaged and retained users.

Delight is a concept that is highlighted well by a framework known as the Kano Model, a product development and customer satisfaction theory developed in the 1980s by Noriaki Kano, a Tokyo University of Science's professor of quality management.[3] Delight is also a psychological and emotional concept, and it is incredibly important to the success of a product or service. People prefer to use products that are pleasurable to use and that makes them feel good (delightful). This is true even if it means giving up bells and whistles (features). Simple and delightful products are almost always better than the opposite alternatives.

---

3 Coppenhaver, Robert. *From Voices to Results - Voice of Customer Questions, Tools, and Analysis: Proven techniques for understanding and engaging with your customers.* Packt Publishing, 2018. *http://bit.ly/2VK9CQ8*

Stickiness basically means that users perpetually continue to use a product after their first use; from the business perspective, this is a measure of user engagement and retention. We are all very familiar with the difference between sticky products and those that are not, even without being aware of this terminology.

Let's begin by talking about delight. Product features which the Kano model categorizes as "delighters" are those that customers don't expect and which provide a huge boost of enjoyment and an element of surprise. Delighters are the secret sauce; they are key product differentiators and generators of competitive advantage. Customer satisfaction increases exponentially with the introduction and enhanced implementation of delighter features. These are the true differentiators that get people to use your product over others, and also produce a great experience and level of enjoyment at the same time.

All companies should try to determine what the delighters for their products are, and then implement them. The potential ROI is *huge*, and can easily result in dedicated customers that also advocate and evangelize a company's products on their behalf. Assuming that you've built a great product that is delightful, eventually the word will spread and the product will be a great success. As Dharmesh Shah (*http://bit.ly/2HDSVlX*) said, "Don't make customers happy. Make happy customers."

One interesting thing to note is that today's delighters are tomorrow's must haves. Think about the iPhone. There are few products that I can think of that were introduced with not just one delighter, but many. A beautiful relatively high resolution touch screen with multiple interactions (e.g., pinching to zoom), a camera and photo library, music player and library, apps, and more. This was delighter city, and phones like this were called *smart phones*.

Now we've dropped the "smart" designation and all of these features are table stakes for all mobile phones—must haves. Also interesting is that AI is now becoming the source of delight in mobile phones with features such as automatic image categorization, facial recognition-based security, animoji, and photo optimization. Thinking ahead, I can easily see the time when phones, tablets, and computers no longer have keyboard interfaces and all interaction is speech driven. The concept of today's delighters becoming tomorrow's must haves is also in line with a concept called the *AI effect*; that is, when certain applications no longer seem to be powered by AI as they become more commonplace (e.g., Google Search). We're seeing this happen now more and more.

Let's discuss stickiness next. You might have a hundred or more apps on your phone. The question is, how many of those do you use every day? Further, how many do you use multiple times per day? How many once per week, and how many once per year? We all have apps on our phones that fall into one of these different groups of usage and frequency. Sticky apps (and products in general) are those that you actually use, and use often. Like delight, stickiness can be a huge driver of product success. In fact, the prospect of understanding what makes products sticky has resulted in people researching and writing about it.

In Nir Eyal's book *Hooked: How to Build Habit-Forming Products*, he presents the *Hook Model*, which he created for building what he calls habit-forming technology. The model consists of four components of a feedback loop. These components are trigger, action, variable reward, and investment. At a high level, the idea is that triggers cause people to perform certain actions and behaviors, which in turn should be rewarded in a nonpredictable and desire-generating way (a concept similar to delight given the element of surprise), and then ending with the user making some sort of investment into improving the feedback loop the next time around. As Nir puts it, "These investments can be leveraged to make the trigger more engaging, the action easier, and the reward more exciting with every pass through the Hook" (*http://bit.ly/3oNV4mC*).

Delight and stickiness should not be ignored or underestimated when building AI-based products, or any products and services in general. In addition to the benefits of innovation and being able to successfully use emerging technologies, these are the key generators of differentiation and competitive advantage.

Now that we've covered the four components that great products should have, let's discuss Netflix in this context.

Netflix and the Focus on What Matters Most

As noted in a MathWork's whitepaper (*http://bit.ly/2HNHhDW*), Netflix points out that as compared to ultimate [AI] model performance—usage, UX, user satisfaction, and user retention are what it finds most important and better aligned with its business goals.

From a product perspective, these statements are extremely interesting, in that optimization for Netflix is much more user centric, as opposed to performance focused. This makes sense, particularly given that Netflix can afford some level of nonperfect performance because the company is not using machine learning for cancer diagnostics, for example.

The really interesting takeaway here is that the four things Netflix points out are directly related to the four things I am proposing that make a product great. Things that just work results mainly in retention, usability results in all three (great UX, satisfaction, and retention), delight results in high satisfaction and retention, and ability to meet human needs and wants results in high satisfaction and retention, as well. Always ask *why* and look to optimize the cause to achieve the desired effect, as opposed to the other way around.

Lean and Agile Product Development

Now that we've established what makes products great and what their purpose is from a human perspective, how do you ensure that you build successful, great products quickly, efficiently, and with minimal risk? It really comes down to two things. The first is ensuring that you have product–market fit and that your product is better than the alternatives, where "better" can mean price, functionality, and delight, for example. The second is that you're actually able to successfully execute and deliver an innovative product that achieves product–market fit.

Figure 8-4 shows The Product-Market Fit Pyramid, the second framework created by Dan Olsen (*https://dan-olsen.com*). Achieving product–market fit is especially important when creating innovative new products such as those powered by AI, and particularly products intended to capture new markets.

The Product-Market Fit Pyramid is logically split into two sections: the market and the product. When all of the levels of the pyramid are satisfied between a product and target customer market, the product is said to have product-market fit. This is what ensures product success.

The bottom two market levels indicate that identification of your target customer and their underserved needs is the foundation by which your product and possibly entire business should be based.

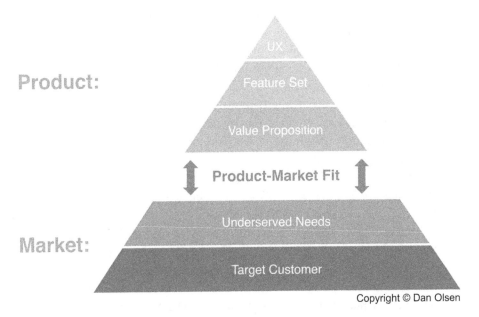

Figure 8-4. The Product-Market Fit Pyramid

The product then is built on this foundation, starting with the product's value proposition. This is the *why* that I've focused on so much throughout this book. It can be framed in the context of needs, wants, goals, or whatever you choose, but ultimately this is the North Star that guides everything else. The value proposition is also where you need to determine why this product is going to be better, as mentioned.

From there, a set of product features and their associated functionality is determined to make the value proposition a reality, and then the UX is created. The UX is what the customer or user interacts with to experience and enjoy the value that the product provides.

Defining everything represented by The Product-Market Fit Pyramid involves creating hypothesis and making key assumptions that must be tested. This is where Lean and Agile product development comes in. In the broader product development sense, Lean and Agile methods such as kanban and scrum are intended to build and iterate quickly in order to test risky assumptions and build working software instead of extensive documentation. The working software mentioned then is able to be tested by actual customers, or nonbusiness people who are as close to customers as possible.

These methods also allow companies to test for product–market fit as quickly as possible and make changes or pivot as needed for success. There are many concepts and frameworks that people have created to help guide this process. They go by names such as *failing fast*, the *build-measure-learn feedback loop*, and the *hypotheses-experiments-test-insights feedback loop*.

Usually, the early part of this iterative process is based on the concept of a minimum viable product (MVP). As discussed earlier in the book, an MVP provides a mechanism to help mitigate risk and avoid unnecessary expenditure of time and cost. The primary idea is that the minimum amount of UX and software functionality should be built and put in users hands as quickly as possible, to properly test the riskiest assumptions and validate product–market fit and user delight.

From a qualitative perspective, an MVP should be delightful, usable, reliable, and functional. Another interesting concept is that of the minimum lovable product (MLP). Sam Altman of Y Combinator (*http://bit.ly/2Ft5HSR*) has said, "It's better to build something that a small number of users love, than a large number of users like." Whether it's an MVP, MLP, pilot, proof of concept, or prototype, the purposes as covered are the same.

Summary

Great products aren't great because of the technology that they're built on alone. Great products should "just work," meet one or more human needs or wants, are easy to use and understand, and are delightful and sticky. Creating an AI vision and strategy to achieve all of these goals will help ensure AI solution success.

In Ben Horowitz's book, *Hard Thing About Hard Things*,[4] he quotes a former boss as saying, "We take care of the people, the products and the profits...in that order." Even though he's referring to company workers, I think this 100% applies to building great products, as well. If products are built with customers and users in mind first and foremost, success and profits will follow.

After these considerations have been incorporated into your AI vision and strategy, it's important to determine how to test your riskiest assumptions and user delight by defining and building an MVP or comparable testable solution. You can effectively facilitate this via Lean and Agile methodologies that will allow

---

4 Horowitz, Ben. *The Hard Thing About Hard Things: Building a Business When There Are No Easy Answers*. New York: HarperCollins, 2014.

you to learn the most information and make any needed changes in the shortest time possible.

Now let's turn our attention to the UX of AI and apply what we've learned, specifically, to creating better human experiences, a primary goal of AIPB.

9

AI for Better Human Experiences

In Chapter 8, we discussed what makes a product great and why understanding that is critical to developing a successful AI vision and strategy. The goal of this chapter is to build on that discussion and build upon the foundation of great products and well-designed UIs as the context for creating better human experiences.

You've probably heard terms like UX, UI, user centric, human centric, and customer centric. Usually these terms are used in the context of digital product design or customer service. These concepts also apply to AI and machine learning applications, and they should be at the forefront of any AI vision and strategy. Emerging technologies like AI do not exist in a vacuum, and therefore proper design considerations and treatment are paramount. This is the basis of the growing concept of the *UX of AI*.

This chapter begins with a few definitions of the term "experience." This will provide context for the rest of the chapter. This is followed by covering how AI can specifically help create better human experiences. We then discuss three concepts: *UX interfaces*; the *experience economy*; and the design methodology known as *design thinking*. Everything discussed is highly applicable to creating an AI vision and strategy.

Experience Defined

We all have an intuitive idea of what the concept of experience means, but what's the formal definition? Here are three definitions from the Collins Dictionary (*http://bit.ly/2wh6rp6*) that I think sums it up best:

- Experience is used to refer to the past events, knowledge, and feelings that make up someone's life or character.

- An experience is something that you do or that happens to you, especially something important that affects you.

- If you experience a particular situation, you are in that situation or it happens to you.

I think that these definitions speak for themselves and require little further explanation. In the context of people, the key takeaway is that the concept of experience exists outside of the context of a specific product or object. We can describe human interaction and usage of products as an experience, and in fact is. The entire field of UX design is based on exactly this.

The Impact of AI on Human Experiences

AI has huge promise for creating better human experiences, as well, and has already been doing so in many applications. Recall from Chapter 7 this nonexhaustive list of outcome categories that people stakeholders might experience as the result of AI-based innovations:

- Better health and health-related outcomes
- Better personal safety and security
- Better financial performance, savings, and insights
- Better UX, convenience, and delight
- Better and easier planning and decisions
- Better productivity and enjoyment
- Better learning and entertainment

AI is able to create better human experiences when used to create one or more of these outcomes. Note that in this book, I use the term "better" in two ways. First, to describe the improvement and emotional aspect of experiences; for example, increased delight, enjoyment, and happiness in the purely positive meaning. Second, I also intend for the concept of better human experiences to include prevention and reduced severity of bad and suboptimal experiences.

Another thing to note is that the designation of "better" is highly personal and in many cases subjective. Some people might think that certain technologies and their impact on their lives is highly beneficial and they couldn't live without, whereas others might find certain technologies or implementations more harmful than beneficial. While I think many people will find much of what follows to represent great potential benefits to humans, ultimately it's up to people to decide for themselves, and that's perfectly fine.

The purpose of this section is to give benefits, approaches, and examples of how AI can create better human experiences for each of these categories. The approaches and examples that I provide are far from exhaustive, and many new real-world use cases and applications are appearing every day, as are advancements in AI techniques and algorithms.

Many of the following examples are built on techniques from AI-based fields such as predictive analytics, prescriptive analytics (automated and/or optimized recommendations, actions, and decisions), and reinforcement learning.

Better health and health-related outcomes

AI has massive potential when it comes to better human health and health-related outcomes, physical and mental. Examples of potential AI-based health benefits include the following:

- Prevention of ailments
- Early diagnosis and treatment of diseases (both physical and mental)
- Personalized and optimized treatment plans and effectiveness
- Better health outcomes and increased life expectancy
- Assistance to people with disabilities
- Reduced accidents and injury

Physical health Real-world examples include:

- Perfectly matched paired kidney donation (*http://bit.ly/2wdSKHd*)
- Retinal scan-based cardiovascular disease and stroke risk assessment (*http://bit.ly/2En8IDB*)
- Early lung cancer diagnosis and personalized treatment (*http://www.optel lum.com*)
- Echo-based coronary disease diagnostics (*http://bit.ly/2VJVgPN*)
- Optimizing medication dosing (*http://bit.ly/2VMQOjo*)
- Sudden cardiac death prevention (*http://bit.ly/2W1CBEn*)
- Intensive-care unit equipment settings optimization (*http://bit.ly/2HwFELG*)
- Image-based skin cancer detection and diagnosis (*https://go.nature.com/2JzVJTo*)

Mental health Real-world examples include:

- Suicide flagging and prevention (*https://cnb.cx/2QoB1q4*)
- Depression and psychosis prediction (*http://bit.ly/2MkoP8v*)
- Animal-like therapeutic robots for nonanimal-friendly environments (*http://www.parorobots.com*) (e.g., hospitals)
- Early dementia detection from video-recorded interviews (*http://bit.ly/2YHxNAL*)

Another example is patient life expectancy prediction (*http://bit.ly/2Eu3J3V* and *http://bit.ly/2WXkV9c*).

This is a very active and promising area of AI development. AI can also help doctors and patients make better decisions about what medical treatment option to choose. In the cases of a medical diagnosis that needs treatment, AI is able to provide probabilities of success and recommendations for a given treatment strategy and thus help people make sometimes critical life decisions.

Better personal safety and security

AI is able to better people's personal safety and security in public, at work, and at home, as well as prevent and minimize potential issues around both. Examples of potential AI-based safety and security benefits include the following:

- Reduced accidents and injury
- Improved online, network, and home security
- Improved public security

Real-world examples include:

- Autonomous vehicles (*http://bit.ly/2HOJBua*)
- Improved construction site efficiency and safety (*http://bit.ly/2YR4pbB*)
- Real-time predictive safety and risk for any given location (*https://prn.to/2QiraC4*)
- Predicting natural disasters (*https://go.nature.com/2YIyLNc*) (e.g., earthquake magnitudes)
- Spam and phishing filters for email (*https://tcrn.ch/2VLdDDY*)
- Crime analysis and prevention (*http://bit.ly/2QgehbJ*)
- Predictive maintenance (*http://bit.ly/2WtHSEd*)
- Fraud detection and prevention (*http://bit.ly/2M30Jor*)
- Identity theft detection (*http://bit.ly/2QjXC7d*)
- Personal data protection (*http://bit.ly/2M6kSXB*)
- Facial recognition-based home security (*http://bit.ly/2YINFDa*)

Better financial performance, savings, and insights

AI is able to help people achieve better financial performance, savings, and insights into their wealth over time. Examples of potential AI-based financial performance, savings, and insights benefits include the following:

- Improved financial predictions and forecasts
- Improved financial planning and ability to achieve target financial goals
- Improved cost and general savings

Real-world examples include:

- Growth of low-carbon and green electricity (*http://bit.ly/2HMXyJb*)
- Image-based solar panel energy savings estimation (*http://bit.ly/2HxPuNk*)
- Forecast-based energy-savings decisions (*http://bit.ly/2HMXyJb*)
- Smart devices and homes (*https://nyti.ms/2VG1joE*)
- Discounts and savings from personalized promotions and offers (*https://www.betterment.com*)
- Robo-advisors for portfolio performance (*https://www.wealthfront.com*)

As of this writing, robo-advisers are a great example that is gaining a lot of popularity, and multiple companies are focusing entirely on AI-powered investment portfolio management, which includes investments selection and rebalancing. The idea is that these platforms can achieve better and lower-cost performance and be completely automated as compared to traditional financial advisor approaches.

Not only do users have the potential for better and automated retirement portfolio performance, but they also can have much better analytics and insights into how the portfolio is doing. Going back to the concept of analysis paralysis, having better insights definitely does not usually mean having more data and charts to look at; rather, it's just the opposite. It means having a very simplified and curated amount of data and insights that tell you basically everything you need to know, with the option of seeing more if you choose (think about the concept of the executive summary). AI and machine learning are being used to generate insights in exactly this way.

Better UX, convenience, and delight

AI is able to create better user experiences, convenience, and delight for people when they interact with technology. Examples of potential AI-based UX, convenience, and delight benefits include the following:

- Easier, quicker, and more relevant discovery of products, content, media, information, and services
- AI-optimized UI layouts and interactions
- Simplified and diversified technology interactions
- Increased task convenience

Real-world examples include:

- Personal assistants (e.g., Amazon's Alexa, Apple's Siri, Google's Assistant)
- Reduced search and browsing friction via search engines and recommender systems (e.g., Google, Amazon, Netflix)
- Conversational product recommendations (*http://bit.ly/2VLUUZ8*)
- Specific song and music artist recognition (*https://blog.shazam.com/*)
- Wine ratings and reviews from bottle labels (*https://www.vivino.com*)
- Specific gesture detection and recognition (*http://bit.ly/2X3n1Ez*)
- Real-time multiperson pose detection (*http://bit.ly/30BBqtL*)
- Image-based question-answering (*http://bit.ly/2Mk2Bqb*)
- Chatbot-driven flower (*http://bit.ly/2WjKKno*) and pizza ordering (*http://bit.ly/2VLV7vo*)
- The ability to reduce the travel and steps required for tasks (e.g., depositing checks with a mobile app as opposed to going to a bank)
- Voice- (*http://bit.ly/2JVGVow*) and image-based search (*http://bit.ly/2JxQyTX*) and interactions
- Pocket-size instant language translation (*http://bit.ly/2QiUF6F*).

Both Amazon and Netflix have created personalized recommendation engines that many people are very familiar with. Adding these engines resulted in huge business value. Amazon increased its revenue by 35% with the addition of these engines, and 75% of the content watched on Netflix is generated by their recommendations (*http://bit.ly/2CjeoM5*).

Let's talk about *why* these engines were so hugely successful for these companies. Browsing and searching for things is considered a chore by many people, and therefore an area of friction and time commitment. This only becomes worse as the amount of items grows significantly, to the point that some people begin to experience analysis paralysis. This is the phenomenon whereby there are two many options, which results in a struggle to make a choice or decision and can ultimately lead to abandonment. Recommendations help alleviate this problem.

The better the engine, the higher chance that the recommendations include the exact items that the user would have chosen had they labored through potentially thousands of items. The other benefit is that users are potentially introduced to similar items that they might otherwise not have known about, but could be a great fit; for example, a product to buy or movie to watch. Lastly, users are also able to easily find related items (e.g., batteries to go with a battery charger purchase).

Another benefit is that providing recommendations is a type of personalization, which is becoming more important to people, especially younger generations. People want personalized experiences around what matters most to them. Most software and technology traditionally has been generic and meant to appeal to the masses, which can diminish the overall experience for a significant group of people.

Let's revisit the huge lifts experienced by Amazon and Netflix after the introduction of recommendation engines. Amazon's massive revenue lift was largely due to increased order size. Instead of people buying one product at a time (if any for that matter)—for example due to the search friction, time commitment, and analysis paralysis already described—people can easily find and add items to their carts that go with other items, are new and exciting, or are just readily available (think of this as the digital equivalent of grocery line impulse buying).

With Netflix's introduction of recommendations, people became much more engaged with the platform and were able to more easily and quickly find what they wanted. They were introduced to new movies and TV shows that they didn't know about but ultimately would enjoy. In many cases, people have become binge Netflix watchers since the platform recommends something new to watch as soon as whatever you're currently watching ends. All you need to do is just click to continue.

Ultimately, the introduction of recommendations might have prevented Netflix from failing as a company. Think of all the apps that we try on our mobile devices that aren't very "sticky" (i.e., useful and delightful to use) and therefore are left unused. This could have very easily happened to Netflix. When Netflix first launched, its catalog didn't have a lot of popular titles and wasn't very big, but it was growing. Combining that with users being essentially asked to labor through searching a lot of nonrelevant content could have easily resulted in total abandonment of Netflix, especially depending on how much time and persistence people wanted to spend on it. This obviously did not happen, and it is likely largely due to the introduction of the recommendations experience. Sticky applications can result in significant customer retention increases.

The easier things become, while also providing maximal value, the better the UX and the more users stay engaged. From the business perspective, this results in less customer/user churn and better retention. One thing worth noting is that while some of what we've covered can improve UX, excellent design and usability are still paramount. People like and use well-designed products; conversely, people do not like and totally abandon poorly designed products. Again, this is related to the UX of AI concept mentioned earlier.

Better and easier planning and decisions

AI is able to help make better and easier planning and decisions. Examples of potential AI-based planning and decisions benefits include the following:

- Simplified, more accurate, and automated planning and decision making
- Planning and decision-making assistance in areas outside of expertise
- Better predictions and forecasts
- Avoidance of analysis paralysis
- Removal of nonoptimal options and decisions

Real-world examples include:

- Automated planning and scheduling (*http://bit.ly/2wdEnmx*)
- Augmented intelligence (*http://bit.ly/2HAmmW4*)

- Retirement investing (*https://www.betterment.com*) and portfolio management (*https://www.wealthfront.com*)
- Accurate house price predictions for sale planning (*http://bit.ly/2X4f9CS*)
- ride-sharing estimated time of arrival (*https://ubr.to/2VNTFsB*)

In the business context, but from the human perspective, AI can create better experiences for business managers at companies. Most leaders and managers go to work every day with the goal of making an impact and driving business success, most often through strategic planning and making key decisions. Successfully accomplishing these things usually results in self-fulfillment and satisfaction, rewards and bonuses, promotions, job security, praise from shareholders and the public, and a lot of respect from colleagues and employees. AI is an enabler of all of these things.

It's also a pretty remarkable feeling and empowering when you're no longer making blind or gut-driven decisions with no good estimates of the outcome, and are able instead to make data-driven decisions with a high probability of success and whose outcomes can be anticipated in advance. Lack of innovation, incremental progress, and the status quo are unable to provide these benefits and improved human experiences.

Better productivity, efficiency, and enjoyment

AI can help with better productivity, efficiency, and enjoyment while carrying out tasks. Examples of potential AI-based productivity and enjoyment benefits include the following:

- More productive and enjoyable work (better work)
- Reducing resources required to accomplish tasks
- Increased efficiency
- Improved organization

Real-world examples include:

- Augmented intelligence (*http://bit.ly/2HAmmW4*)
- Image tagging and categorization (*http://bit.ly/2HLprBu*)

- Email category prediction (*http://bit.ly/2VVzzBk*).

Better learning and entertainment

AI is able to help create better and more fun learning and entertainment for people. Examples of potential AI-based learning and entertainment benefits include the following:

- Discovery of new and more relevant media and entertainment options
- Better and more fun learning
- Better and more fun gameplay

Learning-related examples include Adaptive (*http://bit.ly/2QkoAsn*), differentiated, and individualized learning (*http://bit.ly/2Espjpn*).

Real-world media personalization and recommendations examples include:

- YouTube video recommendations (*http://bit.ly/2XtbRfl*)
- Movie and TV show recommendations (*http://bit.ly/2wcaUt8*)
- Music and playlist recommendations (*http://bit.ly/2VN5AH6*)
- Rank-based news recommendations (*http://bit.ly/30DNFGl*)

Entertainment examples include:

- Adaptive and intelligent gaming (*http://bit.ly/2QiWP6g*)
- virtual reality (*http://bit.ly/2WldY4O*)
- augmented reality (*https://adobe.ly/2VZ87CF*)

Now that we've defined and covered concepts, benefits, and examples around experiences and how AI can help create better experiences for humans, let's turn our attention to the interfaces through which humans interact directly with technology.

Experience Interfaces

Most of us are very familiar with the most common interfaces that provide our technology-based user experiences. The top three today are web, mobile, and desktop. That said, with the ongoing rise and proliferation of the IoT and connected hardware devices, many new interfaces now include personal assistants (e.g., Amazon Echo), smart appliances, smart-home devices (e.g., door locks, lightbulbs, HVAC), smart cars, and other innovative interfaces.

It's worth mentioning that speech is becoming more prevalent as a form of user input, and is on a trajectory to becoming totally dominant. As of this writing, most two- and three-year-old children are now pretty much experts at using digital devices such as mobile phones and tablets (e.g., iPhones and iPads). They have experience with typing mostly in a digital sense; that is, on the virtual keyboard interfaces on these devices, complete with emojis and all.

Now imagine a time when young children are still experts at using technology at a very young age, except that all they know about interfaces and interactions with technology is through speaking alone. They just walk around and talk to everything to make things happen. The idea of actually having to type anything would be both primitive and wasteful in terms of time and effort. Why type when you can just talk? Sound familiar? Why send a letter and waste a stamp, envelope, paper, and your time when you can just write an email? We're already seeing speech become more dominant, and the total dominance that I'm referring to is probably not too far in the future.

So to recap, the two major categories that I've outlined so far are traditional software-based interfaces and connected device interfaces, both of which are seeing a dramatic rise of speech as a form of input and interaction. We can use these interfaces to offer AI-powered functionality with which users can interact.

Current examples include personalization, recommendations, automatic portfolio rebalancing and investing, and dashboards containing insights. As also discussed, there are other advanced applications such as helping blind people see, self-driving vehicles, and AI-driven advancement in robotics.

It's worth noting that not all applications of AI have a UI, with automation being the most obvious, but note that everything else around what makes a product great that we've discussed still very much applies.

The Experience Economy

AI solutions that enable great human experiences have the greatest chance of success. Emerging and state-of-the-art technologies such as AI are able to improve existing experiences, create new ones, and eliminate bad ones.

Experience economy is a term used to describe the fact that people nowadays prefer spending their time and money on experiences instead of products and goods. Examples include traveling, going to a concert or sporting event, skydiving, surfing, meeting your favorite author (aw, shucks), watching the Chicago Cubs win the World Series after 108 years (easily one of the top experiences of my life), and you get the point.

This trend is being driven primarily by millennials and the younger Gen Z generation (those born after 1996). Gen Z is the first true native digital generation, comprising more than one-fifth of the US population (*https://bloom.bg/ 2EsSoTp*). Additional research shows that 74% of Americans prefer buying experiences to products, and 49% of Gen Z and millennials would sell some furniture and clothes to be able to travel more (*http://bit.ly/2JYPdER*).

In response to the huge demand for consumer experiences, companies are increasingly designing and promoting them (*http://bit.ly/2JzDNZ1*). Experience-based offerings can also be a key differentiator and generator of competitive advantage. In many cases, certain experiences have existed and been available for a long time but have not necessarily been readily available or at the forefront of people's mind. The experience economy helps with that and also makes experiences easier to schedule, undergo, and share as a result of experience-driven products. This represents a huge opportunity for experience-focused AI products, as well.

People aren't just looking for experiences in and of themselves; rather, they prefer personalized experiences, an area in which AI excels. Personalization such as recommendations are one of the largest drivers of conversions and revenue increases. Likewise, the potential in general of personalized experiences is huge. AI is already being used to drive personalized digital experiences, but can also be used to tailor nondigital experiences, as well.

Design Thinking

Design thinking is a human-centric and needs-centered methodology and set of processes that is especially useful for solving complex problems that are ill defined or unknown, which are those most associated with innovation (*http:// bit.ly/2YKfKtD*). It is meant to be a highly collaborative process between product designers and users. One of the major benefits of design thinking is its human-centric approach. The ultimate goal of design thinking is to build products that are based on how real users think, feel, and behave. Although the concepts have been around since the 1950s, design thinking is now a popular and widely used technique.

Tim Brown says that the design thinking process is a system of overlapping spaces, not a sequence of orderly steps.] The three overlapping spaces he identifies are inspiration, ideation, and implementation. "Inspiration is the problem or opportunity that motivates the search for solutions," he writes (*http://bit.ly/2YKfWJn*). "Ideation is the process of generating, developing, and testing ideas. Implementation is the path that leads from the project stage into people's lives."footnote:[*Change By Design: How Design Thinking Transforms Organizations and Inspires Innovation*. New York: Harper Business. 2009.

Design thinking is a very useful approach to use when developing your AI vision and strategy. Design thinking is able to help solve problems with technology, but you also can extend it to solving problems beyond technology and products. I provide a brief overview of the methodology here based on the five stages of the design thinking process (*http://bit.ly/2YKfKtD*) as presented by the Interaction Design Foundation. This organization and many others derive their design thinking approach from Stanford University's d.school, the leading design thinking educational institution.

The five stages of design thinking are *empathize*, *define* (the problem), *ideate*, *prototype*, and *test*. This might look somewhat familiar to Lean and Agile product development methodologies. That's because it's a similar method, but applied to the design process that precedes the remaining product development process. Figure 9-1 shows the design-thinking process.

Design thinking is a nonlinear and iterative process. It begins with empathizing with humans and their needs or a problem they have. It's supposed to be a form of immersive discovery in the actual environment and with the actual people that the problem exists. A key aspect is that all assumptions must be set aside in order to better understand users and their needs.

The definition stage is fairly self-explanatory, with the key characteristic that the problem definition should take the form of a human-centric problem statement. This follows from a comprehensive analysis of observations made in the empathize stage. The definition stage is the foundation and enabler of the ideation stage. In the ideation stage, the understanding gained about users and their needs is used to rapidly generate ideas and "think outside the box" for solutions to the given problem as defined in the problem statement.

DESIGN THINKING: A NON-LINEAR PROCESS

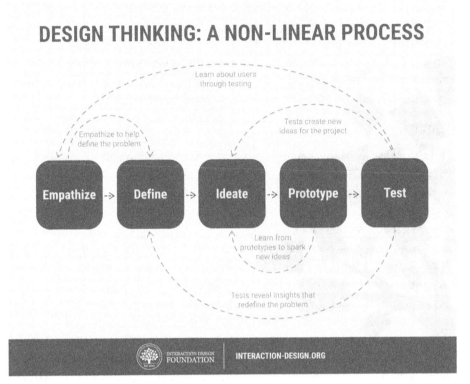

Figure 9-1. The design-thinking process (from Design Thinking: A Non-Linear Process, by Teo Yu Siang and the Interaction Design Foundation. Copyright license: CC BY-NC-SA 3.0. Originally published in http://bit.ly/2YKfKtD)

The ideation stage can employ many ideation techniques, such as Brainstorm, Brainwrite, Worst Possible Idea, and SCAMPER. The first three stages, when completed, become the foundation on which to build a low-cost, scaled-down version of the product. This is an idea similar to that of the MVP. In this case, the prototype is usually built with common design tools, as opposed to creating actual software. The prototype is used to experiment in order to iterate to the best possible solution to the given problem, as defined.

This prototyping stage also helps uncover risky assumptions and any inherent constraints and considerations for the product not yet considered or uncovered. It also helps solidify the potential success of the product in the context of use by real users, particularly in how they would behave, think, and feel when using the product.

The final stage of the process is the test stage, although keep in mind that the process is iterative and not linear. The test stage usually results in modifications to the problem statement, as well as understanding of users and the conditions of use. The end goal is to gain the deepest understanding possible of the product and its users. Design thinking should facilitate a human-centric mapping of the problem space to the solution space, and when done right, should result in successful products that are able to meet human needs.

Summary

The key takeaway of this chapter is that AI is absolutely capable of delivering on the promise of better human experiences. The number-one way to ensure that is by understanding the needs, wants, and likes of actual users and then applying human-centric methodologies like design thinking to create an AI vision and strategy capable of delivering.

Discussing AI's potential in medicine and other areas to improve lives, David Rotman, editor of the *MIT Technology Review*, noted the risk of creating public resentment if AI is not used to benefit as many people as possible. "The danger is not so much a direct political backlash," he wrote, "but rather a failure to embrace and invest in the technology's abundant possibilities."

I couldn't agree more. The primary focus and goal of AI should be to help as many people as possible, and along with AI-based technological advancements, this is how AI will continue to create better human experiences. We've now covered everything that is foundational to developing a successful AI vision, which will also help with AI strategy creation, as well. Chapter 10 concludes Part II of this book with an example of developing an AI vision and resulting vision statement.

10

An AI Vision Example

Now that we've covered AIPB, and how to create an AI vision in detail, let's create an AIPB AI vision using a hypothetical example.

Our AI vision example was inspired by Grant Achatz, a highly renowned chef and restaurateur, famous for his Chicago-based restaurant, Alinea. Alinea was ranked the second best restaurant in the United States and seventh in the world according to *Restaurant* magazine's list of the world's 50 best restaurants (*http://bit.ly/2Rua7NT*). Alinea was also awarded three Michelin stars eight consecutive years (*http://bit.ly/2LfsncC*) at the time this book was published!

Very unfortunately, Mr. Achatz was diagnosed with stage 4b tongue cancer at the young age of 33. Despite most oncology experts telling Achatz that the only treatment option required removing 75% of his tongue and effectively destroying his sense of taste permanently, another opinion provided by a University of Chicago Medicine oncologist named Everett Vokes suggested an innovative treatment option. His plan was geared toward saving Achatz' tongue and taste buds with targeted chemotherapy and radiation, which proved to be successful, although it did result in a temporary loss of his sense of taste (*https://n.pr/2WXucSJ*). Today, Achatz is now cancer free (*http://bit.ly/2N4VVMG*).

Achatz's sense of taste eventually returned, and his story presents a compelling AI opportunity. Let's build an AIPB vision based on this example. What if technology-based mouth sensors could be combined with AI algorithms to map sensory inputs to what we call tastes? Let's try to use AI to create a digital mapping that is similar to the chemical-based sensory mechanism that makes our taste sense work. We want to do this to help people like Achatz, who lose their sense of taste.

Spatial–Temporal Sensing and Perception

Humans perceive tastes such as bitter, sour, salty, sweet, savory, and metallic. This happens when chemical substances make contact with certain nerve cells in our mouths, which then activate other nerve cells. The brain ultimately receives this information and perceives "tastes," or what we also call flavor.[1]

Jeff Hawkins, in his book *On Intelligence*, states: "You hear sound, see light, and feel pressure, but inside your brain, there isn't any fundamental difference between these types of information.... All your brain knows is patterns. Your perceptions and knowledge about the world are built from these patterns.... All the information that enters your mind comes in as spatial and temporal patterns on the axons."

We humans often take our ability to sense and perceive for granted and might think that our brains somehow see, hear, taste, smell, and touch directly. Our brain actually exists in silence and darkness, and senses indirectly only by receiving patterns of signals through sensory organs that are passed through huge numbers of neurons and synapses during their journey deep into our brain (for more information, refer to Appendix A). These spatial and temporal patterns of signals, by the time the brain receives them, are nothing more than neuron activations. In other words, the brain interprets these activations as an image that we see, for example, even though the activations represent nothing to the brain like what we actually perceive that we see. It's like the streaming symbols from the movie *The Matrix* and how they actually represent something else; in this case, what's going on in the matrix.

All of these examples are very analogous to how artificial neural networks and deep learning work. Inputs go in (in this case, sensed chemical substances that trigger nerve activation signals), and the network produces a result such as a prediction or classification. In the case of human sense inputs, outputs could be a specific sound, smell, feeling, visual image, or (you know where this is going) flavor.

AI-Driven Taste

We are interested in creating the world's first technology-based, AI-powered taste-sensing mechanism to help those who are no longer able to taste. Assume that nothing close to this has ever been done before. Moving forward, we refer to

---

1 *https://www.ncbi.nlm.nih.gov/books/NBK279408*

this solution as the Tasterizer, and the hypothetical company is Tasty Co. Notice that we have an initial high-level vision without having performed any assessments or developed a plan. We don't need to do that yet.

Recall our AIPB Framework, as shown in Figure 10-1.

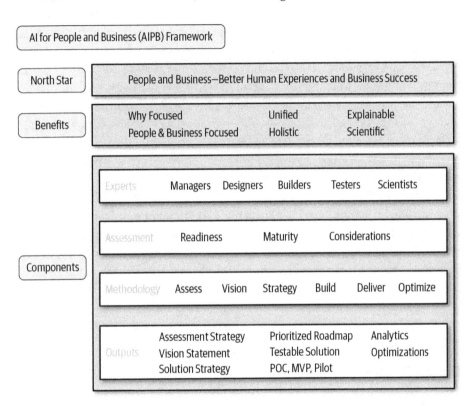

Figure 10-1. The AIPB Framework

We begin with the North Star: better human experiences and business success. So how will this vision address both? Luckily the answer is relatively easy. Getting back the sense of taste clearly results in better human experiences, so done deal for that.

A business that invents this hypothetical solution would be able to achieve business success in many ways, not just sales related. A business based on a product like this, and its employees, can feel really good about how its products are able to help those in need. It's a win-win situation. They also can feel good knowing that they're able to truly innovate and create new products, business models, and capture new markets as a result. Of course, there's also the obvious business benefits such as sales and revenue (assume for this example that there's a big enough market for this business, and you're a first mover).

We've now identified the benefits to both people and business at a high level and are able to move on to developing the vision statement. Remember that all relevant, AIPB-recommended experts should collaborate to develop the intended output of each AIPB Methodology Component phase. For the vision phase, this includes managers (business folks and domain experts) and scientists (AI practitioners). Highest paid person's opinion (HiPPo) methods and design-by-committee are not allowed, and concepts like the *flipped classroom* are highly recommended. Use all sessions as highly productive, effective, actual working collaboration sessions, as opposed to teaching and learning sessions. Let everyone know in advance how to get up to speed, preferably in a way that requires minimal time and effort to accommodate busy schedules.

Also recall that for the AIPB methodology vision phase, and from the AIPB process categories introduced in Chapter 2, I recommend the ideation and vision development category. This includes using recommended methods such as design thinking, brainstorming, and the five *whys*. Note that this is meant to be a high-level and overly simplified example. Developing an AI vision using AIPB in the real world should involve everything vision related that we've discussed so far in this book.

With everything established, and to wrap up our example, let's create our vision statement.

Our AIPB Vision Statement

For those who have lost the ability to taste, we at Tasty Co. are helping to restore people's sense of taste so that they can taste food and beverages once again (why for people). This has enabled Tasty Co. to generate new revenues by capturing an entirely new market while expanding our portfolio of human wellness-benefiting products (why for business). We're able to do that with our patented Taste-Fusion technology, which combines state-of-the-art microsensing hardware with the latest AI techniques in order to map the chemical substances of food and drinks to tastes perceived by the human brain (how). The result is what we call the Tasterizer (what)!

We can modify this statement to be only people focused or only business focused as needed for a specific audience, but the exercise of creating a vision statement that identifies the *why* for both people and business is a must and is something that many companies don't do. As Simon Sinek famously said, "People don't buy what you do, they buy why you do it." Make sure you clearly understand the benefits to the people that use your offering and then build a great product around it.

PART III

Developing an AI Strategy

Using our foundational understanding of how to create an AI vision, including what matters most when doing so, Part III of this book is about developing an AI strategy to make the vision a reality. We focus on concepts such as scientific innovation, AI readiness and maturity, and key considerations for achieving success with AI. You should use these concepts to perform appropriate assessments as defined by AIPB and to develop a strategy to fill gaps and address key considerations, as well as for developing an effective, vision-aligned AI solution strategy and prioritized roadmap to guide the execution of the remaining iterative AIPB downstream methodology phases: build, deliver, and optimize.

Scientific Innovation for AI Success

We now begin laying the foundational framework for developing an effective, vision-aligned AI strategy. This chapter is very important for executives and managers interested in using AI, particularly for strategic planning and appropriately setting expectations.

AI is a highly complex scientific field that is largely driven by exploration, experimentation, and unpredictable outcomes. As a result, you should think of AI as a form of R&D, including expectation setting and budgeting. AI is also a field that is very actively researched and undergoing continuous advancement, applied in increasing and varied ways and at a very fast pace.

I am regularly asked by business executives and managers what value AI can create for them (including ROI), how much time and cost AI solutions will take to build, what solution performance will be achieved, what AI technique or approach will work best, and what exact data is needed to ensure a certain level of performance.

Just as with many R&D initiatives, it is understood that people are usually unable to answer many of these questions upfront (that's the entire purpose of R&D!) AI is no different, although I find that this is largely not yet well understood. The key point is that AI is a scientific field of discovery and not one of design and assembly. Let's discuss why.

AI as Science

Let's revisit the term "science" in the field of data science. Most of us remember the scientific method from school. The *Oxford English Dictionary* defines the scientific method as follows:

A method of procedure that has characterized natural science since the 17th century, consisting of systematic observation, measurement, and experiment, and the formulation, testing, and modification of hypotheses.

Another relevant *Oxford English Dictionary* definition, for the word "empirical," is as follows:

Based on, concerned with, or verifiable by observation or experience rather than theory or pure logic.

Finally, the *Oxford English Dictionary* defines nondeterminism as follows:

Of, relating to, or designating a mode of computation in which, at certain points, there is an unpredictable choice of ways to proceed.

All three definitions apply to AI, machine learning, and data science. These fields, based on statistics and probability, are scientific, empirical, and nondeterministic by nature. This means that success in these fields comes not from logic, theory, or pure subject matter expertise, but from experience, trial and error, and the application of the scientific method, or a very similar process.

I can't state this enough. AI, machine learning, and data science are not fields that will allow you to know exactly what you will get, what is required, how much time it will take, and what it will cost for a given application, without a certain amount of experience, sophistication, and competency (concepts we'll return to in the next chapter) with the exact (or extremely close) set of data and techniques needed for the application to be successful. We use the phrase "new AI project" (includes machine learning) for the rest of this chapter to refer to the scenario in which a data team works on a project involving data and/or techniques that are relatively new in the context of experience, sophistication, and competency.

Take building a simple to-do list mobile app, for example. Assume that all it does is allow users to sign up for an account and then use the app to create and manage to-do lists. Designing, developing, and deploying the mobile app to the iTunes (iPhone) and Google Play (Android) app stores is all relatively deterministic and does not require application of the scientific method, nor empirical observation and data gathering. UX and UI designers will develop the interface and experience, developers will build the app based on designs and other requirements, QA and automation testers will verify the app quality and absence of bugs, and DevOps engineers will submit the app to the app stores for release.

Assuming that you have an experienced team, everyone involved should be able to roughly estimate the amount of time, effort, and specific tasks required to build the mobile app. This is a great example of something deterministic and nonscientific in technology development.

On the contrary, when beginning a new AI project, it's impossible to know how much data preparation (e.g., cleaning, processing) is required without first accessing and exploring the data. It is likewise impossible to know whether the available data (prepared or not) is well suited to solve the problem at hand or whether it requires additional data processing, feature engineering, and data augmentation. Determining all of these things requires exploration, experimentation, and experience. Let me explain why.

There is a concept often referred to in the context of AI and machine learning known as *tractability*. *Merriam-Webster* defines tractable as being "easily handled, managed, or wrought," and it is synonymous with the word "malleable." Some problems are simply intractable, meaning that they are extremely difficult or impossible to solve. In AI and machine learning, intractable projects or tasks are normally due to choosing the wrong approach (i.e., model, algorithm, or technique) or not having the "right" data or features. Usually this becomes obvious from the inability to create a suitable model with a given approach and data. Advanced techniques such as deep learning are able to overcome some intractability issues given their feature extraction capabilities; that is, deep learning does not require humans to manually perform feature selection and feature engineering, but in other cases, more and/or better data or better-suited algorithms might be required.

There is also a concept called the "no free lunch theorem," which is based heavily on the mathematics of optimization (*http://bit.ly/2Fso1sh*). Many people interpret this theorem in machine learning applications to mean that there is no way to determine in advance which exact model and model configuration will perform best for a given application. You must undergo an empirical (experimental) process in order to determine this, and even if a well-performing model has been found, it is not guaranteed to be the best performing model. Luckily there is strong demand among AI tool vendors and machine learning practitioners to help with these facts of AI development. In particular, tools are actively being developed to help accelerate the exploratory discovery process in order to get initial model performance estimates, to better understand the ability of the data on hand to get the job done, and to help more quickly select the best model or algorithm.

For a new AI project (again, "new" as previously discussed), requiring that everything be known upfront, including time, cost, performance and requirements, is a recipe for failure and disappointment. Failure to understand this often results in improperly set stakeholder expectations and also executives either flat-out rejecting to move forward on these initiatives or taking an exorbitant amount of time to make decisions to proceed. All of this can result in missed opportunities, cost-of-delay penalties, and defeat at the hands of the competition.

Another thing to consider comes from looking at this from the 80/20 Pareto Principle perspective; that is, 80% of target (good enough) model performance is relatively easy to achieve (e.g., with model selection and model configuration), whereas the other 20% requires an exponential increase in uncertainty and unpredictable time, cost, and effort (e.g., data augmentation, feature engineering). The exact proportions will depend on the specific application and how critical performance is for it. Not all AI solutions require the same level of performance (e.g., medical diagnosis versus product recommendations).

Given everything covered in this section and in general, innovation involving scientific fields such as AI should be referred to as scientific innovation. Simply adding the word scientific is better suited to reality and should help set expectations appropriately, which can ultimately lead to more successful initiatives. Here is a simple formula that I've created that I think represents this best:

Scientific + Empirical + Nondeterministic = Scientific Innovation Success

Scientific innovation requires a shift in mindset and approach similar to switching from waterfall to agile. Companies have made, or are still making (it can take a while) this shift as a result of significant waterfall failures, and also from understanding the many benefits of lean and agile methods over waterfall. Adopting a scientific innovation mindset and approach sooner than later is key to AI success.

The TCPR Model

Everything described so far is so critical to understand that I've developed a model and some analogies to better illustrate it all. When it comes to new AI projects, these are the questions I hear most often in advance of starting.

- How long will it take to deliver the solution, and for what cost (time and cost)?

- How good will the solution be (performance)?
- What exactly do you need in advance to deliver your target performance level (requirements)?

All of these questions when combined basically ask: In advance of starting a new AI project, and without first providing a view into the readiness and quality of the data that's available, I want to know what I'm going to get exactly, how much it will cost, how long it will take, and what exact data (remember the "right" data?) I need to ensure mitigated risks, timely delivery, and ultimate success.

Unlike the known quantity of traditional business intelligence (BI), for example, we usually can't answer these questions in advance for new AI projects. The key phrase here is "known quantity." In Chapter 12, we discuss how the ability to answer these questions in advance is actually a function of maturity, and I present models that I created to better illustrate it.

For now, let's explain why these questions are very difficult, and sometimes impossible, to answer in advance for new AI projects. We do so by putting it in the context of project management and a relevant analogy. The project management field often refers to a triangle model of scope, cost, and time for a given project level of quality. It is balanced, a balanced equation in fact, because one component cannot be changed without affecting or adjusting another. Figure 11-1 shows this triangle.

Figure 11-1. The project management triangle

If you're not familiar, the idea is that if one component is fixed (most often cost due to budgets), the other two become trade-off levers. In the case of a fixed budget (cost), the number of resources (people) is fixed by the budget and therefore so is the amount of work (scope) that can be done in a given amount of time.

Requiring the work to be completed faster (less time) necessarily requires an increase in cost because more people will be needed to reduce the time to delivery (assuming that adding more people will actually reduce the time to delivery—in reality it often doesn't). Alternatively, requiring increased work to be done (increased scope) necessarily requires more time for a fixed number of people (cost).

So, to summarize: this is a balanced system; that is, requiring an increase in scope or decrease in delivery time can be achieved only by a corresponding increase in cost. Very critically, this applies only to projects that are deterministic —that is, they do not fall under the umbrella of scientific innovation. In fact, AI and machine learning projects will likely not go any faster nor will model performance be increased to acceptable levels by simply throwing more data scientists at it.

Given that, and returning to the questions posed, I have developed a new and better-suited dependency model as related to AI, machine learning, and data science. The components are time, cost, performance, and requirements, referred to collectively as *the TCPR Model*, as illustrated in Figure 11-2. Here are the questions again for reference, followed by the TCPR Model:

- How long will it take to deliver the solution, and for what cost (time and cost)?

- How good will the solution be (performance)?

- What exactly do you need in advance to deliver your target performance level (requirements)?

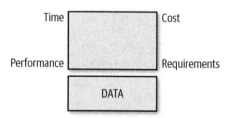

Figure 11-2. The TCPR Model

The TCPR Model represents what is known as an *indeterminate system* (i.e., more than one solution exists), and a famous example of this in engineering is the calculation of forces in the legs of a four-legged table. Unless the table and floor upon which the legs sit are absolutely perfect, it is not possible to calculate the simultaneous forces at all four legs, and the table is likely resting most of its weight on three legs (think of all the wobbly tables you've come across). This is what makes this an indeterminate system. A three-legged table, on the other hand, represents a *determinate system*, and is therefore balanced and predictable like the project management triangle.

Notice that the TCPR Model includes a data foundation. This is critical because there is no point even talking about the four TCPR-related questions without having an initial understanding of the data sources and data fields that are available first. They all depend on some amount of data discovery, exploration, and understanding.

That bears repeating in another way. Determining the TCPR of an AI solution requires data upfront, no matter what, and also some amount of actual exploration and experimentation. This is part of what makes AI and machine learning nondeterministic. Let's go over a couple of analogies to help better understand the concepts behind the TCPR Model and its dependency on having data upfront.

A TCPR Model Analogy

Let's turn the discussion to an analogy that will help explain more. Let's imagine a baker who is interested in creating a new, fancy, and complex cake for her bakery. A group of renowned food critics from prominent food magazines and newspapers will assign a rating to the cake on a scale of one to five stars. If the average critic rating is high enough, the baker will be given a very prestigious baking award.

Let's discuss this in terms of the TCPR Model, and keep in mind that much of this might be obvious when it comes to baking, but in the context of AI seems to not be obvious at all to many people. This despite AI and baking being comparable in this context.

TIME AND COST

The precise baking time is very important because only a few minutes short or too long will ruin the cake quality and the resulting star ratings. Despite the time importance, the baker is unable to determine the precise time in advance to bake the cake because that will depend on the final selection and proportions of ingredients (recipe) and require many baking trials to figure out. The exact cost of one cake is also unknown until the final recipe is determined.

Likewise, the exact time and cost required to develop and deploy a new AI solution is impossible to know upfront unless it's something that a given group of practitioners have done before with the same-ish data (a measure of maturity, discussed in Chapter 12). After they have the data, they can begin experimenting with different models and techniques in order to better determine potential time and cost. They might be able to give a general idea of time based on experience if, and only if, they're confident that they know exactly what data is available and of its adequacy for the given application.

PERFORMANCE

The critics' individual ratings and the overall average rating of the cake are essential. That said, the baker has no way to predict what the individual or average ratings will be until she's created a cake that she believes is as perfect as possible. Even then, the baker and individual critic's tastes likely differ (Top Chef anyone?), so the average rating is virtually impossible to predict in advance.

Likewise, AI practitioners are unable to guarantee how good the results of a new solution will be (e.g., model performance) in advance, nor can they guarantee 100% predictive accuracy, for example. First, no predictive model is 100% accurate, period. Second, it's impossible to know in advance what model or algorithm will perform best, or whether the data is adequate enough to meet a given target performance. Data and time is needed to experiment with different algorithms in order to get a better idea of achievable performance.

REQUIREMENTS

The impact of the final recipe and cooking approach (e.g., time, temperature, oven position) on the individual and average critic ratings is huge. Still, the exact ingredients, amounts of each, and cooking approach must be empirically determined by experimentation and trial and error. If the final cake doesn't get good enough reviews from the critics, the baker must still continue to modify the ingredients to keep improving it over time for her customers and future critics.

Likewise, it is impossible to determine the exact recipe (data, features, and techniques) needed for a new AI solution that meets your performance requirements. Again, data and time are required to experiment in order to find the best performing approach.

A Data Dependency Analogy

People often ask why data is needed upfront in order to answer questions about time, cost, performance, and requirements. The reason is simple, and I use one last analogy to demonstrate. Prior to the invention of cameras, family members were captured in hand-painted portraits. We can assume that the painter was hired without having first met or seen the family members. Exact determination of TCPR components without first having data in hand is like asking a painter to paint a family portrait without having the family present or having any idea what the family looks like.

I find that all of this can be extremely difficult for some people to understand. Often the reason is that many people are used to building deterministic digital technology products like mobile apps, websites, and SaaS applications. In those cases, the software engineers choose the programming language and "stack," and they themselves write the code for the applications (deterministic and does not involve statistics and probabilities). The code that they write creates, reads, updates, and deletes (CRUD) data that previously didn't exist; that is, it doesn't require data upfront.

Data scientists and AI engineers, on the other hand, don't build applications like web and mobile apps that create data—they train and optimize statistical-based models that require data as a mandatory dependency, and where the best performing algorithm is impossible to know in advance. All of this is makes data science (and scientific innovation) different than deterministic digital development and therefore nondeterministic.

The Human Requirement of Certainty

It's human nature to want everything to be stable and predictable, and thus avoid uncertainty if possible, and often at all costs. This was especially true of Albert Einstein, a bona fide scientist. He basically invented quantum theory and the field of quantum mechanics based on his Nobel Prize–winning discovery of the photoelectric effect (not relativity), which essentially states that light is both a wave and a particle, referred to as the wave-particle duality of light.[1]

---

1 https://www.scientificamerican.com/article/einstein-s-legacy-the-photoelectric-effect/

Although Einstein didn't realize it until other scientists built on his discovery of the photoelectric effect, he had discovered that much of physics and our universe is based on statistics, probabilities, uncertainties, and lack of causal explanation. This bothered him so much that he is famously quoted as saying, "I, at any rate, am convinced that He [God] does not throw dice."

Many people don't realize that most of Einstein's key accomplishments such as the photoelectric effect, general relativity, and special relativity were actually discovered by him as a relatively young man. He was born in 1879 and won the Nobel Prize a few years into his forties in 1921. He'd already published his theories on relativity earlier between 1905 and 1915.

From 1925 onward, Einstein began to publicly refute and debate many aspects of quantum theory for which he himself helped provide the basis. Some have said that the last 30 years of Einstein's life were wasted because of his inability to accept the uncertainty and lack of causal explanation of quantum theory. Imagine the additional pioneering, innovation, and discoveries Einstein would have been responsible for during his last 30 years had he continued with his work and been more willing to accept uncertainty.

Summary

If everything was deterministic, the fields of statistics and probabilities wouldn't exist. The real world and our universe is largely based on random variables and events, and is quite often best described using statistics, probabilities, and other nondeterministic methods. Insisting nondeterministic things be deterministic is the same as trying to fit a square block into a round hole.

This is becoming better understood, and it is part of the reason why there's been an exponential explosion in the fields of data science, machine learning, and AI. That said, and based on my experience, I think we still have a way to go before everyone naturally understands and is comfortable with this. Also, and as we will see in Chapter 12, it's not that simple.

The level of uncertainty risk associated with AI projects follows a maturity model. Some projects might be more deterministic and estimatable upfront based on adequate experience and technical competency with similar projects, but also can be commoditized. Chapter 12 looks at the model I created to illustrate these concepts. In my opinion, innovators, differentiators, and disrupters win, period, and usually when the journey starts with uncertainty and taking a leap into the unknown. If everything is perfectly known upfront, someone's already done it.

If you are a decision maker when it comes to pursuing AI initiatives, it is critical that you understand the concepts in this chapter because they will help your organization achieve forward progress, innovation, differentiation, competitive advantage, and ultimately success. It also allows for setting expectations properly and generating a better shared understanding. Lastly, it is the first step in developing a successful AI strategy. The next steps defined by AIPB for creating an AI strategy—the topic of the next chapter—involve the concepts of AI readiness and maturity, both of which we must properly assess and plan for, as outlined by AIPB.

12

AI Readiness and Maturity

As part of creating an AI strategy, and in order to successfully pursue and generate real value from AI initiatives, companies must have a certain degree of AI readiness and maturity. I have created an AI Readiness Model that breaks AI readiness into four categories, and I have also created three models related to maturity.

In this chapter, we go over AI readiness and AI maturity, and their respective models in detail. Recall that the AIPB Assessment Component defines three categories: readiness, maturity, and key considerations. This chapter focuses on the first two categories; Chapter 13 looks at key considerations.

You should carry out assessment of all three categories during the initial assess phase of the AIPB Methodology Component, which should result in an assessment strategy. This strategy should identify AI readiness and maturity gaps, with a plan to fill them, and also address key considerations that should be taken into account and planned for when pursuing AI initiatives.

Let's begin our discussion with the concept of AI readiness.

AI Readiness

Figure 12-1 shows the AI Readiness Model that I created, a simplified version of which was first introduced in Chapter 3.

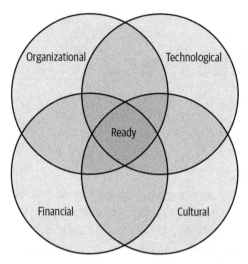

Figure 12-1. The AI Readiness Model

These four categories—organizational, technological, financial, and cultural—when combined, are the primary factors contributing to an organization's readiness and ability to execute a successful AI initiative, and therefore to capitalize on the opportunity and benefit from the initiative as intended. AI readiness is complicated, as you'll see, and there are many things to consider.

Although being "ready" in every way presented in this chapter is the ideal scenario, companies certainly should not wait to pursue AI initiatives until after this is achieved. In reality, often companies are never able to accomplish everything discussed in the AI readiness parts of this chapter, but the more gaps that you can identify and fill, the better.

Let's discuss each readiness category in turn.

ORGANIZATIONAL

I break the organizational category of AI readiness into four subcategories. These are organizational structure and leadership, shared vision and strategy, adoption and alignment, and sponsorship and support.

Organizational structure, leadership, and talent

Organizational structure, leadership, and talent are important components of AI readiness. Specifically, the organization should be structured such that it has strong leadership around data and advanced analytics, ideally at the highest executive level. Often this person has the title chief AI officer (CAIO), chief analytics officer (CAO), chief data officer (CDO), or something similar. In my opinion, this data and advanced analytics leadership is so critical that I consider it to be a hard prerequisite for developing and executing any AI vision and strategy; the only hard prerequisite in this chapter, in fact. I will note, however, that this is often easier said than done. There are not many leaders or manager-level people available to fill such roles, and certain projections indicate a growing and mass shortage of such people over time.

Again, in my opinion, AI, machine learning, and data science should sit organizationally only under an executive leadership role with the requisite expertise such as the aforementioned (doesn't need to have a C-level title). I personally don't recommend organizing AI, machine learning, and data science under software engineering or other product development disciplines. Leadership and managers in these disciplines will likely not have the requisite expertise, and therefore not be able to make critical decisions involving key AI considerations and trade-offs, and everything else discussed so far.

Most non–data scientists in general do not have the relevant background and experience to understand everything needed for data science and advanced analytics. Just as virtually all technology companies have a CTO, a company that is serious about taking advantage of its data with techniques including AI and machine learning should have an equivalent analytics leader. It is as important as having any other C-level functional leader, if not more for companies that are serious about becoming more data-driven or data-informed.

Further, and most important, data and advanced analytics leadership is critical for bringing the right AI expertise and strategic direction to the table at the highest level of the company. Also, for developing an AI vision and strategy, you need to ensure that everyone has a shared vision and understanding around both, that expectations are properly set and managed (which can be very challenging given the scientific nature of the work, as discussed), that you effectively communicate initiative progress, and that you make sure that the right opportunities are pursued. This includes determining whether AI is the right tool for the job. AI could be a sledge hammer when you only need a push pin. An analytics leader with the appropriate expertise can help determine whether AI will solve a given problem or provide a certain UX in a unique and warranted way.

Without this organization, the burden and responsibilities are placed on individual contributors, regardless of whether they have the appropriate leadership or business skills. Normally, the following happens with enterprises that do not have the proper organization as described. The CEO, CTO, or whomever asks an AI or machine learning practitioner, in advance of starting an AI project and without the practitioner first accessing and exploring the data that's available, "What will I get exactly, how much it will cost, how long it will take, and what exact data is needed to ensure mitigated risks, timely delivery, and ultimate success?" (Sound familiar from the last chapter?)

The practitioner responds that they'll need to explore and analyze the data, and then experiment with many different approaches to try to achieve the best performance possible. The executive's response is something like, "great, so what am I going to get exactly, how much it will cost, how long it will take, and what exact data is needed to ensure mitigated risks, timely delivery, and ultimate success?" Data scientists are already unicorn-ish enough as it is. Let's not ask them to also have business leadership and strategy skills that they might not have. Ensure that you have the appropriate data and advanced analytics leadership in place, and organize your business accordingly.

This is a perfect segue into the characteristics and responsibilities of an effective data and advanced analytics leader. Most data scientists and machine learning engineers need direction. It is highly unlikely that you'll get the outcome you want simply by handing data to these folks and telling them to have at it. In the worst case, hiring data scientists without anyone who is an expert in data science and advanced analytics who can lead and manage may be doomed from the start.

This person should have strong and demonstrable skills in effective communication, data science, advanced analytics, and stakeholder management. They should also have the critical soft skills that we discussed earlier in the book. AI is a very dynamic field that is changing and becoming more advanced every day. It is crucial to have somebody who is able to keep pace with trends and state-of-the-art techniques in the field, and who also has the ability to determine how to utilize this information to create the best AI vision and strategies possible while keeping initiatives on track for ongoing success.

Given the complexity and scientific nature of AI and machine learning, this leader must be able to properly communicate and educate on complex topics that are scientific in nature, in an easy-to-understand way, and in the context of business and what matters most to executives. This person must understand and avoid the "curse of knowledge," a form of bias that causes people to assume that lesser-informed people have the background to understand something as well as they do. The goal is to make no assumptions and present complex information with childlike clarity.

This person must also be excellent at providing insight into AI initiatives, project status, and, most important, the ability to properly manage expectations. Expectation management is a critical skill, particularly for the scientific initiatives associated with data science and advanced analytics.

In addition to the responsibilities already covered, this person should also be responsible for data and analytics P&L (or just analytics if there's a separate data-specific organizational structure), performing strategic assessments (such as those defined by AIPB) and developing associated strategies, talent hiring and development, tooling and best practices, and more. Lastly, talent is also a critical component of AI readiness, which we'll discuss again in Chapter 13.

Vision and strategy

Creating an AI vision and strategy is a core part of AIPB and has been an ongoing theme in this book. We have also discussed the concept of generating a shared vision and understanding and its importance in being able to produce successful AI initiatives.

Here, we examine vision and strategy development through the lens of AI readiness, as some amount of readiness is needed to both create and execute successfully. With the appropriate analytics leadership in place, a company should be able to develop a benefit-driven AI vision and strategy. At a high level, and as previously discussed, the vision covers the why, how, and what for a particular AI initiative to benefit both people and business. The strategy, on the other hand, is the plan for executing the vision to make it a reality.

Both of these involve creating appropriate business and individual use cases for key strategic initiatives. The business case is the business-level *why*, which should outline the vision, goals, and potential ROI for a given initiative. Business cases can also include identification and development of potential new business models, products, and services, and/or capturing greater market share and expanding into new markets.

After you've established one or more business cases, the next step is to identify and specify individual use cases for specific AI solutions. This means identifying the users who will benefit from the solution (or specific features), defining why (benefit) and how (user flow) the user will interact with the solution to accomplish a certain task, and determining what the outcome will be for all potential user interactions in a given scenario.

In the field of product management, and assuming a product vision has been created, a technology-based solution strategy is manifested as a prioritized product roadmap and backlog of ideas. The solution strategy should take into account any assessments and corresponding strategies, as well. For cases in which an AI solution is either standalone or will be deployed as part of another application (e.g., to automate a process, augment human intelligence, or integrate with an existing mobile or web-based application), the strategy will involve generating a product roadmap, with the initial focus usually on first building a MVP or comparable entity (e.g., prototype, proof of concept [PoC], or pilot) to test the riskiest assumptions, validate the product–market fit, and verify usage as intended.

For needs that are time sensitive or require timed coordination, and for which an AI solution must be developed, tested, and deployed to a production environment, you must keep in mind the scientific, empirical, and nondeterministic nature of data science and advanced analytics tasks, as previously discussed. This is important because it can affect the ability to create estimations and deliverable timelines. It also results in a certain amount of budget uncertainty because it is impossible to know in advance the exact resources needed (e.g., cloud compute for model training and optimization) and time required to achieve the desired result. This all requires a shared vision and understanding, along with proper expectation management among key stakeholders. Again, increased maturity, as we'll discuss soon, will help decrease general uncertainty.

Adoption and alignment

Having developed an AI vision and strategy and thus having established the goals and plan to successfully execute key AI initiatives, the next step is to gain company-wide adoption and alignment around both, which means it must become a "shared" vision and strategy.

New initiatives, especially those involving data from across a company, can require buy-in, participation, and resources from senior executives and multiple LoB owners. Business owners might include the CEO, head of marketing, head of product, and head of sales, for example. Adoption means that all relevant stakeholders commit to the initiative and take ownership of a certain aspect of it and its overall success.

Adoption typically results from stakeholders understanding the vision, value (benefits), and potential ROI. Stakeholders who understand these things are more likely to be interested in adopting initiatives.

Adoption is not enough, however. Alignment is required, as well. Alignment means that all stakeholders not only share the same vision, understanding, and strategy, but are also aligned on what is needed to execute on the strategy, what to expect throughout the process, and ultimately on making the solution and its intended benefits a reality. This includes alignment around who is responsible for what, potential phases and milestones, key deliverables, and timing of involvement.

Sponsorship and support

Given the proper organizational structure and leadership and a shared vision and strategy that has company-wide adoption and alignment, the next step is to establish initiative sponsorship and support.

Sponsorship means having key stakeholders commit to providing the resources (e.g., money, data, people) necessary to ensure initiative success and as needed at the right time. Support means providing ongoing support in helping define requirements, getting tasks done (e.g., providing access to data), answering questions, collaborating as needed, properly setting expectations, and communicating progress.

TECHNOLOGICAL

I break the technological category of AI readiness into three subcategories: infrastructure and technologies, support and maintain, and data readiness and quality (the "right" data).

Infrastructure and technologies

The infrastructure and technologies component of AI readiness refers to having the appropriate technology-based resources and processes in place, which includes cloud infrastructures and services (e.g., AWS and GCP), DevOps and site reliability engineering (infrastructure as code; tools for build, integration, and deployment; scalability), oversight of regulations and compliance (e.g., Europe's General Data Protection Regulation [GDPR]), and effective software development processes and methodologies (e.g., Agile, Kanban, CI/CD). This category also includes the people required to set up infrastructure components and who can design solutions built on top. Note that some new infrastructure development might be required for new AI initiatives.

Infrastructure can also include data warehouse and/or data lake setup and maintenance, including all data acquisition; ingestion; integration; extract, transform, and load (ETL); extract, load, and transform (ELT); and data pipeline–related processes.

Technologies in the context of AI readiness refer to having core competence and expertise with using requisite technologies for any given AI project. In the context of AI applications, the technologies category includes common programming languages (e.g., Python, R, Java), software packages and libraries (e.g., Jupyter Notebooks, TensorFlow, scikit-learn, Spark), version-control systems (e.g., Git), testing tools (e.g., A/B testing), and databases (e.g., PostgreSQL, Hadoop, MongoDB).

This list is nonexhaustive and not small, and that's part of the reason why building software solutions is difficult.

Support and maintain

After any AI solution (and software solutions in general) is developed, it needs to be supported and maintained. These solutions should be regularly monitored to ensure proper functioning and health.

Supporting software involves creating processes to capture bug reports with proper severity (e.g., critical, high, medium, low), soliciting and capturing customer feedback and new feature requests, and handling customer support requests. When any of these items are captured, a system should be in place to track progress if action is to be taken as well as to provide visibility in order to communicate progress and status updates to those submitting the support requests.

Also, there are usually multiple levels, or tiers, of support that represent increasing degrees of escalation as needed to resolve a certain issue. Finally, support might be governed by a service-level agreement (SLA), and therefore must adhere to specific response and resolution times or face certain penalties.

Maintaining a solution means addressing anything support or enhancement related, and making appropriate changes or improvements and deploying them to production. In addition, programming languages and software (e.g., libraries, frameworks) are usually updated regularly. Code bases should therefore also be updated regularly to take advantage of the newest programming languages, software, and frameworks, which usually offer improvements such as bug fixes and performance and security enhancements.

Maintenance also includes technical debt reduction and improving nonfunctional requirements such as scalability, reliability, and maintainability. Time should always be alloted (usually 20%) to software development teams in order to continuously work on this type of maintenance. As with support, systems and processes should be in place to effectively carry out both on an ongoing basis.

Data readiness and quality (the "right" data)

Data readiness and quality was discussed at length earlier in the book. Having the "right" data is a critical element of the technological category of AI readiness. Recall from Chapter 4 that I use the phrase "data readiness and quality" to collectively refer to the following:

- Adequate data amount
- Adequate data depth
- Well-balanced data
- Highly representative and unbiased data
- Complete data
- Clean data

If you need a refresher, refer to Chapter 4.

FINANCIAL

I break the financial category of AI readiness into three subcategories: budgeting, competing investments, and prioritization.

Budgeting

People and technology cost money and require resources. Budgeting in this context refers to money to spend on resources such as people and technology.

As such, AI initiatives cost money as well, and you need to budget for these costs. In the context of AI readiness, this means that money should be earmarked for making a company's AI vision and strategy a reality. One very common challenge is that a given AI initiative might require a budget from multiple business owners, something that companies aren't necessarily set up to easily handle. Getting buy-in and commitment across business functions to contribute budget monies to the same initiative is a cross-functional effort that can be very challenging, and is therefore highly related to the sponsorship and support element of AI readiness, as well. Part of the reason for this is differing LoB incentives, and also that the potential value and ROI might not be easily attributable in a quantified way to a specific LoB, which means that P&L implications might not be straightforward or desirable for that LoB, and can potentially cause barriers to progress. Potential benefits and ROI should be considered at the company-wide level—this should apply to any cross-functional form of innovation and transformation.

Suppose that marketing is championing a new AI initiative and is therefore willing to allocate budget to it. It might be that a certain amount of infrastructure and people's time are required from the IT department. Usually different business functions are incentivized differently, and they usually have differing priorities and initiatives as a result. This can result in alignment, priority, and budgeting challenges. This is one of the reasons having a strong leader in data and analytics is critical. This person should be tasked with generating the shared vision and understanding that we've talked about, and therefore help people across business functions see the value to their departments and, more important, to the company as a whole, and ultimately get the necessary buy-in and participation (e.g., money, time, and resources).

Competing investments and prioritization

Depending on the size of a company and its internal departments, there are usually many different potential initiatives to prioritize within each of those departments, in addition to the high-priority company-wide initiatives that need to be addressed. This all results in competition for resources; as a result, financial decisions and prioritization are required around competing investments.

Nothing seems to succeed in securing the funds to pay for a given initiative better than a compelling argument around how much money will be generated as a result of the initiative. In other words, presenting convincing ROI estimates is very powerful when possible, and that includes crafting a very effective story on how a given initiative can generate the proposed ROI. Story telling is often a key skill here, and, again, having a data and advanced analytics leader is critical.

CULTURAL

I break the cultural category of AI readiness into four subcategories: scientific innovation and disruption, gut-to-data driven, action ready, and data democratization. Cultural readiness is largely about creating a culture, mindset, and established set of processes that enable and foster pursuit of data-driven initiatives such as those associated with AI and machine learning.

Scientific innovation and disruption

Companies are often not set up or incentivized for innovation and disruption. Many companies are mostly incentivized and driven by short-term, quarter-by-quarter gains such as company profits and growth. This usually results in incremental thinking and action, and means that significant progress and improvement can take a long time.

Creating a culture of innovation and disruption is very important in terms of AI readiness for developing and executing an AI vision and strategy. In incremental-thinking companies, creating this culture can be very challenging, and there are usually many forces opposing it. Creating this culture begins with big-picture, long-term, and high-risk-versus-reward thinking. It also begins with a willingness to be agile and experimental.

Keep in mind that you might have very agile competitors that have prioritized and embraced a culture of innovation and disruption from day one. Sticking to the status quo and thinking in small incremental steps is the quickest way to fall behind and not remain competitive.

Also, large enterprise companies often have a "buy versus build" mentality—the attitude of "Why invest time, money, and resources into customized advanced analytics, for example, when I can just buy a product like a popular CRM right off the shelf, right?" Wrong.

When trying to sell people on the idea of data science and advanced analytics, this has come up time and time again. I hear things like, "But XYZ already has an analytics dashboard." This might be true, but third-party tools that have built-in analytics are catering to the masses, are very generic, and are not customized to your business or needs. If you're looking for shallow insights, that's the analytics solution for you. But if you want differentiated, very deep, and actionable insights, and want to have the ability to make predictions and have optimal actions automatically taken for you, look elsewhere. In fact, AI and machine learning represent opportunities that are well beyond—even unachievable with—traditional analytics, and are universally applicable throughout business. You should approach AI and machine learning as a new core business competency in the same way that marketing and sales are. The more you think of your company as a data company, and data as a core advantage, the better off your company will be.

Another thing to consider that many don't realize is that by generating deeper insights, you can more easily develop new ideas and strategies around potential new business models, services, and products. You can also find innovative ways to capture new markets and expand your current market. Again, in ways that are unachievable with traditional analytics.

Companies that embrace scientific innovation and disruption have the best chance of differentiating themselves while also generating competitive advantage. AI represents a massive opportunity in this respect. Innovation creates barriers to entry, provides commoditization protection, and ultimately increases your chances of long-term success. As of 2018, seven of the top ten publicly traded companies in terms of market capitalization are technology companies, and they have recently replaced major incumbents that had previously enjoyed the top ten designation, including ExxonMobil, General Electric, Wells Fargo, and Wal-Mart.[1]

Gut-to-data driven

Certain physical laws such as those describing gravity, motion, and electricity often boil down to taking the path of least resistance. Humans are no different, and as a result, decision making is often entirely driven by experience and historical precedent; for instance, what happened in similar situations in the past, simple analytics, and gut feel. Although many decisions have been made with success using this approach, not only can we significantly improve the success rate and outcomes by incorporating data into decision making, but analytics-based decision making also enables predictions of the potential impact (e.g., ROI) for a given decision. In other words, it unlocks the ability to be better able to understand and plan for the exact outcome in advance.

The concepts of being data driven and data informed are highly applicable here. It is not necessary, or possible, in some cases for decisions to be made solely based on data (data driven), but we should definitely incorporate data and analytics, when available, into the process of making all important decisions (data informed). The outcomes will almost certainly be better.

Becoming a data-driven organization requires a cultural and mindset shift, along with a data democratization shift. People can't make data-driven or data-informed decisions without having access to the "right" data as well as the ability to properly analyze, derive insights, and take actions from such data. Companies must invest heavily in functionally appropriate talent (e.g., analysts, data scientists, and AI and machine learning engineers) for this purpose. This is again a cultural shift in terms of seeing the value of the investment into data and analytics and its potential return and prioritizing it accordingly.

---

1 *https://en.wikipedia.org/wiki/List_of_public_corporations_by_market_capitalization*

Action ready

Being "action ready" means being committed to prioritizing the generation of actionable insights and then being willing to take the actions (e.g., make decision, augment intelligence, automate) needed to realize the potential value and benefits. This is a cultural thing and cannot be overstated. For any given goal such as increasing revenue, companies can create different initiatives to help accomplish the goal and often have multiple levers that can be pulled, as well. This includes having the ability to create new and innovative levers that don't yet exist (i.e., products, features, services). There is not much point in generating highly actionable deep insights if nobody is willing to pull any levers that are suggested by these insights.

I won't delve into more detail on the types of actions that can be taken here, because that list would be massive, very company specific, and also industry and business function specific in many cases. The point is that if your company is going to become culturally ready to pursue generating deep actionable insights, become culturally ready to take appropriate action, as well.

Data democratization

Data is not very useful if it is siloed and unavailable. Many companies build silos around entire departments in general, and especially each departments data. LoB owners often have an "it's my data" mentality and approach. Let's be clear—it's the company's data, and data is most effective when combined with other data and when it is accessible by anyone who can benefit from it without violating data governance rules, privacy, and security in particular.

Tear down silos and democratize data. This is critical. I'm not suggesting that you run out tomorrow and build a data warehouse or data lake (I've definitely seen this become a barrier to advanced analytics adoption, as well), but work hard to ensure that everyone has access to data within the company who can benefit from having it. Not only that, consider making data available externally (ethically of course, and without aforementioned violations), as well.

In an *MIT Sloan Management Review* article, "Analytics As a Source of Business Innovation" (*http://bit.ly/2Rtx7ws*), the authors discuss how Bridgestone wants to transform its business by taking advantage of shared third-party data (e.g., data from car manufacturers) in order to sell proactively by encouraging and reminding consumers to come in for tire inspections, new tires, and other services before a problem develops; in other words, predictive maintenance. Tire manufacturers currently have no way to know how many miles have been driven on a given set of tires for a given car, so data democratization could change this, and this idea is applicable to many industries and companies.

Like many things, data is better democratized than siloed and restricted. Getting to this point requires a cultural shift as well as the gut-to-data-driven shift, as discussed. LoB owners and any employee who is trying to make effective and company-improving decisions should instinctively think to access relevant data in order to gain insights and produce outcomes, and do so.

Now let's switch gears and discuss AI maturity in the context of AIPB and assessments.

AI Maturity

AI maturity is highly relevant to successfully developing and executing an AI vision and strategy. I have created multiple maturity-related models that we cover in this section, two of which I first introduced in Chapter 3.

I break AI maturity into both *data maturity* and *analytics maturity* subcategories. This is due to the fact that data-specific and analytics-specific roles, processes, and tools can be different, and so can the corresponding levels of maturity for each.

Data maturity means having an increasingly advanced data capturing, collection, processing, integration, and analytics-optimized storage foundation in place (data pipelines and infrastructure). Analytics maturity refers to applying increasingly advanced analytics to existing and new data, which ranges from simple and traditional analytics (e.g., statistical analysis, visualization, descriptive analytics, and business intelligence) to more complex advanced analytics (e.g., AI, machine learning, predictive analytics, prescriptive analytics). To keep things simple in this discussion, and unless otherwise noted, I use the term "AI maturity" to include both data maturity and analytics maturity.

Before discussing AI maturity as related to data and analytics specifically, let's first discuss a more general Technical Maturity Model that I've created, as shown in Figure 12-2. This provides the criteria for measuring the degree of maturity for each level of sophistication covered in the AI Maturity Model (Figure 12-3) that follows.

I define technical maturity, in general, as a mixture of individual levels of maturity characteristics (i.e., maturity measurement criteria). Specifically, I define technical maturity as a collective measure (mixture) of the level of experience, technical sophistication, and technical competency around a given technical field or technology at a given point in time; in this case, AI. Figure 12-2 shows this.

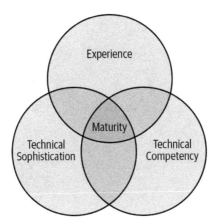

Figure 12-2. The Technical Maturity Mixture Model

Experience represents the collective amount of experience that the relevant team has with the technical field or technology involved. Technical sophistication is a measure of the team's ability to utilize advanced and state-of-the-art tools and techniques related to the given technical field or technology (e.g., deep learning, reinforcement learning, natural language understanding). Technical sophistication is usually directly related to the team and its individual members' experience (for example, perhaps only one team member knows how to use reinforcement learning techniques). Finally, technical competency is a measure of the ability to successfully execute and deliver on related initiatives and projects.

The proportions of each maturity characteristic contributing to the collective measure (mixture) of technical maturity can be somewhat subjective and constantly changing based on advancements in technology. Here is a formula that I've created to indicate that increased technical maturity according to this model results in increased certainty and confidence (remember scientific innovation and the TCPR model?) and, ultimately, better outcomes and success.

↑ Maturity = ↑ Certainty and Confidence = Better Outcomes and Success!

In the context of the technical maturity mixture highlighted in the previous model, maturity can be progressively measured by a field-specific (AI in this case), predefined number of levels of sophistication. Figure 12-3 shows a model that I've created to illustrate this in terms of AI maturity.

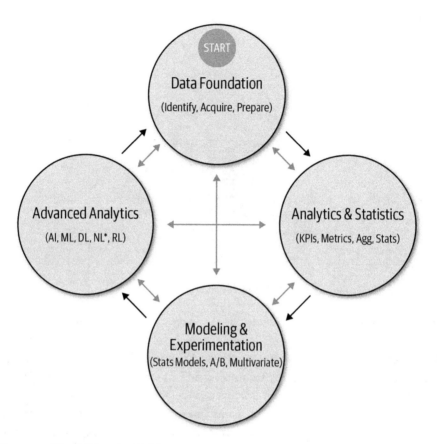

Figure 12-3. The AI Maturity Model

The model shows the starting point as building a data foundation to fuel progressively increasing levels of analytics sophistication, as indicated by the green arrows. Building a data foundation means identifying, acquiring, and preparing the "right" data, which we discussed earlier in the book. Acquiring data includes capturing and integrating data, potentially from many different sources and systems.

After a data foundation is either partially or entirely built, we can measure AI maturity as a progression from traditional analytics and statistics, to more sophisticated modeling and experimentation, and finally to advanced analytics, which includes state-of-the-art AI and machine learning techniques.

Similar to Maslow changing his mind about his hierarchy requiring a strict and ordered progression, I don't think that it's mandatory to gain complete competency at every level of maturity according to this model before moving to the next level, and particularly before beginning to use AI and machine learning. Also, the red arrows indicate that the outputs of each level of sophistication can influence or power one or more of the other levels in some way. For example, all three analytics-specific levels can create data output that can be integrated into your data foundation. Likewise, the outcomes resulting from AI and machine learning applications should be understood using traditional analytics and statistics, particularly in terms of the solution's impact on key success metrics and KPIs.

Figure 12-4 shows the final maturity model that I've created, the Innovation Uncertainty Risk versus Reward Model, which is highly relevant to AI maturity. It presents a nontechnical, strategic, and business-focused perspective.

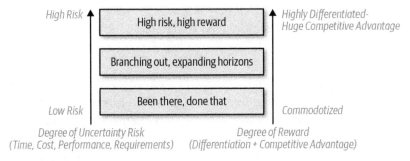

Figure 12-4. Innovation Uncertainty Risk versus Reward Model

The model shows the relationship of technology-based maturity (again, AI in this case) as a function of innovation uncertainty risk versus reward, where uncertainty is around time, cost, performance, and requirements (again, the TCPR Model!), and the reward is differentiation and competitive advantage.

Time and cost uncertainty should be obvious, as already discussed. Performance uncertainty refers to error-based performance in AI and machine learning applications (e.g., accuracy, although note that not all applications are error based), for which the solution might be a predictive model, for example. In contrast, performance for more deterministic applications such as a mobile app would be KPI or UX based; for example, conversions, customer retention, or delight. Finally, requirements uncertainty is around the data, features, and techniques required to achieve target performance.

Notice that I've intentionally omitted specific data and analytics subject areas from the model (e.g., ETL, A/B testing, AI) or any specific technologies, for that matter. I've done this because what is emerging or state-of-the-art in terms of data and analytics techniques today might be commoditized, automated, or obsolete tomorrow. Also, maturity is a moving target and is technical area specific; that is, you might have varying degrees of maturity with respect to business intelligence as compared to AI techniques such as deep learning.

In the context of analytics maturity level, "been there, done that" represents low uncertainty risk, and thus it is very easy to estimate time, cost, performance, and requirements for a specific project. This results from having the requisite experience, sophistication, and competency to effectively erase any uncertainty and resulting risk. It also means that the technology being used and resulting outcomes might be commoditized and not able to help generate significant differentiation and competitive advantage (minimal rewards, if any).

BI is a good example, although as is often the case, it's not that simple. Certain industries are generally very slow to make the data and analytics cultural shifts covered earlier in the context of AI readiness. In those cases, significant BI competency can create appreciable competitive advantage relative to the competition.

"Branching out, expanding horizons" is the process of building on existing data and analytics experience, sophistication, and competency to increase the level of maturity for either or both. This usually means that uncertainty risk is increased because there are new areas of exploration, experimentation, and unpredictable outcomes; or, put another way, scientific innovation. It also means that there is greater potential for generating increased differentiation and competitive advantage.

The final category, "high risk, high reward," is as it sounds. It represents taking risks and gambling, venturing into the great unknown, pushing boundaries, and any other comparable way of thinking about pursuing true scientific innovation to reap potentially huge rewards. This means pioneering and leading with emerging and state-of-the-art technology instead of following.

It also means assuming a large amount of uncertainty risk but with the upside of massive rewards. The way that venture capitalists operate is a great example. Most strategic investments are expected to fail, but those that succeed usually do so in a huge way. For successful VCs, though, the successes more than financially cover the greater number of failures. R&D programs at pharmaceutical companies work in the same way.

A final note on this model. At a glance, the model seems to indicate that low uncertainty risk always implies commoditized data and analytics technologies and competency, and vice versa, for high uncertainty risk. In reality, it is not that simple and depends on many factors. For example, some tech giants (e.g., Google, Amazon) have a lot of experience, sophistication, and competency with certain AI and machine learning techniques, which therefore carry low uncertainty risk for them, and yet those techniques are nowhere near being commoditized in the general market. The model is therefore a relative one and applies more so to the majority of companies outside of the AI-forward tech giants.

Summary

We divided AI readiness into four categories—organizational, technological, financial, and cultural—as shown by the AI Readiness Model. Although companies are unlikely to be completely "ready" in all categories, as described, you should pursue AI initiatives nonetheless. We have also defined AI maturity in terms of different concepts and multiple models, particularly the Technical Maturity Mixture Model, the AI Maturity Model, and the Innovation Uncertainty Risk versus Reward Model.

Overly focusing on mandatory and progressive steps to data and analytics maturity before moving forward is similar to establishing barriers to entry, where some barriers can take a very long time to break down (e.g., building a data warehouse). Get started now, and make decisions based on needs and desired outcomes, not on your data and analytics maturity.

The key is to assess your AI readiness and AI maturity as a subphase of the assess phase of the AIPB Methodology Component, and identify gaps and a plan to fill them as you go. This becomes part of your assessment strategy. To help complete your AIPB assessments and create your assessment strategy, an important part of your overall AI strategy, we next discuss AI key considerations.

13

AI Key Considerations

This chapter covers the third and final category of the AIPB Assessment Component: the many key considerations that you need to take into account, and plan for, when developing an AI strategy. Readiness, maturity, and key consideration assessments should be completed as part of the assess methodology phase to create your assessment strategy. Figure 13-1 shows specific key considerations that we cover in this chapter.

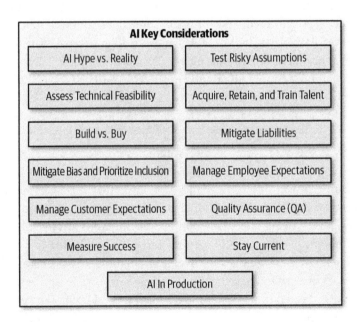

Figure 13-1. AI key considerations

Other critical considerations, not noted in Figure 13-1, are ethics and human values. You should never lose sight of these two things. AI-based solutions should be ethically designed and built to benefit people. With that as our foundational key consideration, let's discuss the other key AI considerations.

AI Hype versus Reality

Many people are under the impression that AI is very close to, or has already achieved, AGI. This is partly due to some of what we see in science-fiction TV shows, movies, and comic books. The *Terminator* movie franchise is a classic example, and other good examples include *Ex Machina*, *Westworld*, and C-3PO from *Star Wars*.

These incorrect impressions are also largely due to product marketing, over-promising, and the tendency of many people and companies to call just about anything AI—what I collectively refer to as *AI hype*. You see this a lot with software products, particularly SaaS. Having a few metrics in a dashboard does not qualify as being AI powered, and yet many companies continue to say that they "do" or "have" AI with analytics not much more sophisticated than that. "Real" AI is intelligence exhibited by machines. If a machine doesn't learn, generate some degree of understanding, and then use the knowledge learned to do something, it's not AI.

The reality of AI is that, as discussed earlier in the book, it is currently a one-trick pony that is mainly used to solve highly specialized problems, and as of this writing, AGI is still a long way off. AGI might never become a reality in our lifetimes.

AI as a field is also still in its infancy, and the real-world use cases and applications are growing daily. AI is advancing at a rapid pace, and there is a lot of important research being done. One of the main questions around AI is whether current techniques such as deep learning can ever be adapted to multitasking and, ultimately, AGI, or whether we need to find and develop a completely new approach to AI that doesn't yet exist.

AGI is also related to a question of AI for human automation versus AI for augmented intelligence, and currently most executives and companies are interested in augmented intelligence over automation. Also, there is something very interesting known as the *Paradox of Automation* (*http://bit.ly/2xcktsk*). The paradox says that the more efficient an automated system becomes, the more critical the contribution of the human operator becomes.

For example, if an automated system experiences an error (machines are never perfect; bugs exist), the error can multiply or spiral out of control until it is fixed or the system shuts down. Humans are needed to handle this situation. Think about all of the movies or TV shows you've seen in which an automated process (e.g., on a spaceship, on an airplane, in a nuclear power plant) fails and humans are deployed to find workarounds and heroically solve the problem.

Lastly, given all of the AI hype and proliferation of AI tools, there are some people who seem to think that starting an AI project should be relatively easy and that they can quickly expect big gains. The reality is that planning and building AI solutions is difficult, and there's a significant talent shortage. There's a major shortage of data scientists and machine learning engineers in general, particularly those who have AI-specific expertise and skills.

Even when you have the right talent, AI initiatives can still be very difficult to execute successfully. That said, achieving success with highly custom and difficult-to-build AI solutions will likely generate significant differentiation and competitive advantage. This was highlighted by the Innovation Uncertainty Risk versus Reward Model covered in Chapter 12.

Also, there aren't many simple automated ways to build many types of AI applications, or to access, move, and prepare data. That said, luckily there are new automation tools, techniques such as transfer learning, and shared models that can offer sufficient accuracy out of the box, or with only minor modifications.

In addition, large gains from AI can take significant time, effort, and cost. Some of those costs can be sunk by unsuccessful projects. Also, although there are many people working on simplifying AI for general use, AI research and techniques are still quite complex. Take a quick look at some of the latest AI research papers published to Cornell's Arxiv (pronounced "archive") digital library to see for yourself.

A concept worth mentioning is that of the *AI winter*, which refers to periods of time in which financial and practical interest in AI is reduced, and sometimes significantly. There have been multiple rounds of AI winters since the early 1970s, due to many factors that we won't discuss here. The AI winter concept is associated with the fact that technologies and products are subject to hype cycles that relate to their maturity, adoption, and applications.

This law certainly applies to AI and is the reason why we're seeing so much hype about AI as of this writing. Ultimately, AI has enormous potential to drive real value for people and companies, but we are nowhere near the full realization of all of the potential capabilities, applications, benefits, and impacts. Regarding another AI winter possibly caused by unmet expectations due to the hype, renowned AI expert Andrew Ng does not think there will be one of any significance (*http://bit.ly/2L7Tkz3*). This is simply because AI has come a long way and is now proving its value in innovative, exciting, and expanding ways in the real world.

Testing Risky Assumptions

Risky assumptions are made by people all of the time about many things. When building companies, products, and services, assumptions often represent potential risks that increase depending on the degree to which they're incorrect, including potential costs (e.g., time and money) and lack of product-market fit and adoption, for example. Common assumptions and risk types associated with technology and innovation are around value, usability, feasibility, and business viability. Related questions include: for [insert any technology-based product or service here], will anyone find enough value to buy or use it, will users know how to use it and understand it without assistance, can it be built given our resources and time available, will this product achieve product-market fit and be profitable, and can we execute a successful go-to-market strategy?

The Segway is a great example of this. Dean Kamen and many others assumed that the product was going to disrupt and transform transportation for a very large number of people, and therefore quickly built a huge number of units. A lot of the public hype around the Segway's release seemed to support that assumption, as well. Although Segway vehicles are still sold for highly specialized applications, they certainly did not have the expected massive impact and sales that Kamen and his company were hoping for.

By the time it was determined that the Segway assumptions were incorrect, a large amount of time, money, and other resources were spent. Approximately $100 million dollars in R&D costs (*http://bit.ly/2Xo1uvM*), according to some estimates.

For an AI-specific example, a six-year-old girl in early 2017 accidentally ordered a $170 dollhouse and four pounds of cookies (*https://fxn.ws/2Zzej1M*) just by having a conversation with Alexa about dollhouses and cookies. In this case, a potentially risky assumption is that consumers are aware of and will set up safety settings (e.g., add a passcode or turn off voice activated ordering) for these devices to prevent accidental orders by children.

The concept of the MVP stems from Lean manufacturing and software development, which provides a mechanism to help mitigate risk and minimize unnecessary expenditure of time and cost. The primary idea is that the minimum amount of UX and software functionality should be built and put in users' hands as quickly as possible to properly test the riskiest assumptions and validate product–market fit and user delight. Feedback and metrics from MVP pilots are then used to drive iterative improvements until a product or feature is "de-risked." You should use this framework, or similar Agile and Lean methodologies when developing AI solutions.

Assess Technical Feasibility

We discussed different goals for people and business stakeholders at length earlier in the book. The discussion was kept at an appropriately high level, although in reality, high-level goals driving real-world AI solutions must be broken into more granular goals or initiatives that are better suited at guiding the technical approaches to be used.

Machine learning models don't fundamentally increase profits or reduce costs as outputs, for example. Machine learning models make predictions, determine classifications, assign probabilities, and produce other outputs based on the chosen technique as well as the data being leveraged, which must be appropriate and adequate for each of the possible output types (i.e., the "right" data, which we covered earlier in the book). Further, each of these output types could be used to achieve the same goal, albeit from a different angle—there's usually more than one way to get the job done. Determining which approach and output type to use to best achieve a more granular goal (e.g., personalized podcast recommendations), which in turn will help achieve the top-level business goal (customer retention), along with having the "right" data on hand are what technical feasibility is all about.

Let's assume that our top-level business goal is customer retention. Let's further assume that our collaborative team of business folks, domain experts, and AI practitioners decide that AI-based personalization of a podcast app's feed is likely to have the most potential ROI and retention lift out of the options being considered. In this case, the podcasts shown in each individual user's feed can be displayed and ordered based on a predictive model that calculates the likelihood that the particular user will like it (a probability), or listed without a specific order based on a classifier that classifies each podcast as relevant or not relevant (only the ones classified as relevant are shown), or through some other method.

The point is that a technical feasibility assessment involving an appropriately assembled, cross-functional team must be used to determine which approach will work best and whether the data can get the job done for the given choice. Think of a technical feasibility assessment as being the next, more granular, step of opportunity identification. This might require preparing data, and testing many possible options (remember this is scientific innovation!).

Acquire, Retain, and Train Talent

An incredibly important consideration is acquiring and retaining talent. AI, machine learning, and data science are difficult. There's a lot of work being done by people and organizations to try to simplify and automate aspects of these fields, but they are still challenging and require very specialized expertise and experience.

The ideal data scientist is an expert programmer, statistician and mathematician, effective communicator, and MBA-level businessperson. This is a uniquely difficult (read, unicorn) combination to find in any one person. The reality is that people are often good at some of these things and less so at others. In addition, although most universities offer computer science degrees, education has not yet caught up to the demand for data science and advanced analytics talent, and therefore not many quality degree programs exist.

The end result is a significant shortage of highly competent and experienced talent. This includes leaders, managers, and practitioners alike. LinkedIn reported in August of 2018 that there was a national shortage of approximately 152,000 people with data science skills, and that the data science shortage was growing faster (accelerating) than the shortage for software development skills.[1] Not having the necessary internal expertise, skills, and leadership while executing your AI strategy can result in unsuccessful initiatives, sunk costs, and wasted time.

As someone who has spent a lot of time recruiting data scientists and machine learning engineers, I can honestly say that it's not easy. The vast majority of applicants that I've seen are either fresh out of college or in the process of switching careers. This type of applicant is often well suited for large organizations that have the infrastructure needed to nurture and train very junior talent. This can be more difficult for smaller to midsized data science teams, and for

---

1 *https://economicgraph.linkedin.com/resources/linkedin-workforce-report-august-2018*

startups in general. Smaller companies also need to fiercely compete with larger and established tech companies for AI talent.

The good news for many small- to midsized companies is that many data scientists are very interested in working with a promising company that has a great value proposition and culture. In addition, people are often driven by the need to have a direct impact on a company's success and are therefore attracted to smaller companies and data science teams. Companies that fit this description should tailor their messaging accordingly to better attract and retain top talent.

Another consideration is that data science and advanced analytics talent is expensive, and companies might need to spend a substantial amount of money depending on their needs and the talent market at the time. It is very important to ensure that you have the best talent and therefore the best chance for success and most return on dollars spent. Companies should thus prepare and budget accordingly. AI talent is not cheap. Multiple prominent articles have been published by the *New York Times* and others on the relatively high costs of AI talent.[2]

Given the shortage, competition, and relatively high costs for AI talent as described, a company must develop a strong recruiting, hiring, and/or staffing augmentation strategy. There are multiple options to consider when it comes to finding and hiring talent. Many include typical business considerations such as hiring contractors versus full-time employees, staff augmentation using a specialized firm, and hiring on-shore versus off-shore.

It's worth noting that for talent hired outside of your organization and country, there can be a nontrivial risk of exposing and sharing your intellectual property and data outside of your organization, particularly in a different country with different laws, where you are not well equipped to monitor everything. This is becoming especially important given the focus on data privacy and security these days, including needing to be compliant according to regulations such as Europe's GDPR.

Some of these regulations and standards are very specific about who can have access to sensitive data, and how and where they can access it. This can be exponentially more challenging to monitor and control with off-shore companies, so you must take extra care to ensure trust, compliance, and accountability. Whichever way you find and hire talent, be sure to properly vet candidates and

---

2 https://www.nytimes.com/2018/04/19/technology/artificial-intelligence-salaries-openai.html and https://www.nytimes.com/2017/10/22/technology/artificial-intelligence-experts-salaries.html

potential partner firms, and assess and mitigate any potential risks. Strong leadership and expertise in data and advanced analytics is key here.

Another option to consider is an *acquihire*; that is, buying a company primarily to acquire its data science and advanced analytics talent. Acquihires can require a significant amount of money and present a unique set of challenges, but might be a viable option for obtaining talent in a hurry, and has been a strategy employed by many companies.

The last potential option is training talent internally, which can be an excellent choice for overcoming talent shortage challenges. In many ways, this option is ideal but can require a lot of upfront training infrastructure setup and development, talent, cost, and time, particularly when developing an effective and structured curriculum.

Creating an internal advanced analytics training program allows a company to train for exactly what's needed, both in terms of expertise and tools. It should include training for programming, mathematics, statistics, data science principles, machine learning algorithms, and more.

As someone who has taught and trained thousands of people, and developed curriculum from scratch, this is easier said than done, although it is certainly doable. Going this route requires making certain decisions, as well. What education, experience, skills, and background are required to get into the training program? How are those things assessed? Ultimately, you are trying to assess potential more than actual skills and expertise given that your company will be the one filling those gaps.

Other things to determine are how to assess progress and knowledge learned throughout the training process, which includes assessing hands-on projects, optimal training length, and whether trainees should work on actual business projects. You must also determine what the path for the employee looks like following training and whether there will be ongoing training.

Developing an effective and successful training program like this would be amazing and hugely powerful. This can also become increasingly necessary as AI becomes more predominant in the workplace, and people might need to be reallocated to new jobs that require specialized training as a result.

An alternative, or an option for curriculum augmentation, would be to take advantage of many existing online training tools and courses (e.g., MOOCs).

One final thing to note. In addition to hiring and/or staffing augmentation, a strong emphasis should also be placed on employee onboarding, training, engagement, mentorship, development, and retention. Given the relative shortage and competition around talent, care should be given to providing the best work environment (e.g., safe, diverse, inclusive), culture, and opportunities possible in order to keep your best talent around for a long time.

Build Versus Buy

When it comes to employing technology for products, services, and operations, companies often need to determine whether to build versus buy. This is a very legitimate question.

To come to the "right" answer and make the corresponding decision, you can use common business and financial analysis techniques such as cost-benefit analysis (CBA), total cost of ownership (TCO), return on investment (ROI), and opportunity cost estimation. These techniques might require financial estimates and forecasting that can be imprecise and difficult to obtain. I would argue that you can answer the build versus buy question in a much simpler way in most cases.

First, is there a buy option available? If not, the answer is simple: you must build. Second, do you want to develop specific technologies as a core part of your business, or use technology to innovate, differentiate, and generate competitive advantage? If yes, you must build some or all of the total solution. It's definitely worth determining, however, whether anything existing is available to use without you having to reinvent the wheel. When building technology solutions, it's often best to use open source software and other tools such as APIs when available and at a reasonable cost, especially when free.

If innovation isn't your goal and you're mainly interested in applying technology to help improve business KPIs only, or to facilitate business operations and processes, there might be off-the-shelf solutions available that make more sense to buy. In this case, you need to very seriously weigh the buy benefits against potential disadvantages such as vendor lock, very high costs, data ownership, data portability, and vendor stability. There are few, if any, cases in which I would recommend any technology solution in which you do not own your data, or have the ability to move your data at will.

Generally speaking, I find that buying most often results in an inferior product that costs far more than building and is not customized to your specific business or needs. It also means that you're buying a commoditized product that's available to every one of your competitors, too, which means you have absolutely no advantage beyond being better at configuration or are more of a power user.

I'm always amazed at how many company executives will say that they must increase sales and profits, cut costs, and truly differentiate themselves from their competitors, and yet at the same want to buy off-the-shelf solutions and avoid pursuing innovation. More and more every day, you can't have both. They also realize how unhappy they are with aspects of a specific product or vendor and migrate to another as a result. I've seen this over and over. In many cases, the product or vendor that these executives migrate to presents some of the same problems they had before, and thus the cycle repeats. That tends to become pretty expensive pretty quickly, and incurs a ton of nonfinancial costs, as well. When the dust settles, they would have been better off building.

Ultimately, it comes down to whether you want to lead, differentiate, and truly strengthen your unique value proposition, or just simply follow and do what everyone else is doing. This is analogous to the ideas behind *red ocean* and *blue ocean strategies* for those familiar. Red oceans are characterized by fierce and dense competition and commoditization. Blue oceans, on the other hand, represent new and uncontested markets, free of competition, and where the demand is created as opposed to being competed for.

In that respect, it's less of a question of build versus buy, but rather lead or follow. Leaders build and followers buy, almost always. Likewise, leaders are successful at finding new profit and growth opportunities through innovation and differentiation, whereas followers fight to stay afloat and maintain the status quo. I think that in today's technology age, it's become abundantly clear that innovators and leaders continue to disrupt and displace incumbents and those slow to innovate and embrace emerging technology.

One final note. We discussed scientific innovation already at length as well as the scientific, empirical, and nondeterministic nature of AI and machine learning. If these are insurmountable challenges for your company, it can be very difficult to pursue AI initiatives. In that case, using data is still critical and should be centered more on commoditized business intelligence and descriptive analytics until you're able to innovate and build versus buy.

Mitigate Liabilities

There are many potential liabilities and risks when it comes to data and analytics, including those associated with regulations and compliance, data security and privacy, consumer trust, algorithmic opaqueness, lack of interpretability or explainability, and more.

Starting with regulation and compliance, most new initiatives are primarily centered on increasing data security and privacy. Companies publishing privacy policies is standard practice, but very few people read these policies, nor are they able to understand all the details, given the legal jargon.

The EU's GDPR (*https://eugdpr.org/*) is a major change in data privacy regulation that went into effect on May 25, 2018. GDPR currently applies only to the EU, but many US-based tech companies operate globally, and therefore need to be in compliance in the EU. According to the official GDPR website, stronger rules on data protection mean that people have more control over their personal data, and businesses benefit from a level playing field.

It is yet to be seen whether the GDPR will be adopted by the United States or if it will its own comparable data privacy regulation. In 2018, the state of California passed the California Consumer Privacy Act (AB 375) (*http://bit.ly/2FtAKhb*). This could certainly be a step closer to the United States adopting stricter consumer privacy regulation in general.

In addition, trust is very important to most consumers. Consumer trust with respect to data means that consumers do not want their data to be used in ways they are unaware of or would not approve of. Examples include using people's data in ways that benefit only business and not the consumer, and selling data to third parties without oversight or regard of its use after it's transferred.

Customer inquiries and complaints can occur when people feel that their data is not properly secured or used. Lack of consumer trust can be a form of liability. It is critical that we use data in ethical ways while respecting consumer privacy, security, and trust. Again, the goal should always be to benefit people and business, not just business.

We can establish trust through transparency and disclosure. Potential areas of transparency for customers include transparency into a business in general—how and why certain business decisions are made—as well as transparency into technologies, algorithms, and third-party partners that use consumer data. This is particularly important in highly regulated industries like insurance, financial services, and health care.

In addition to the considerations discussed so far, explainability, algorithmic transparency, and interpretability can be critical in certain scenarios. These are not the same things, and it's important to understand the differences. Explainability is the ability to describe very complex concepts, such as those very common with AI, in simple terms that almost anyone can understand. This means abandoning complex statistical, mathematical, and computer science jargon in exchange for easy-to-understand descriptions and analogies.

Algorithmic transparency means that any algorithms used, along with their intention, underlying structure, and outputs (e.g., decisions, predictions) should be made visible to any stakeholders (e.g., business, user, regulator) as needed. This can help build trust and provide accountability.

Interpretability refers to the ability of people to interpret exactly how certain algorithms and machine learning models make predictions, classifications, and decisions. Some algorithms and models are very difficult, if not impossible, to interpret and are usually referred to as "black boxes." This can cause a problem; for example, someone deciding to sue a company based on a decision made or action taken that was carried out by an algorithm.

In court, for example, it can be very easy to explain why a person was algorithmically turned down for a financial loan if the decision was made using a highly interpretable decision tree–based algorithm. If the loan decision was made using a neural network or deep learning approach (covered more in Appendix A), on the other hand, all bets are off. You likely wouldn't be able to justify and convince the judge as to why the decision was made exactly—a situation that would not be in your favor. It is for these reasons that highly interpretable and explainable algorithms are often chosen over their black-box counterparts in highly regulated industries, despite the potential model performance penalty.

Additional potential issues with black-box algorithms are lack of verifiability and diagnostic difficulty, as noted by Erik Brynjolfsson and Andrew Mcafee in their *Harvard Business Review* article (*http://bit.ly/2Xv1SGW*). Lack of verifiability simply means that it can be almost impossible to ensure that a given neural network will work in all situations, including those outside of how it was trained. Depending on the application, this could present a serious problem (e.g., in a nuclear power plant).

Diagnostic difficulty refers to potential issues with diagnosing errors, some of which might arise from similar factors that cause model drift, and subsequently being able to fix them. This is largely due to the complexity and lack of interpretability with neural network algorithms, as discussed.

Despite the aforementioned potential downsides of black-box algorithms, neural networks and deep learning techniques have many significant benefits that can outweigh the downsides. Some of these benefits include potentially much better performance, the ability to produce outcomes not possible using other techniques, and also the ability to do something that most other machine learning algorithms are unable to do (e.g., automatic feature extraction). This means that the algorithm removes the need for a human machine learning engineer to manually select features or create new features for model training. This can be a huge benefit, although it might not be clear what features a given neural network automatically generates and leverages, and therefore adds to the degree to which the neural network is a black box. In either case, the trade-offs between potential lack of interpretability and the benefits discussed present key considerations for which you must account.

Lastly, errors in general present a potential liability that you must consider, and in some cases, certain errors can have life-and-death consequences. Let's discuss error types and potential consequences a bit more. As discussed earlier in the book, most AI and machine learning models are error based, which means that the models are trained using a training dataset until the chosen performance metric (and accompanying error) is within acceptable range when the model is tested against a test dataset.

Depending on the application, acceptable range can mean predicting something 85% of the time correctly, or it might mean making a choice between a lower false positive (type 1 error) rate over a false negative rate (type 2 error). Let's look at two examples to explain the difference between these error types and their potential impact. The first example looks at email spam detection; the second examines diagnosing cancer from a medical test. In the spam detection case, an email is considered positive if it is spam, and in the cancer case, the test results are considered positive when actual cancer is diagnosed. False positive (type 1) errors occur when a predictive model incorrectly predicts a positive result (spam or cancer in our example), whereas false negative (type 2) errors occur when a predictive model incorrectly predicts a negative result (not spam or not cancer in our example).

In email spam detection, it's more important to ensure important emails wind up in the inbox, even if that means letting a little bit of spam in, as well. This means that those building and optimizing the model will tune it to favor making false negative (type 2) errors over false positive (type 2) errors, and therefore some emails might be incorrectly classified as being not spam and sent to the inbox when they should have been sent to the spam folder.

In cancer detection and diagnosis, however, this trade-off and decision is significantly more important and carries potential life or death consequences. In this case, it's much better to falsely diagnose someone with cancer (false positive —type 1 error) and ultimately find out it was a mistake, as opposed to telling a person they don't have cancer when they actually do (false negative—type 2 error). Although the former case can cause the patient undue stress, additional expenses and medical tests, the latter case can cause the patient to leave the doctor's office and go about their lives with the disease undiscovered and untreated until it's too late.

In other applications, another type of error trade-off is referred to as precision versus recall, and similarly, decisions must be made about which is more important to favor. Google's Jess Holbrook advises making a determination about whether "it's important to include all the right answers even if it means letting in more wrong ones (optimizing for recall), or minimizing the number of wrong answers at the cost of leaving out some of the right ones (optimizing for precision)."[3]

There are many types of performance metrics and errors associated with machine learning, which can sometimes carry significant consequences if not tuned for correctly. It is very important that executives and managers understand the different types of potential errors and their impacts, as most practitioners (e.g., data scientists) are usually not in a position to properly assess, manage, or make key decisions around the potential risks involved.

Mitigating Bias and Prioritizing Inclusion

Another key consideration—and one that is becoming much more widely talked about—are the potential biases that AI applications can learn and exhibit. This is commonly called *algorithmic bias* and can include biases and potential discrimination based on race, ethnicity, gender, and demographics. Clearly, you need to avoid this.

Algorithmic bias is largely a data problem. Data can be biased due to the factors and conditions that the data stems from (e.g., socioeconomic and low-income communities), and therefore isn't an AI problem per se, but a real-world systemic issue that is represented in the data and infused into AI solutions (from training) as a result. The data might be biased in a way that reflects very poorly and inaccurately on a certain subset of people and therefore might not model reality. This data, when used without careful consideration of bias, can result in trained models that can make very poor and unfair decisions. These decisions

---

3 *https://medium.com/google-design/human-centered-machine-learning-a770d10562cd*

can further bias both reality and subsequent data, and therefore create a negative feedback loop.

Inclusion, or lack thereof, is related to algorithmic bias, as well. It is very important to prioritize inclusion from the outset of a project. This means making sure to gather and use as widely a diverse and inclusive dataset as possible. The ultimate goal is to ensure that a given AI solution provides benefits to all people, and not just one or a few select groups.

Another consideration is known as *confirmation bias.* Confirmation bias is when people see what they want to see if they look hard enough. An example of confirmation bias is when you're interested in buying a new car and are considering a specific make and model. Often, people in this situation begin to notice that exact make and model on the roads much more than previously, and this helps confirm that they are making the right decision. This despite the fact that the number of cars with the specific make and model hasn't changed, and also that many other car models might be equally, if not more, represented on the roads.

I have seen confirmation bias many times when it comes to data. This type of bias can occur in different ways. One is that people simply think the data supports an idea or hypothesis they have even though that support is not concrete and largely subject to interpretation. Another possibility is that the data is manipulated in some way to include only supporting data while discarding the rest.

Regardless of how confirmation bias can occur, it is critical to let the data tell you what it has to say, assuming that you or your data science colleagues have the requisite expertise and skill set to extract key information and insights from the data. It is just as important to learn that a given hypothesis is wrong as it is to learn that it is right. Understanding what nonmanipulated deep insights the data contains is a critical step in utilizing the data in meaningful, high value, and optimal ways.

The final type of bias covered here is *selection* (aka sampling, or sample selection) bias. Selection bias occurs when data is not properly randomized prior to use with techniques such as statistics, machine learning, and predictive analytics. Lack of proper randomization can result in unrepresentative data that does not properly reflect the full data population.

Managing Employee Expectations

AI is good at making some people feel like either killer robots will take over the world, or in the less dramatic case, that they will be replaced at work by AI robots or automation. As such, it is quite possible that there will be deep employee concern and resistance to AI initiatives, particularly those that could potentially automate parts or entire jobs.

Another potential employee concern is how and why AI is being used in certain applications, which ultimately stems from some people's ethics, morals, and values. In some cases employees can feel very strongly against a particular AI application and protest the company as a result.

The main point here is that empathy and sensitivity should be given to these potential concerns and addressed accordingly. Again, trust often results from transparency, so it is very wise to educate employees on why certain AI initiatives are being pursued as part of an overall vision and strategy, and what employees can expect as a result. Great internal data and advanced analytics leadership is critical here, particularly in terms of the messaging (conveying value and vision), impact, rollout, and timing.

Managing Customer Expectations

As discussed, AI hype largely supersedes its current state-of-the-art and actual real-world use. As a result, many people's expectations of AI are unrealistic, and this can lead to disappointment and lack of appreciation for the many already-existing benefits of AI.

The impact of hype on people's perception and expectations of AI solutions is especially notable for personal assistants such as Amazon's Alexa, Google's Assistant, and Apple's Siri. Tons of hype and marketing around these technologies when initially launched gave people the impression that these tools were able to carry out a large number of useful tasks and also provide accurate information and answers on demand. It wasn't long before people realized that their capabilities were actually quite limited, and that a large proportion of requests weren't able to be filled or the results were simply wrong. Additionally, the user experience (e.g., conversationally) of using these devices for many people leaves something to be desired, although it is getting better over time.

For these personal assistants to truly rise to the hype and meet people's expectations, they will need significant improvements in natural language understanding (NLU), which if you recall is a very difficult problem in AI. Expectations should be set accordingly; personal assistants currently provide very useful features and functionality that are relatively limited at the moment, but new capabilities are being actively developed and overall functionality and usefulness should improve significantly over time.

AI and machine learning are capable of many things, and the list is growing, although many people are still not sure what these technologies can do specifically or how we can use them in real-world applications. In addition, many people think of AI in very narrow and often industry- or business function–specific terms, which is usually a function of the person's role in a company. If you speak with marketing people about AI, for example, they might be aware of, and focus on, segmentation, targeting, and personalization. There are, however, many other potential uses of AI and machine learning in marketing, and that's not always obvious.

Additionally, often people and businesses do not know exactly what they want or what is possible in software, which is something I've encountered especially in consulting. A well-known quote attributed to Henry Ford, is[4] "If I had asked people what they wanted, they would have said faster horses." This can be a result of many things, including lack of technical background, lack of imagination, or not knowing what's technically feasible.

This means that most nontechnical people tend to have a limited ability to influence the way technology impacts their experiences and lives. People must therefore rely on those of us who do understand how to design and build technological solutions, including those using AI. It is then up to us to make sure that we respect that and put people at the center of our solutions.

A potential outcome of this, and another consideration around customer expectations, is that customers might believe that off-the-shelf software can get the job done. In this context, you might hear things like, "My CRM can do that." In most cases the reality is that the CRM cannot do that. Software built for the masses such as SaaS CRM applications are usually built to appeal to the average of the masses, although this might include some specific feature customizability in the form of plug-ins and modules.

In either case, most built-in analytics are very generic and not customizable enough. Data can also become potentially much more useful when combined with other data, which is usually not possible with off-the-shelf solutions without extensive export and ETL processes. Everything discussed in the section on building versus buying is pertinent here.

---

4 It turns out that there's no actual proof that he ever said this (*https://hbr.org/2011/08/henry-ford-never-said-the-fast*), but it makes a good point.

Quality Assurance

All software applications must be properly tested for quality. The industry term for this is *quality assurance*, or *QA*. This is no different for AI-based solutions (e.g., generating deep actionable insights, augmenting human intelligence, automation). In particular, QA is paramount to ensuring intended and high-performing outcomes as well as inspiring confidence in the results and deliverables among key stakeholders and end users.

Have you ever been given a report full of metrics, data visualizations, and data aggregations in which you or a colleague noticed that some of the values didn't seem to be correct? Often the person who generated the report looks into it and finds that a set of feature values was counted twice, left out all together, or something similar. The aggregation and data transformation logic might have been incorrect, and therefore the software that generated the report was buggy. In either case, nothing is better at shaking people's confidence in data applications more than being presented with incorrect and error-ridden results. In these cases, creating a successful AI solution on which people rely on data for insights can become an uphill battle.

Finding errors like these when doing complex data queries, ingestions, transformations, and aggregations can be very difficult, and often requires substantial QA and even hand calculations to replicate the analytics being automated to ensure that everything is calculated properly. That's assuming that it can even be done.

Previously, we explored black-box and complex algorithms. In those cases, it can be virtually impossible to do QA and reproduce what they are doing in any other way. The only measure of correctness might be the model's performance itself, which is subject to change over time, and not even applicable in the case of unsupervised learning. In either case, ensuring accurate analytics, predictions, and other data-based deliverables is critical for maintaining stakeholder confidence and for promoting a data-informed and data-driven cultural shift; in other words, for getting people to become reliant on data for insights and decision making.

Measure Success

The purpose of becoming data informed or data driven is to transition from historical precedent, simple analytics, and gut feel, as discussed, but also to gain much deeper actionable insights and maximize outcomes and benefits from key business initiatives. Using data in decision making should be done on both sides of the decision-making process. You should use data to inform better decisions and suggest or automate actions, and you also should use it to measure the effectiveness and value of actions taken.

Given the importance of data in the decision-making process, there is not much point in pursuing and deploying AI solutions without having a way to measure impact and success. In other words, be sure to know whether you achieved your goals, and whether the intended benefits were realized and by how much.

After a particular AI-based solution is chosen, built, and deployed in the real-world, it is very important to be able to measure success. There are a variety of business and product metrics (KPIs) that are often used. Let's discuss business metrics first. Business metrics are direct measures of the state and health of a business, either as a snapshot, or tracked over time to make comparisons, determine trends, and enable forecasting. These metrics are based primarily on company financials and operations, and are measured outside of the context of specific products and services.

Top examples include total revenue (top line), gross margin, net profit margin (bottom line), earnings before interest, taxes, depreciation, and amortization (EBITDA), ROI, growth (both revenue and new customers), utilization rate (for billable time), operating productivity (e.g., revenue per sales employee), variable cost percentage, overhead costs, and compound annual growth rate (CAGR). Business metrics include funnel and post sales metrics as well; things like qualified lead rate, cost of customer acquisition (CAC), monthly and annual recurring revenue (MRR, ARR), annual contract value (ACV), customer lifetime value (LTV), customer retention and churn, and lead conversion rate.

Product metrics are those intended to measure the efficacy and value of specific products and services, often for both the business and user. These metrics are ideal for better understanding customer engagement (type and frequency of product interaction), customer satisfaction and likelihood to recommend, customer loyalty, and sales driven by product interactions (conversions).

Dave McClure coined the phrase "Startup Metrics for Pirates: AARRR!!!" (*http://bit.ly/2FtLrQK*). This phrase represents a model that he created for a metrics framework to drive product and marketing efforts. The "AARRR" part stands for acquisition, activation, retention, referral, and revenue. This is a type of funnel that represents the journey of a new exploring, nonpaying customer through conversion to becoming a paying customer.

Acquisition is the first site visit or app download. Activation is a result of an initial positive experience with the product, and willingness to return. Retention is repeated visits and use. Referral is the act of telling others about a product because of liking it so much, and revenue means that the user performs actions with the product that result in money spent and business revenue received.

Although not all stemming from the AARRR model, specific product metrics include net promoter score (NPS), app downloads, number of accounts registered, average revenue per user, active users, app traffic and interaction (web and mobile), conversions (both revenue and nonrevenue generating), usability test metrics, A/B and multivariate testing metrics, and many quality- and support-related metrics.

These metrics are not only important for measuring success, but you can use some of them as features for training machine learning models. We can use certain metrics, such as those associated with user engagement, to predict future sales, for example. These metrics can also be used to create new AI visions, drive decisions, and guide AI strategy modifications in order to improve success metrics and maximize desired outcomes.

One thing worth mentioning is that you should avoid emphasizing vanity metrics. These are metrics that look great and make people feel good, but have very little quantifiable impact on business outcomes. A great example is the number of followers you or your company have on a social media platform. The more the better, of course, but that doesn't mean that your company's top line grows in proportion to your followers.

I want to finish this section by briefly mentioning the concept of customer delight. This is arguably the most difficult thing to measure, and yet has the most potential to make or break a product or service. People pay for products and services they like, and avoid those they don't. Not only that, liking something isn't good enough, especially for premium and relatively more expensive products. The additional cost must be justified, particularly when there is a lot of competition, by going from like to delight. People will give up bells and whistles (features) for a product that is delightful and pleasurable to use.

Stay Current

It is incredibly important to stay current when it comes to AI, particularly for those involved in a creating a company's AI vision and strategy, making related decisions, and for those involved in execution (i.e., practitioners). This is true in terms of specific fields such as deep learning, natural language, reinforcement learning, and transfer learning, all of which are being actively developed at a very fast rate, with advancements being made almost daily. This is also the case for AI-related hardware, tools, and compute resources.

How best to stay current? Because I can't speak to your individual needs and optimal way of learning, I can simply let you know my preferences and primary sources of information. I have Twitter lists and Reddit feeds that I follow. I am also subscribed to many relevant email newsletters, delivering great and current content directly to my email inbox. I also regularly read books and take online courses when I have the time. For staying updated on very technical and academic research and advancements, I use Cornell University Library's arXiv.org. I also try to keep up with general industry and market research. Finally, I do good old-fashioned research, as needed.

My advice is to find what works best for you and stick with that. It's very difficult to keep up with everything, so pick a manageable set of topics and filter everything else out in order to stay up to date on your interests.

AI in Production

There is a very big difference between exploratory machine learning and AI development, as compared to creating production-ready AI solutions that require actually deploying, monitoring, maintaining, and optimizing. This is represented by the build, deliver, and optimize phases of the AIPB Methodology Component.

There are many key differences and challenges that you should consider, which deserve a chapter of their own. As such, and given the more technical, subject matter-specific nature of this topic, a thorough discussion of considerations and differences associated with AI in production and development can be found in Appendix C.

Summary

This chapter covered key considerations that represent the third and final subphase of the assess phase of the AIPB Methodology Component and final category of AIPB assessment. The three AIPB assessments should be completed to create your AIPB assessment strategy, which should be incorporated into your overall AI strategy.

At this point, we've covered a lot when it comes to planning for and executing a vision-aligned AI strategy. Chapter 14 presents an example of developing an AI strategy and the resulting outputs: a solution strategy and prioritized roadmap.

14

An AI Strategy Example

Now that we've covered information and considerations necessary for creating an AI strategy in detail, let's create one using a hypothetical example. Recall that an AI strategy guided by AIPB should take the form of a solution strategy and prioritized roadmap.

Podcast Example Introduction

Let's assume that I want to build a simple, podcast listening app that allows users to get podcast recommendations based on their preferences and past listening history. Users with unpaid accounts will be shown ads, whereas users with paid accounts will not see ads. Stakeholder-wise, I represent the business because it's my company and app, the users are those who use the app to find and listen to podcasts, and the customers are the companies that use my app for advertising to unpaid users.

All three (business, users, customers) can have many goals for the app, and each goal could have multiple initiatives that can help achieve them. Let's assume an AI vision exists for which this strategy is based, that defines the *why*, *how*, and *what*, as previously discussed. (I cover this example in greater depth in Appendix B, so we leave the vision aspect as is in this chapter in order to focus on AI strategy development.)

AIPB Strategy Phase Recap

Before diving into our discussion and development of a solution strategy and prioritized roadmap for our example, recall from Part I that all expert categories are recommended for developing an AIPB strategy. This is because developing an end-to-end, AI-based innovation strategy from the AIPB North Star through to production solution optimization may require some expertise across many functional areas of a business. All expert categories should therefore be collaboratively involved, as applicable and as needed, with oversight and management as the responsibility of the manager group of experts (especially product managers given the prioritized roadmap output).

For the AIPB methodology strategy phase and from the AIPB process categories introduced in Chapter 2, I recommend the following:

- Ideation and vision development (e.g., design thinking, brainstorming, five *whys*)
- Business and product strategy (e.g., strengths, weaknesses, opportunities, and threats [SWOT], cost-benefit analysis [CBA], Porter's five forces, The Product-Market Fit Pyramid)
- Roadmap prioritization (e.g., cost of delay, CD3, Kano model, importance versus satisfaction)
- Requirements elicitation (e.g., design thinking, interviews)
- Product design (e.g., design thinking, UX design, human-centered design)

Each of these recommended process categories and specific methods will be applicable to certain respective steps covered as we progress through this chapter and example.

As mentioned in the AIPB AI vision example chapter, HiPPo (highest-paid person's opinion) methods and design by committee are not allowed, and concepts like the flipped classroom are highly recommended. Use all sessions as highly productive, effective, actual working collaboration sessions, as opposed to teaching and learning sessions. Let everyone know in advance how to get up to speed, preferably in a way that requires minimal time and effort to accommodate busy schedules.

Now let's discuss creating the AIPB strategy phase outputs. Both are guided by an AI vision, which again defines the *why, how*, and *what* to which the strategy should be based and aligned.

Creating An AIPB Solution Strategy

Creating an AIPB solution strategy can range from simple to extensive, and involve many different disciplines and considerations. Recall that the solution strategy should define the people, processes, and resources required (i.e., the plan) to do the following:

- Make your AI vision a successful reality

- Execute your assessment strategy initiatives while executing your AI strategy

- Iteratively execute the Five Ds

Iteratively executing the Five Ds includes answering all questions and addressing all considerations outlined in the AIPB methodology strategy phase section of Chapter 3. Refer to that chapter and section for a detailed refresher.

Our example solution strategy will be kept at a very high level given the vast depth and types of solution strategy deliverables that could be involved. Deliverables could be in the form of one or more documents, diagrams, or presentations, for example, and the relative nature of each could be business level, technical (e.g., software architecture, data models), product related, design related, data- and analytics-related, and so on.

For the purposes of this example, our high-level solution strategy provides our plan, as represented by the following list:

- Develop and execute a prioritized roadmap (representing a MVP) leveraging the Five Ds process.

- Conduct user research in the context of podcasts and our app vision to help guide design and development.

- Take advantage of best-in-class designers and modern design methods to ensure the best UX possible.

- Use an appropriate, modern tech stack and software architecture to build mobile apps for both iOS and Android devices.

- Develop and integrate a new recommender engine that will be built and deployed as a cloud-based API endpoint.

- Ensure proper monitoring and analytics after the apps are made available on the iTunes and Google Play app stores.

- Properly assess app usability and UX, and make changes according to our findings.

- Develop success metrics and a plan to evaluate them to help drive future data-driven decisions and improvements.

- Develop a data feedback loop that can guide ongoing recommender engine improvements and optimizations.

Creating an AIPB Prioritized Roadmap

For creating an AIPB prioritized roadmap, my recommended approach is to create a tiered roadmap, in which each tier is aligned to the tier above it. The tiers that I recommend using are shown in Figure 14-1, and your prioritized roadmap will ultimately look something like this. A product manager should be able to help with this process.

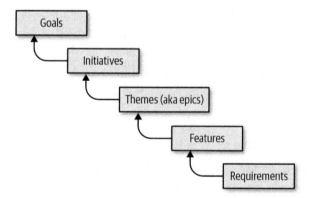

Figure 14-1. AIPB prioritized roadmap tiers and alignment

Goals are the *why*, benefits, and outcomes that we've been talking about throughout this book, and should be given for people and business, one of the primary unique aspects of AIPB. An example of this was presented when creating our example AIPB AI vision statement in Chapter 10.

Initiatives are specific, individual strategies for achieving an aligned goal. We referred to these earlier as goal-aligned initiatives. Themes (also called epics) are high-level product features that can include many lower-level features. Both themes and individual features should be defined through discovery, ideation, and creation of resulting Agile requirements that will guide design and development work.

In this example, let's assume that the primary goals on the business side are to increase customer acquisition, engagement, and retention. These are actually multiple goals, but we've rolled them into one for simplicity. We can come up with multiple aligned initiatives, themes, and features to achieve these goals.

For example, we can create preference-based, personalized incentives and promotions to encourage users to sign up for an account as opposed to using the application anonymously. In this case personalization is the initiative, while incentives and promotions are themes, each of which could have multiple specific features. We could also strategically create high-quality content (e.g., podcasts, images, copy, features) and recommendations that are personalized to each individual user. Personalization helps make things more relevant to the individual. These approaches should help achieve our goals of customer acquisition, engagement, and retention.

From the user perspective, one goal for users is to be able to quickly find new podcasts that they're likely to enjoy. This should include podcasts that have similar characteristics (e.g., length and format) and topics as those that they already listen to, while also introducing users to new, nonsimilar podcasts. This allows users to discover new content that they'd otherwise not know about. Initiative-wise, we could accomplish this with personalization, as discussed, to achieve our business goals. This is a great example of "for people and business," for which the same strategic initiative and outcome is a win-win for both.

Lastly, the customer's primary goal is to produce the highest ROI possible on their mobile app ad spend. We can accomplish this through a variety of methods such as segmentation and targeting. Figure 14-2 shows a generalized visualization of a goal-aligned prioritized roadmap.

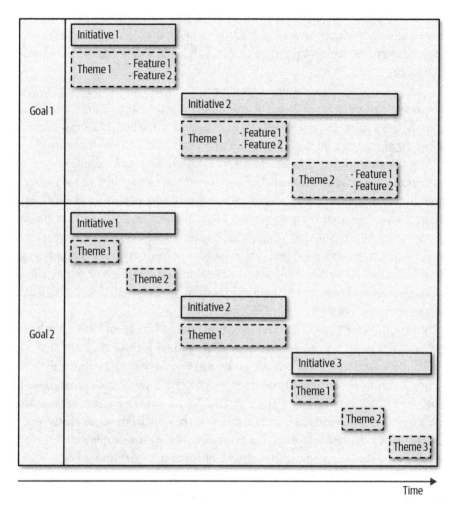

Figure 14-2. Goal- and initiative-aligned prioritized roadmap

Here is a more specific bulleted version of a prioritized roadmap, tailored to our example, and assume that this is a work in progress. Also assume that anything related to segmentation, personalization, and recommendations is intended to be AI-powered. Note that I've used more words than I normally would to describe some items (e.g., goals and initiatives) for clarity, and also that some roadmap items will need design and non-AI software development work as well since we're integrating AI solutions into an app with a user interface and non-AI powered features.

ALIGNED GOALS, INITIATIVES, THEMES, AND FEATURES

- Business goal: Increase customer acquisition, engagement, and retention

  — Initiative 1: Personalization

    — Theme 1 Incentives

      — Feature 1: Incentivized signup

    — Theme 2: Promotions

      — Feature 1: Segmentation-based targeted promotions
      — Feature 2: Preference-based targeted promotions

- User goal: Quickly find new podcasts likely to be enjoyed that are both similar to podcasts I currently listen to, and also introduces me to nonsimilar podcasts that I might not know I would like until giving it a try.

  — Initiative 1: Personalization

    — Theme 1: Podcast feed

      — Feature 1: Personalized messages
      — Feature 2: Personalized images
      — Feature 3: Personalized layout

    — Theme 2: Recommendations

      — Feature 1: Recommendations based on similar users
      — Feature 2: Recommendations based on similar podcasts
      — Feature 3: Recommendations based on nonsimilar podcasts or users

- Customer goal: Achieve above average ROI on mobile app ad spend

  — Initiative 1: Targeting (increase likelihood that ads are relevant to each user)

    — Theme 1: Segmentation-based, targeted advertising

Notice that certain themes and features might align; that is, roll up to more than one initiative or goal. That's perfectly fine. Requirements-wise, I recommend defining requirements at the theme and feature level, which will guide the design and development process. In the case of software, requirements should be associated with Agile and not waterfall methodologies.

Lastly, prioritizing all levels is key because you can't accomplish everything at once (unless you have a huge team and budget). I recommend starting at the goal level—prioritize goals at each of the people and business levels and then collectively (there will be some overlap as in our example). Then, prioritize the initiatives aligned to each goal, followed by prioritizing the themes aligned to each initiative, and finally by prioritizing each feature aligned to each theme. This will result in an optimal, prioritized roadmap to drive the rest of the AIPB downstream process of build, deliver, and optimize. I recommend cost of delay, CD3, Kano model, and importance versus satisfaction methods for prioritization.

From an Agile perspective and my own experience, I find that roadmaps with nonexistent (or very loose) time ranges (for long-term planning and/or scientific innovation) or those covering at most 90 days (roughly estimated) worth of work are best. Anything beyond 90 days is likely to be highly inaccurate and will improperly set expectations (again, this is Agile, not waterfall).

From my suggested roadmap tiers, themes and features are the roadmap items that will need to be designed (for items with a user interface) and built during the AIPB build phase. Goals and initiatives are used for strategic, planning, and alignment purposes. A prioritized roadmap will guide the product development team and all downstream AIPB Methodology phases with a prioritized order of development tasks.

PART IV

Final Thoughts

At this point we've covered the AIPB Framework and how to develop a winning AI vision and strategy. Part IV concludes with a discussion of the potential impact of AI on jobs, the importance of executive leadership on pursuing AI initiatives, and the future of AI, particularly trends and what to expect and watch out for.

15

The Impact of AI on Jobs

The power and promise of AI is huge for both people and businesses alike, although applications of AI should take into account human needs, wants, and psychology. The goal of this chapter is to discuss the potential impact of AI in the context of human needs as related specifically to jobs.

AI, Job Replacement, and the Skills Gap

One of the biggest concerns about AI that I hear from people—aside from killer AI robots taking over the world—is the fear of losing jobs, a topic definitely worth examining further. When humans believe that their ability to meet their basic needs is under threat, a fight-or-flight response usually ensues. In the context of AI, a flight response is probably well suited for a terminator or killer robot–like scenario, but we're not even close to that yet, and might never be. So fight responses, usually in the form of fear or pushback, are the most common at this time.

Although some jobs are being replaced now by AI and/or automation, and others might be replaced in the future, we are currently nowhere near job replacement happening on a mass scale in the immediate future. The vast majority of people and companies pursuing AI are interested in other applications such as augmented intelligence. Also, according to Erik Brynjolfsson, a professor at the MIT Sloan School of Management, "Even with rapid advances, AI won't be able to replace most jobs anytime soon. But in almost every industry, people using AI are starting to replace people who don't use AI, and that trend will only accelerate."[1]

Unemployment is the greatest concern in the context of job replacement by machines, and it comes in two main forms: technological (*http://bit.ly/2Kxd1AO*) and structural (*http://bit.ly/2IWcchO*) unemployment. Technological unemployment results from technological change such as AI and automation. In this case, certain tasks are performed by new technology, and a human worker is no longer needed to carry out those tasks. This means that any reassignment or reskilling will need to be around a different set of tasks and responsibilities. Structural unemployment on the other hand is a result of mismatched skills between workers and available jobs; in other words, the skills and expertise needed to fill available roles.

This is also known as a *skills gap*, and we're seeing that today across technology-related roles such as AI researchers, machine learning engineers, data scientists, and software engineers. The problem is made even worse in the case of data scientists and machine learning engineers given how broad the fields of AI and data science are. You might find a data scientist who excels at data preparation, visualization, and advanced statistical analysis but is not very strong in machine learning modeling, and vice versa.

In terms of AI, people are becoming more specialized every day given the lack of unicorns. We're beginning to see AI and machine learning engineers who specialize in natural language techniques, deep learning, reinforcement learning, or other techniques, but not all at once. This presents a real challenge because despite the demand to fill these roles, AI and data science are difficult and require programming, statistics, mathematics, computer science, and machine learning expertise. These are challenging topics to learn for many people, regardless of market demand, and are simply not for everyone.

The Skills Gap and New Job Roles

Given the growing need for specialization, the proliferation of AI and machine learning applied to real-world applications and bigger and more diverse data, we are seeing many new roles come into existence, with a specialized set of responsibilities. Some of these include DataOps, data engineers, and data product managers. We are also seeing an increased interest in having humans-in-the-loop to

---

1 *https://sloanreview.mit.edu/projects/reshaping-business-with-artificial-intelligence/*

provide human reasoning capabilities, a strength of humans, but not of today's AI. As a result of the increasing importance and emphasis on data and analytics, we're also seeing increasing involvement and diversification of roles such as software engineers, DevOps engineers, site reliability engineers, and BI specialists.

Another consideration is that technology has historically created new and different jobs, and AI should be no exception. In fact, the World Economic Forum in its 2018 *Future of Jobs Report* estimates that by 2022, as the Fourth Industrial Revolution unfolds, "75 million jobs may be displaced by a shift in the division of labor between humans and machines, while 133 million new roles may emerge that are more adapted to the new division of labor between humans, machines and algorithms."[2] This represents a net gain of 58 million jobs.

The report also points out that this net gain and positive outlook will require a series of shifts in the workforce to accompany new technologies. Figure 15-1 shows examples of roles across industries categorized as either stable, new, or redundant. The report uses the term redundant to refer to roles that are most susceptible to technological advancements and process automation over the period between 2018 and 2022. These jobs are expected to be increasingly redundant and characterized as routine based, middle skilled, and white collar.

Many other sources of research indicate that AI will actually create significant increases in economic growth and create more jobs than it will replace, albeit disproportionately by industry. Manufacturing, for example, is likely to lose a lot of jobs, whereas other industries such as health care will gain jobs. Here are some interesting findings:

- Gartner predicts that AI will create 2.3 million jobs and eliminate 1.8 million jobs by 2020, a net gain of 0.5 million jobs.[3]

- McKinsey posits that AI has the potential to increase global economic activity by $13 trillion by 2030, resulting in 16% higher cumulative GDP than today, and 1.2% additional GDP growth per year. It further reports

---

2 The World Economic Forum indicates that this estimate and the assumptions on which it's based should be treated with caution.

3 https://www.itpro.co.uk/automation/30463/gartner-by-2020-ai-will-create-more-jobs-than-it-eliminates

that by 2030, total full-time-equivalent-employment demand might remain flat, or experience a slightly negative decrease.[4]

- PwC estimates that by 2037, AI will create 7.2 million jobs in the UK while displacing 7 million, for a net gain of 200k jobs[5] and also that AI, robotics, and automation will add 93 million jobs to the Chinese economy.[6, 7]

Table 3: Examples of stable, new and redundant roles, all industries

Stable Roles	New Roles	Redundant Roles
Managing Directors and Chief Executives	Data Analysts and Scientists*	Data Entry Clerks
General and Operations Managers*	AI and Machine Learning Specialists	Accounting, Bookkeeping and Payroll Clerks
Software and Applications Developers and Analysts*	General and Operations Managers*	Administrative and Executive Secretaries
Data Analysts and Scientists*	Big Data Specialists	Assembly and Factory Workers
Sales and Marketing Professionals*	Digital Transformation Specialists	Client Information and Customer Service Workers*
Sales Representatives, Wholesale and Manufacturing, Technical and Scientific Products	Sales and Marketing Professionals*	Business Services and Administration Managers
	New Technology Specialists	Accountants and Auditors
Human Resources Specialists	Organizational Development Specialists*	Material-Recording and Stock-Keeping Clerks
Financial and Investment Advisers	Software and Applications Developers and Analysts*	General and Operations Managers*
Database and Network Professionals	Information Technology Services	Postal Service Clerks
Supply Chain and Logistics Specialists	Process Automation Specialists	Financial Analysts
Risk Management Specialists	Innovation Professionals	Cashiers and Ticket Clerks
Information Security Analysts*	Information Security Analysts*	Mechanics and Machinery Repairers
Management and Organization Analysts	Ecommerce and Social Media Specialists	Telemarketers
Electrotechnology Engineers	User Experience and Human-Machine Interaction Designers	Electronics and Telecommunications Installers and Repairers
Organizational Development Specialists*	Training and Development Specialists	Bank Tellers and Related Clerks
Chemical Processing Plant Operators	Robotics Specialists and Engineers	Car, Van and Motorcycle Drivers
University and Higher Education Teachers	People and Culture Specialists	Sales and Purchasing Agents and Brokers
Compliance Officers	Client Information and Customer Service Workers*	Door-To-Door Sales Workers, News and Street Vendors, and Related Workers
Energy and Petroleum Engineers	Service and Solutions Designers	Statistical, Finance and Insurance Clerks
Robotics Specialists and Engineers	Digital Marketing and Strategy Specialists	Lawyers
Petroleum and Natural Gas Refining Plant Operators		

Source: Future of Jobs Survey 2018, World Economic Forum.
Note: Roles marked with * appear across multiple columns. This reflects the fact that they might be seeing stable or declining demand across one industry but be in demand in another.

Figure 15-1. Stable, new, and redundant roles. (Source: The Future of Jobs Report 2018, World Economic Forum, Switzerland, 2018)

---

4 https://www.mckinsey.com/featured-insights/artificial-intelligence/notes-from-the-ai-frontier-modeling-the-impact-of-ai-on-the-world-economy

5 https://www.theguardian.com/technology/2018/jul/17/artificial-intelligence-will-be-net-uk-jobs-creator-finds-report

6 https://internetofbusiness.com/robotics-a-i-will-create-jobs-but-decimate-middle-class-careers-wef/

7 https://www.pwc.com/gx/en/issues/artificial-intelligence/impact-of-ai-on-jobs-in-china.pdf

At least for now and the foreseeable future, AI does not appear to be even remotely close to a total replacement of jobs. AI is still relatively narrow in its abilities, and is nowhere near capable of human comprehension. AI is also not able to multitask, self-learn from its environment outside of a single task that it's been trained on, or deal with any appreciable variations in the conditions from which it is trained. Yet variations occur constantly in the real world, and humans are usually able to handle them seamlessly and with ease. Most of what humans are able to do as infants is impossible for AI today.

The point is that it is less about everyone's jobs being replaced for now and the forseeable future; rather, it's about what jobs are being replaced, what new jobs will be created, and what groups of people will be affected most and to what extent.

The Skills of Tomorrow

Jobs today require two primary things: hard skills (includes expertise) and soft skills. I would argue that soft skills are at least as important, if not more important, than hard skills. Soft skills usually contribute most to an employee's ability to succeed at their job.

Unlike hard skills, soft skills are extremely difficult to teach. Even when they are taught, there's no guarantee that an employee will adopt, master, and continue to demonstrate these skills. In addition to the continually growing demand for technical skills (e.g., AI and data science), real-world jobs increasingly require soft skills such as critical thinking, problem solving, flexibility, adaptability, collaboration, and resourcefulness.

These skills are not being significantly developed by students in today's educational system, which means that there's a demand for skilled labor that is being largely unmet. Additionally, modern AI is not able to perform most of these soft skills now and might never be able to.

That's worth repeating. AI cannot demonstrate virtually any of the soft skills listed. This means that as a result, AI can not replace or automate a huge variety of jobs, and that means that there are a ton of job opportunities for people who have virtually zero competition from machines. Without humans who have the skills to fill these roles, we will continue to see large-scale talent shortages, just like we see today with roles such as data scientists and software engineers.

The Future of Automation, Jobs, and the Economy

It should be clear now that there is a lot to consider outside of just whether or not AI will replace everyone's jobs. Technology has been used to make people's lives better and easier for a long time, and will continue to do so. People's primary concern shouldn't be that AI kills jobs, but rather how governments, societies, businesses, and educational institutions will change to ensure that people are best equipped to succeed in an increasingly technological world. This includes not only changes in policy and education, but also in workforce job reassignment, retraining, or reskilling. The reality is that humans need to be able to work with machines more and more, not that machines need to work completely without humans.

Let's finish this section with two quotes and a very brief discussion about the impact of job automation on the economy.

"The basic fact is that technology eliminates jobs, not work. It is the continuous obligation of economic policy to match increases in productive potential with increases in purchasing power and demand. Otherwise the potential created by technical progress runs to waste in idle capacity, unemployment, and deprivation."[8,]

"Producers will only automate if doing so is profitable. For profit to occur, producers need a market to sell to in the first place. Keeping this in mind helps to highlight the critical flaw of the argument: if robots replaced all workers, thereby creating mass unemployment, to whom would the producers sell?"[9].

Think about it: What's the point of businesses automating everything to the point that everyone is out of work and without financial means? As the second quote points out, who will buy their goods and services? Unfortunately it might not be that straightforward given the increasing economic inequality we've seen, and which could lead to an extreme case of the haves and have-nots if left unchecked. In that case, the haves would make and buy things, whereas the have-nots would be left out. Again, we must be aware of these issues and try to avoid them. This is not purely an AI problem either.

Ultimately technology will not cease to advance and there's no reversing the technological progress that's already been made. This has been true in the past

---

8 National Commission on Technology, Automation and Economic Progress, Technology and the American Economy, Volume 1, February 1966, pg. 9.

9 Larry Elliott, quoting Kallum Pickering in "Robots will not lead to fewer jobs – but to the hollowing out of the middle class," *http://bit.ly/2Fr8DiP*

(e.g., the era of the Luddites), and will continue to be true in the future. We must therefore be proactive in discussing and addressing potential large-scale job automation, and take any steps necessary to ensure that people and technology are able to live harmoniously and in mutually beneficial ways as we move into the future.

Lastly, and somewhat interestingly, there are people who view the possibility of AI replacing everyone's jobs as actually a good thing. The idea is that it will free everyone to live happy and meaningful lives doing whatever interests them, as opposed to working constantly to meet economic and societal demands, especially if that means working jobs that aren't interesting or enjoyable (which is unfortunately the case today for many people).

If total human work replacement actually happened across the board, it could alternatively be an extremely bad thing without proper precautions and infrastructure in place. A related idea is that of a universal basic income (UBI) available to everyone to compensate for lack of jobs requiring human workers, and intended to keep people from suffering from poverty. These considerations are definitely important to keep in mind as AI progresses, although most indications suggest we're nowhere near this, nor will be for quite some time.

Summary

Humans naturally react with a fight-or-flight response when threatened, and the perceived threats posed by AI are no different. Although there might be significant pushback to AI as a killer of jobs, indications from current research, historic precedent of technology-enabled job creation, along with a focus on education and training reform, can go a long way toward better understanding the possibility of and preventing large-scale loss of jobs and adverse economic impact. As in the past, technology and AI will continue to be able to meet human needs, wants, and likes and ultimately create better human experiences. This is a core goal of AIPB.

We finish the book in the next chapter with final thoughts and an overview of AI trends and future predictions.

16

The Future of AI

At this point of the book, I hope that you're inspired and ready to leverage AI within your organization guided by AIPB. In this chapter, I share some final thoughts on the importance of executive leadership, followed by an overview of AI trends and a look ahead at the future.

AI and Executive Leadership

If you are a senior-level executive, I would like to extend an extra thanks for reading this book. Why? Two reasons. First, executive leadership understanding and buy-in is critical to advancing AI initiatives as well as helping ensure initiative success. Second, because many senior executives become far removed from the areas they oversee in their business and rightfully become mostly concerned with strategy over tactics and subject matter expertise. For good reasons, businesses need people to own strategy, P&L, operations, and other executive-level responsibilities for the business and each function. There is a definite downside, however, to this removal and focus only on the 30,000 (or whatever thousand) foot view. It is often expressed as a need for an executive summary for everything.

It's very important in my opinion for executive leadership to have an appreciable amount of subject matter expertise in areas core to the businesses offerings and respective lines of business. This is especially true in the case of AI, machine learning, and data science. These fields can be difficult for people to understand, and when decision makers are those who don't understand, it can be very difficult to move forward with advanced analytics initiatives.

As a counterpoint, it's fine if your understanding of these fields is only at the executive-summary level, but that means delegation of trust and decision making must be given to those with greater expertise. The reason is simple. I strongly believe that a major reason why many companies are still apprehensive to adopt

AI, despite knowing that they need AI to achieve certain goals, produce certain outcomes, or to remain competitive, is that key decision makers don't understand it well enough. That's understandable. Myself and others are working on demystifying and simplifying AI, but more work still needs to be done.

I also think that it's extremely important for executive leadership to have an appreciable amount of product acumen, as well. Companies are built around a product, including when the product is a service. The product is in fact the company glue, especially when viewed in terms of a hub-and-spoke model that I have created, in which the product is the hub and everything else are spokes. Figure 16-1 presents the Tech Product Hub-and-Spoke Model. Note that the AIPB expert categories are the spokes.

Figure 16-1. Tech Product Hub-and-Spoke Model

In general, executives and managers build and run businesses around a product or suite of products, designers design the product, builders build the product (e.g., software engineers), testers test the product, and scientists help build, understand, and optimize the product. The Hub-and-Spoke Model holds for entire business functions, as well—marketers market the product; sales folks sell the product; customer success folks support the product; product development designs, builds, and tests the product; operations operate a business around a product; finance and accounting track and manage money invested in or generated by the product; and product managers manage almost everything related to the vision, strategy, development, and success of the product.

Some of the greatest technology companies were created and/or run by CEOs that were former product managers and/or subject matter experts. Steve Jobs is an obvious example, but the list also includes Sundar Pichai (CEO, Google), Satya Nadella (Microsoft CEO), Marissa Mayer (CEO, Yahoo), and Indra Nooyi (CEO, PepsiCo).[1]

So, let's move on to final thoughts about AIPB and AI-based scientific innovation. To stay relevant, remain competitive, and especially to get ahead of the competition, companies must continue to innovate, particularly around data and analytics. With exploding increases in data generation and decreases in costs to store, process, and analyze the data, there has never been a more important time to develop a vision and strategy on how you will harness and use your data to create better human experiences and business success.

As we've covered, advanced analytics techniques such as AI and machine learning offer amazing opportunities for innovation and value creation. That said, many people still struggle to understand what exactly AI and machine learning are, how they differ from data science, and how all of these fields can drive real-world value. Additionally, pursuing AI offers huge possibilities for success but also failure for the many potential reasons discussed.

The key is to begin today. Don't wait, don't create barriers to entry, and, most important, don't get left behind. A great quote from Andy Weir is, "A good plan today is better than a perfect plan tomorrow." Make a plan today for incorporating AI into your business. Certain aspects of AI readiness such as leadership, cultural shift, and executive level buy-in are a must; the rest can be worked on as you go. Ensure that readiness-related gaps are filled and required shifts are prioritized and made. Also, approach data and analytics in terms of increasing levels of maturity, along with the maturity dependencies and tradeoffs among uncertainty, risk, and reward. With the required leadership, cultural shift and executive buy-in, start small and increasingly incorporate machine learning and other AI techniques in real-world applications for your business.

Also, keep in mind that value comes not only by way of ROI, but also as improvements to human experiences and delight. Optimize for this as much as you do for business objectives and KPIs. The benefits to your customers and users will benefit your business as a result.

AIPB, and the guidance in this book, will help executives and managers ensure beneficial and successful AI pursuits due to its unique and purpose-built North Star, benefits, structure, and approach. Build great AI-driven products, services, and solutions—period!

---

1 *https://www.mckinsey.com/industries/high-tech/our-insights/product-managers-for-the-digital-world*

What to Expect and Watch For

Let's discuss the future of AI and the things you should expect to hear more about and watch for in the coming years.

Unlike many established and more stable digital technologies such as mobile and web, AI is an incredibly dynamic and advancing field, and is literally changing on a daily basis. Not only from a technical and capabilities perspective, but as an explosion of AI use cases and applications in the real world. AI is making a significant transition from being something that offers huge potential, to something that is actually driving real and significant value for both people and business.

This will certainly continue as the capabilities and potential applications of AI expand in the future, and just as important, as people and companies better understand what AI is, how it can create value, and how to realize that value successfully. Hopefully, this book and AIPB have provided a framework to help develop that understanding and guide the process of AI-based scientific innovation. As I said in Chapter 1, if by simply understanding the concepts presented by AIPB and the contents of this book, executives and managers are able to progress further ahead with advanced analytics than where they are today, that's a win.

With that, let's discuss the future of AI in categories. The coverage here is high level and brief. You are encouraged to further research specific areas of interest, and don't worry if you're not familiar with some of the jargon that follows. My goal is to provide you with a big picture view of what's in store for the future of AI in both the short and long term.

INCREASED AI UNDERSTANDING, ADOPTION, AND PROLIFERATION

AI is still in its infancy, and we're only now beginning to see a major increase in real-world applications and use cases. Many of these new applications come from either the most prominent tech companies such as Amazon, Google, and Netflix, or from much smaller innovative and disruptive companies.

Many large enterprise companies have the resources to hire AI talent and pursue AI initiatives but aren't able to, or worse, experience failure due to factors such as lack of data and analytics readiness, maturity, and inability to properly understand and address many key considerations associated with AI. This puts these companies in a precarious position because there are some very small and highly agile startups that are more than happy to pursue AI and disrupt incumbents and industries.

As a result of these challenges, there is an increasing demand for data and advanced analytics leadership to help facilitate better understanding and drive the creation of visions and strategies around AI, but also for making AI more understandable in general to both businesses and consumers. This means an increasing demand for easy-to-understand AI and machine learning training for executives and managers that will help shed light on how advanced analytics can be used within their organization and help facilitate opportunity identification, ideation, and vision development around AI.

Although the technical details might be well understood by only highly specialized AI researchers and machine learning engineers, executives and leaders need to get to a point where they can think of ways to achieve goals by using their data to create deep actionable insights, augment human intelligence, automate repetitive tasks and decision making, predict outcomes, quantify feedback, and much more. From a maturity perspective, this means gaining a better understanding as described, and also graduating from traditional BI and descriptive analytics to more advanced predictive and prescriptive analytics. This is the only way to unlock the true potential of data—an impossible task if you employ only simpler, traditional analytics.

Part of the increased understanding around AI includes the realization that data is gold, and that you cannot place enough value on data readiness and quality. You can't build a brick house without bricks, just like you can't use AI to create new sources of value, differentiation, and competitive advantage without high-quality data. Companies are beginning to better understand this, and the next step is toward data democratization. Data silos stifle AI innovation and progress. Becoming a data-driven and/or data-informed organization requires data and access to as much as possible across data sources and business functions.

There's also a severe shortage of AI and machine learning talent. To address the talent shortage, many companies are working on developing tools to help democratize, simplify (reduce complexity through abstraction), and even automate some of the work normally carried out by data scientists and machine learning engineers. Automated machine learning (AutoML) is one of those areas undergoing active development and advancement. AutoML enables those who have limited expertise to train and optimize machine learning models, with examples including AWS SageMaker and Google's AI Hub. Google also released Kubeflow Pipelines to help simplify machine learning workflows.

Some of the automated aspects of AutoML are really useful, especially for those who have the requisite expertise, although I'm personally very wary about handing someone the keys to a Ferrari with a manual transmission who has never driven before and doesn't have a driver's permit. There's a lot of potential for those without the requisite expertise to make poor decisions due to not knowing what trade-offs, considerations, and different techniques to try when training models, which can result in sunk costs, lost time, and failed initiatives. In the worst case, this can mean taking on a significant amount of liability risk, with potentially life-or-death consequences.

Analytics democratization and open data are also areas of increased focus. There's been a massive proliferation of freely available data, machine learning models, and open source code. Models are also more portable and shareable thanks to the advent of tools like the predictive modeling markup language (PMML).

Lastly, today's advanced AI techniques such as deep learning require significant computing resources, training costs, and time. There are a lot of people focused on improving efficiency through algorithmic and hardware advancements, as covered earlier. This will help accelerate model learning and training, which results in reduced costs and time. It also enables quicker experimentation and hypothesis testing, and a more Agile approach overall.

Everything discussed in this section will enable increased understanding, much more widespread adoption at the manager and practitioner levels, and ultimately a proliferation of many more real-world AI use cases and applications.

ADVANCEMENTS IN RESEARCH, SOFTWARE, AND HARDWARE

Research

AI and machine learning are very hot and active areas of research. The latest research mostly involves advancements in algorithms and techniques. Some of the most exciting areas of research include natural language (NLP, NLG, NLU, machine translation), deep learning, reinforcement learning, transfer learning, personalization, recommendation systems, generative AI, and information retrieval (e.g., speech and visual search). Refer to Chapter 5 for a refresher.

Also, techniques such as deep reinforcement learning are exploring ways to create AI that is self-directed and able to self-learn over time, whereas other approaches are trying to make AI better able to solve multiple problems simultaneously; or in other words, multitask. Other techniques are being developed to help solve the cold-start problem that we previously discussed. Also, advanced approaches to causal inference traditionally carried out with A/B and multivariate testing are being developed using new AI techniques.

In addition, researchers are trying to find ways to make applying AI easier and more efficient. All advanced analytics techniques require data. Large amounts of high-quality, prepared data can be difficult and/or expensive to come by. As such, techniques such as *few-shot learning* (*http://bit.ly/2KujNHL*) are being developed to enable AI with relatively small amounts of data and without having the same data quality requirements. Researchers are also trying to find ways to improve algorithmic efficiency (e.g., neural networks) in order to train models faster and reduce costs. This includes developing simpler algorithms and models that can achieve the same or better results as the state-of-the-art algorithms in use today and that require less data.

Another very interesting area of development is around how machines learn in general. This includes online learning, incremental learning, and out-of-core (aka external-memory) learning. All of these techniques allow learning to happen on an ongoing and incremental basis as new data is fed back into the system, or in situations where datasets are too large to allow training on a single computer.

Software

In the age of big data and with today's huge datasets getting exponentially bigger with the proliferation of technologies such as IoT, scaling AI is becoming more important than ever. This includes moving and processing enormous datasets for consumption by AI algorithms as well as in terms of deploying production AI solutions that are able to perform reliably and consistently at scale. There are ongoing software advancements to help with this.

There is also a proliferation of open source, proprietary, and cloud-based software available for building AI solutions. This includes software packages, libraries, platforms, frameworks, APIs, SDKs, and collaboration tools. It also includes databases and data management systems such as those used for efficient analytics (e.g., data warehousing and data lakes).

Hardware

Modern, advanced AI and machine learning techniques such as deep learning, along with training these models on large amounts of data, are increasingly requiring highly specialized and performant hardware, nowadays referred to as *AI chips*.

One of the major recent hardware advancements for meeting the demands of today's AI was to use GPUs instead of traditional CPUs for processing large amounts of data and AI model training. GPUs are much better suited for dealing with large amounts of data and performing the underlying mathematical computations that today's AI algorithms require. Other specialized hardware in this category include application-specific integrated circuits (ASICs) and field-programmable gate arrays (FPGAs).

Certain companies have created branded and proprietary AI chips for these applications. NVIDIA is very well known for its GPUs, for example. Google has created an ASIC it calls a tensor processing unit (TPU) for intensive machine learning tasks. Intel has its own chip called the Intel Nervana Neural Network Processor (NNP), and it is teaming up with Facebook to create a new "inference" chip called the NNP-I (*http://bit.ly/2Iz9lMC*) (the I is for "inference").

ADVANCEMENTS IN COMPUTING ARCHITECTURE

Client/server and cloud computing have been the primary computing architectures for quite a while. As the internet and technology in general has grown exponentially in terms of scale, computing has advanced accordingly in order to scale with it. That includes both horizontal and vertical scaling.

With today's increasing focus on mobile devices and performance in general, new computing architectures are becoming much more relevant and popular. This includes increasing demand for offline computing abilities; for instance, the ability to use and benefit from applications even when offline.

Two very exciting areas of future development that are both highly relevant to AI are *edge* and *fog* computing. In traditional cloud-computing architectures, data is passed back and forth between clients (e.g., mobile devices, web browsers) and servers (cloud based or on-premises). The time required for data transmission and processing between clients and cloud servers is overhead that can be significant and nonperformant in some cases.

To meet increasing demands for performance and powerful real-time computing closer to the source of data (e.g., client, sensor), edge and fog computing are gaining steam. Edge refers to devices themselves; for example, a mobile phone, tablet, or sensor. Fog typically refers to the gateway between devices and the cloud; for example, an internet gateway. In these cases, computing and data storage are shifted from the cloud to closer to the devices and other generators of data. This can result in major speed and performance increases.

TECHNOLOGY CONVERGENCE, INTEGRATION, AND SPEECH DOMINANCE

As AI continues to advance and evolve in its applications, it is beginning to converge with other technologies, and people are recognizing the potential value of integrating AI into a multitude of technology solutions. For me, convergence is most apparent when certain applications no longer seem to be powered by AI, a phenomenon called the *AI effect* (discussed further shortly).

Personal assistants (e.g., Alexa, Siri) are becoming more like that all the time —they are thought of more as assistants than AI. These assistants represent the convergence of AI, audio hardware such as mics and speakers, electronic hardware, and internet connectivity (IoT). AI is also becoming increasingly integrated in established technologies, as well. Examples include recommendation engines and personalization in eComm and mComm experiences.

There are many current and future areas of AI convergence and integration. Examples include the following:

- Autonomous machines and vehicles

- Robots and robotic process automation (RPA)

- Control systems

- Checkout-free and line-free shopping (e.g., Amazon Go and sensor fusion)

- IoT and intelligent systems (e.g., smart cities, smart grids)

- Computer vision using specialized cameras, light detection and ranging (LiDar), and other forms of sensing

- Fog and edge computing (e.g., AI deep learning models on mobile devices)

- Blockchain

- Quantum computing

- Simulation and digital twins

Predictive, prescriptive, and anomaly detecting AI is also being integrated into more traditional processes associated with information technology, supply chains, manufacturing, transportation, and logistics.

Lastly, speech is poised to dominate human interactions with technology in the future. We're seeing that already, but not at the levels I expect will come in the not-too-distant future. People are interacting with technology and devices increasingly by speaking to them and having the technology speak back. This includes the assistants that we see today as well as other applications of conversational and question-answering AI. There will be a generation of children at some point who will have no concept of what it's like to type on a physical or digital keyboard. They will have grown up simply talking to everything.

SOCIETAL IMPACT

AI is certainly becoming more publicly prominent. Not only is there hype about it seemingly at every corner, but there is an ongoing proliferation of TV commercials about AI solutions, and people are interacting with AI now more than ever in their daily lives; including encountering AI in mobile apps, web apps, assistants, chatbots, IoT, robotics, augmented intelligence, and automation.

As a result of this newfound attention and relevance, people are beginning to raise serious and legitimate questions around the ethical and responsible use of AI, if and how AI should be regulated, what AI means politically, and, finally, how AI will affect society, and will that impact be good, bad, or both? These are good questions, and more attention from people and organizations is being directed toward answering them every day.

Because we covered the impact of AI on jobs at length in Chapter 15, let's turn our attention to other ways that AI will likely have increasing effects on society.

As we discussed earlier in the book, a primary concern for people at the data level is data privacy and security, which are key areas of data governance. It's worth mentioning that data governance is not new and was the responsibility of companies and IT departments long before AI was on anybody's radar or was being used in any appreciable way. That said, people's privacy, security, and trust around data matters a lot, and AI and machine learning initiatives create additional demand for data, so we're now seeing increased attention on this in the context of AI. Business leadership along with analytics, IT, and security experts need to work collaboratively to be able to take advantage of data to create better human experiences and business success while also providing transparency where possible and ensuring maximum privacy, security, and trust.

Additionally, governments at the national and local levels are increasingly regulating around privacy and fair use with the goal of helping to protect consumers. Europe's GDPR went live in May 2018, and the California Consumer Privacy Act is coming in 2020. Government attention, politics, and imposed regulations in this area will likely grow over time, so keep an eye out for future developments.

Fairness, bias, and inclusion are very important considerations for the future of AI, as well. AI can potentially and unwittingly be used in unfair, biased, and noninclusive ways. This is a topic gaining prominence and will definitely receive further attention as AI progresses. One step in that direction was the "Toronto Declaration: Protecting the right to equality and non-discrimination in machine learning systems," (*http://bit.ly/2N5IPPz*) launched on May 16, 2018 at RightsCon Toronto.

To better measure and track everything discussed so far, a premium is being placed on AI transparency, interpretability, and explainability as discussed in depth in Chapter 13, and as a result, many people are focused on creating interpretable and explainable AI. Expect to see many more developments there.

To wrap up this section, it's worth mentioning a few organizations on the frontlines of these issues and future considerations. There are many people and organizations that want to help ensure the ethical, fair, inclusive, transparent, and safe use of AI that is aligned to human values and that benefits all of humanity. Safe use refers to the growing concept of AI safety (*http://bit.ly/2XoxDrL*). Some of them include the following:

- The Future of Life Institute (FLI) (*http://bit.ly/2IyQhy4*)—Asilomar AI Principles on AI research issues, ethics and values, and longer-term issues

- The Partnership on AI to Benefit People and Society (*https://www.partner shiponai.org/*)

- Brookings Artificial Intelligence and Emerging Technologies Initiative (*https://brook.gs/31R2ZjB*)

- IEEE Standards Association (*http://bit.ly/2J5tJnX*)—Global Initiative on Ethics of Autonomous and Intelligent Systems

- OpenAI (*https://openai.com/*)—AI research for safe artificial general intelligence

- Google's Responsible AI Practices (*http://bit.ly/2XuPpmu*)

- Microsoft's Fairness, Accountability, Transparency, and Ethics in AI (FATE) group (*http://bit.ly/2X2N7vB*)

I find all of this to be very important because my interest is entirely in ethical and beneficial use of AI, and so is this book. It's about using AI to benefit people and businesses alike and to create better human experiences and business success. When pursued through that lens, AI represents a game-changing opportunity to transform and improve peoples lives as well as extend and save them.

AGI, SUPERINTELLIGENCE, AND THE TECHNOLOGICAL SINGULARITY

Work continues on making progress toward solving AI-complete (AI-hard) problems, with the goal of ultimately achieving strong AI; aka artificial general intelligence (AGI). This might require the combination of many existing techniques, creation of an entirely new technique, or something else.

A concept and model called *comprehensive AI services* (CAIS)[2] approaches the solution of general intelligence as the integration of superintelligent highly specialized AI services working together, similar to the concept of service-oriented architecture (SOA) in software architecture.

Solving the AGI problem is considered "difficult" for many reasons. It means huge advancements in AI with capabilities that are way beyond anything we have today. Here's a nonexhaustive list of required advancements:

- Acquire the ability to multitask across different tasks types

- Emulate human understanding, reasoning, and logic

- Emulate cognitive functions and processes in general

- Learn from observation and the environment in the same way babies and animals do

- Become self-directed, self-learning, self-improving, and self-modifying

- Emulate causal inference (cause and effect predictions) in the way humans naturally do

This is a ridiculously tall order at the moment, and we shouldn't expect a ton of progress on this in the near future. Also, historically, people tend to very much overestimate progress and adoption of new innovations and technologies. Think about AI; although adoption is certainly increasing, it's nowhere near the pace that many thought. Even if amazing advanced technology exists and is available for use, this doesn't mean that everyone will use it.

There are a lot of forces that actually prevent adoption, as we've discussed. This is covered in depth in the *Innovator's Dilemma* by Clayton Christensen, and is also made clear by Everett Rogers seminal work on his diffusion of innovations

---

2 Drexler, K.E. (2019): "Reframing Superintelligence: Comprehensive AI Services as General Intelligence," Technical Report 2019-1, Future of Humanity Institute, University of Oxford.

theory, in which he categorizes adopters as innovators, early adopters, early majority, late majority, or laggards. In my experience, it doesn't matter what the state of the technology is, per se, but rather what the level of widespread adoption is. In that context, I'd say that AI in still early in its diffusion and adoption.

Ultimately, estimates vary wildly across the board on when we can expect anything close to resembling AGI, and who knows at this point about adoption rates after AGI is available, so I will just leave it at that.

THE AI EFFECT

Another concept worth discussing is the AI effect. The AI effect describes the case in which after an AI application has become somewhat mainstream, it's no longer considered by many as AI. It happens because people's tendency is to no longer think of the solution as involving real intelligence and only being an application of normal computing. This despite the fact that these applications still fit the definition of AI regardless of widespread usage. The key takeaway here is that today's AI is not necessarily tomorrow's AI, at least not in some people's minds.

This makes perfect sense if you think about it. At one point in time, when Steve Jobs and Apple first launched the iPhone, it was truly amazing to people that a phone could be a one-stop shop for music, pictures, phone calls, messaging, games, and more, all while introducing touch-based interactions and a gesture-sensitive screen. Now people just expect all of that to be a part of any mobile phone, and most don't give much thought to it anymore. It's table stakes. The same can be said for C-3PO in *Star Wars*. In the film, it is portrayed that protocol droids are commonplace and there is nothing particularly special about the technology or machine intelligence. I almost lose sight of how impressive C-3PO would be if he was a real robot because I'm a huge *Star Wars* fan and am so used to that character. Who knows, maybe some day humans will think of AGI in the same way?

Amazon and Netflix recommendations are another good example of this. People are so used to these recommendations that they might not think of it as a remarkable bit of technology and application of AI. These systems are in fact very remarkable and drive a huge proportion of both company's revenue, user engagement, and retention. Some estimates indicate that 35% of Amazon's revenues are generated by its recommendations, and 75% of everything watched on Netflix comes by way of recommendations.[3] This is obviously far from trivial.

---

3 *https://www.mckinsey.com/industries/retail/our-insights/how-retailers-can-keep-up-with-consumers)*

Summary

As I've said many times in this book, AI is absolutely able to benefit both people and business and create better human experiences and business success. To realize these benefits and outcomes, the right experts must collaborate to perform the proper AI assessments and create appropriate strategies to ensure success when pursuing AI initiatives. They must also collaboratively create an effective AI vision and strategy that is highly likely to succeed, and be able to execute the strategy to build, deliver, and optimize successful AI solutions.

The AIPB Framework and its unique and purpose-built North Star, benefits, structure, and approach to AI-based, scientific innovation will help many people and companies navigate this process and better undergo a successful applied AI transformation. For additional assistance, remember to visit *https://aipbbook.com* to check for the latest AIPB information, resources, and to sign up for the mailing list. Lastly, if you enjoyed and learned something new and useful from this book, please leave a positive review wherever you bought it.

Best of luck in all of your AI pursuits, and I can't wait to see what the future of AI holds.

AI and Machine Learning Algorithms

Even though human-like deductive reasoning, inference, and decision making by a computer is still a long way away, there have been remarkable gains in the development and application of AI techniques and algorithms. We can use these techniques to create incredibly powerful and exciting AI-based solutions to real-world problems.

The algorithms that power AI and machine learning, along with properly selected and prepared training data, are able to create these solutions in ways that are not possible for humans to create any other way. There are many different goals of AI, as discussed in this book, with different techniques used for each.

This appendix is written for anyone interested in learning more about the technical nuts and bolts of AI and machine learning at a high level, including biological neural models that have inspired and helped form the field of AI. Although perhaps more technical than other content in this book, my goal is to present the information in a way that nontechnical folks can understand.

The primary topics of this chapter are how machines learn, biological neurons and neural networks, artificial neural networks, and deep learning. Deep learning is one of the most exciting and promising algorithmic techniques used to build AI solutions; it represents a special type of neural network architecture, which we discuss further in this chapter. First, let's begin by learning more about how machines learn.

Parametric versus Nonparametric Machine Learning

A more technical way to describe machine learning is that it represents algorithm-based learning techniques that learn a target (or mapping) function that maps input variables (feature data) to one or more output variables (targets).

Learned functions can be either parametric or nonparametric. Parametric functions are characterized by a model that has an assumed form upfront, where the form includes the number and types of terms, functions, and parameters.

Here is the equation of the straight line that some of us learned when we were young:

$y = mx + b$

The model is parametric because it has a predetermined form that includes two parameters (m and b), where one of the parameters m is given in a single linear function of x in the term mx. In this case, y is modeled as a linear function of x, where m represents the slope of the line (change of y for a corresponding change of x), and b, the y-intercept (value of y when x equals zero).

Figure A-1 shows the straight-line equation again in a form more common to statistics and machine learning, usually referred to by the name *simple linear regression*.

$$Y_i = \beta_0 + \beta_1 X_i$$

Target   Param 1   Param 2   Data/Feature

Figure A-1. Straight-line equation

The equation represents a target function where Y_i is the target, and X_i is the feature data. The value of Y is therefore dependent and modeled as a function of X.

Two parameters (β_0, β_1) are needed to properly model the exact relationship between X and Y. This is the equivalent to m and b in the earlier straight-line equation. Note that we can create other predefined parametric functions that include x raised to different exponents (e.g., x^2) and/or where each term is either added, subtracted, multiplied, or divided, for example. Here is an example of a parametric model of increased complexity:

$y = \theta_0 x - \theta_1 x^2 + \theta_2 x^3$

Nonparametric models have no assumed form upfront and therefore no predefined parameters, functions, or operations. Figure A-2 summarizes the difference between parametric and nonparametric machine learning models.

Parametric

Non-Parametric

Type of optimization problem
- Assumed model form (params, functions, ...)
- Learn optimal parameters (aka coefficients)

No assumed model form

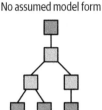

$$Y_i = \beta_0 + \beta_1 X_i$$

Target   Param 1   Param 2   Data/Feature

Figure A-2. Parametric versus nonparametric models

Let's discuss how the learning mechanism works at a high level for different types of machine learning techniques.

How Machine Learning Models Are Learned

In the case of supervised machine learning applied to parametric functions, the machine learning algorithm has the goal of finding the optimal parameter values —for example, β_0 and β_1 in the simple linear regression example—that create the best performing model; that is, the model that best describes the true relationship between the target variable and feature variables. Finding the optimal parameter values is the "learning" part of machine learning, and the learning is possible given the machine learning technique (algorithm) used and the data provided.

Nonparametric supervised machine learning functions are characterized by having no assumed form. The machine learning algorithm actually generates the model form during the learning process in some cases (e.g., decision trees), whereas in other cases the machine learning model is based on data similarity; for instance, determining the output based on similarity to existing data examples. K-nearest neighbors is a common and specific algorithm used for similarity-based, nonparametric machine learning applications.

Unsupervised learning is carried out by a variety of algorithmic approaches that depend on the type of application. Clustering applications are based on advanced data grouping algorithms, whereas anomaly detection are based on algorithms that specialize in finding abnormal data outliers.

All of the examples discussed so far fall into two additional categories: either *error-based* or *similarity-based* learning. Error-based learning works by choosing a performance metric that indicates how well a machine learning model is performing; that is, how often it predicts correctly in the case of predictive analytics (e.g., accuracy). The algorithm works by trying to minimize (via a loss function) the errors produced by the model, which is done by finding the optimal parameters in the case of parametric learning, or by finding the optimal model and parameters in the case of nonparametric learning. Similarity-based learning works by determining the greatest similarity between data points as opposed to using an error-based model.

It's worth noting that statistical learning is a term sometimes used synonymously with machine learning, and other times to differentiate statistical and probability-based learning techniques such as linear regression. We use the term machine learning here as a catch-all for any applications involving machine-based learning from data without requiring explicit programming.

Biological Neural Networks Overview

The human brain is exceptionally complex and quite literally the most powerful computing machine known.

The inner workings of the human brain are often modeled around the concept of neurons and the networks of neurons known as biological neural networks. It's estimated that the human brain contains roughly 100 billion neurons, which are connected along pathways throughout these networks.[1] Figure A-3 shows a complete biological neuron cell diagram.

At a very high level, neurons interact and communicate with one another through an interface consisting of axon terminals that are connected to dendrites across a gap (synapse), as shown in the figure. Some estimates indicate that the human brain has between 100 and 500 trillion synapses (*http://bit.ly/2XqYmx1*), which is enough to store all information learned and memories developed in an entire human lifetime.

---

1 *https://www.ncbi.nlm.nih.gov/pmc/articles/PMC2776484/*

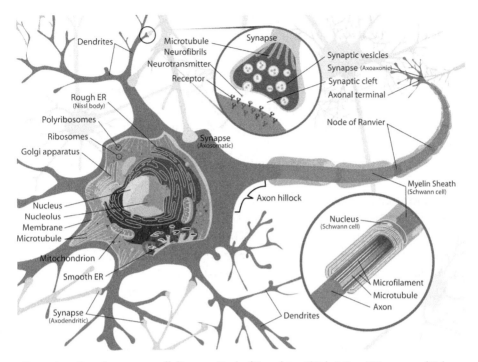

Figure A-3. Complete neuron cell diagram (LadyofHats, http://bit.ly/2RwrAW3, accessed February 25, 2019)

In plain English, a single neuron passes a message to another neuron across the synapse if the sum of weighted input signals from one or more neurons (summation) into it is great enough (exceeds a threshold) to cause the transmission. This is called *activation* when the threshold is exceeded and the message is passed along to the next neuron.

The summation process can be mathematically complex. Each neuron's input signal is actually a weighted combination of potentially many input signals, and the weighting of each input means that that input can have a different influence on any subsequent calculations, and ultimately on the final output of the entire network. Each neuron also applies a linear or nonlinear transformation to the weighted inputs.

These input signals can originate in many ways, with our five senses being some of the most important, as well as ingestion of gases (breathing), liquids (drinking), and solids (eating), for example. A single neuron might receive hundreds of thousands of input signals at once that undergo the summation process to determine whether the message is passed along and thus ultimately cause the brain to generate actions and cognitive functions.

The "thinking" or processing that our brain carries out and the subsequent instructions given to our muscles and organs are the result of these neural networks in action. In addition, the brain's neural networks continuously change and update themselves, which includes modifications to the amount of weighting applied between neurons. This happens as a direct result of learning and experience.

Given this, it's a natural assumption that for a computing machine to replicate the brain's functionality and capabilities, including being "intelligent," it must successfully implement a computer-based or artificial version of this network of neurons. This is the genesis of the advanced statistical technique and term known as artificial neural networks (ANNs).

Before moving on to ANNs, it's worth revisiting how humans learn. It turns out that the brain, particularly the neocortex, starts at birth as an initialized massive biological neural network, but one that has not yet learned and subsequently developed any significant understanding and memories.

As children begin observing their environment and processing stimuli by sensing the world around them, the billions of neurons and trillions of synapses work together to learn and store information. This results in our ability to understand and comprehend information, recognize spatial and temporal patterns, have thoughts and make mental predictions, recall information and memories, drive motor actions based on recall and prediction, and continue to learn throughout our lifetime. This is what makes humans intelligent.[2]

Let's now discuss how humans have tried to mimic this natural phenomena with machines.

An Introduction to ANNs

ANNs are one of the primary tools used to build AI applications, and they are being used in many powerful and exciting ways, many covered throughout this book.

ANNs are statistical models directly inspired by and partially modeled on biological neural networks. They are capable of modeling and processing nonlinear relationships between inputs and outputs in parallel. The related algorithms

---

2 Hawkins, Jeff, and Sandra Blakeslee. *On Intelligence*. New York: Times Books/Henry Holt. 2008.

are part of the broader field of machine learning, and we can use them in many applications such as prediction, natural language processing, and pattern recognition.

ANNs are characterized by parameters that can be tuned by a learning algorithm (parametric learning) that learns from observed data in order to build an optimized model. Some of these parameters include weights along paths between neurons and also values referred to as bias. Hyperparameters (tunable model configuration values) such as the algorithm's *learning rate* can also be tuned for optimal performance. When using an ANN, the practitioner must choose an appropriate learning algorithm and what is known as a *loss* (or *cost*) *function*.

The loss function is what's used to learn the optimal parameter values for the problem being solved. Learning the optimal parameter values is usually done through optimization techniques such as *gradient descent*. These optimization techniques basically try to make the ANN solution get as close as possible to the optimal solution, which when successful means that the ANN is able to solve the intended problem with high performance; or, put another way, predictive accuracy.

At a very high level, gradient descent works by trying different combinations of parameter values in an algorithmic, strategic way in order to iterate to the optimal overall parameter combination, and thus model. Although a bit oversimplified, the algorithm is able to determine when it has approached the best possible parameter combination and will stop the iteration process as a result.

Architecturally, an ANN is modeled using layers of artificial neurons, or computational units able to receive input and apply an activation function along with a threshold to determine whether messages are passed along, similarly to biological neurons and neural network information-propagating mechanisms.

In a *shallow* ANN, the first layer is the input layer, followed by one hidden layer, and finally by an output layer. Each layer can contain one or more neurons. The term "hidden" is used to indicate that the layer is between the input and output layers, and that the layer transforms its own input values into input values for the next layer. The term also refers to the fact that hidden layer output values are neither easily interpreted nor explainable relative to the human understandable input and output values of the network.

Figure A-4 shows an example of a simple ANN.

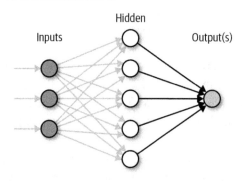

Figure A-4. An artificial neural network

ANN model architectures can be modified to solve a wider and more complex set of problems by adding hidden layers and/or neurons in any given layer, for example. Note that an increased chance of *overfitting* can also occur with increased model complexity, which means that the model performs well on training data, but not on new and unseen data (e.g., test data and/or real-world data).

The chain of transformations that occur from input to output is known as the credit assignment path, or CAP. The CAP value is a proxy for the measurement or concept of "depth" in a deep learning model architecture, and is the number of hidden layers plus the output layer. Deep learning (*http://bit.ly/ 2ICH3kx*) generally refers to a neural network architecture that has a CAP greater than two; that is, more than two nonlinear transformation (hidden) layers.

Model architecture and tuning are therefore major components of ANN techniques, in addition to the actual learning algorithms themselves. All of these characteristics of an ANN can have significant impact on the performance of the model.

Additionally, ANNs are characterized and tunable by the activation function used to convert a neuron's weighted input to its output activation. There are many different types of transformations that can be used as the activation function.

One thing worth noting is that although ANNs are extremely powerful, they can also be very complex and are considered black-box algorithms, which means that their inner workings are very difficult to interpret, understand, and explain.

Choosing whether to employ ANNs and deep learning to solve problems should therefore be considered with that in mind.

An Introduction to Deep Learning

Deep learning, although sounding flashy, is really just a term to describe neural networks with two or more hidden layers. Deep learning is further characterized by the consumption of raw input data and by different types of architectures and associated algorithms. These deep networks process data through many layers of nonlinear transformations in order to calculate a target output in the supervised case. Deep learning is able to do things with data that humans are unable to do using other techniques, and, as of this writing, is a very hot area of AI research and development.

More generally, deep learning represents a group of techniques known as *feature learning* or *representation learning*. Feature learning algorithms are able to learn features from raw data, or, stated another way, are algorithms that learn how to learn! This characteristic of deep learning is incredibly useful when it is extremely difficult or impossible for humans to select or engineer the appropriate features for a given application. The benefits of feature learning algorithms are realized most when learning from unstructured data such as images, video, audio, and language in the form of digital text. In these cases, deep learning algorithms automatically learn features and use them for a specific task such as image classification.

For deep learning neural networks, the number of layers are greater than in learning algorithms referred to as shallow. Shallow algorithms tend to be less complex and require more upfront knowledge of optimal features to use, which typically involves feature selection and engineering. In contrast, deep learning algorithms rely more on optimal model selection and optimization through model tuning. They are better suited to solve problems where prior knowledge of features is less desired or less necessary, and where labeled data is unavailable or not required for the primary use case.

Image recognition is a good example. It would be very difficult, if not impossible, for someone to write an explicitly programmed algorithm that tests all pixels, pixel groupings of varying sizes (areas) and locations, and color variations of an image to recognize and detect a cat. The reason is that the algorithm would need to know how to look for many different features of a cat in the image; for example, whiskers, pointy ears, and cat-like eyes. These features differ in many ways such as size and shape depending on the type and age of the cat.

In reality, the algorithm would need to detect even smaller and more simple features first, such as lines (vertical, horizontal, diagonal), curves, geometric shapes, and much more. When combined, these simple features could represent the cat's face and head features, as described, and when those features are combined, can represent an image of a cat. Unlike explicitly programmed code that depends heavily on feature selection and feature engineering, deep learning is able to automatically learn and create representations and combinations of these smaller features just from being given an adequate training dataset. The end result is an ANN that is able to recognize a cat in an image, which is truly remarkable.

More specifically, you can think of each layer of the network as being able to learn features and components that contribute to the overall goal of the given neural network. For example, suppose that you are training a neural network to be able to recognize whether an image is of a cat. One layer might simply learn different low-level patterns such as straight lines and curves, whereas the next layer might learn to find different features such as eyes and a nose, the next layer groups of features such as a face or torso, and then finally put it all together to determine whether the image is a cat. The network is therefore able to learn features from simple to complex in a hierarchy and then combine them into an overall solution.

Another important benefit of deep learning algorithms is that they are great at modeling nonlinear and potentially very complex relationships between inputs and target outputs. Many phenomena observed in the physical universe are actually best modeled with nonlinear transformations. A couple of very well-known examples include Newton's law of universal gravitation and Albert Einstein's famous mass–energy equivalence formula (i.e., $e = mc^2$).

It's worth mentioning that deep learning has some potential disadvantages, as well. Most prominently, deep learning can require very large amounts of training data, computing resources (cost), and training time. Also, deep learning algorithms are considered some of the blackest of black-box algorithms in use, which makes interpretability, explainability, diagnostics, and verifiability basically impossible in most cases.

Also worth noting is that single hidden-layer neural networks, the shallow networks we referred to earlier, can carry out many of the same learning tasks as their deep counterparts. That said, to be able to perform the same tasks as deep networks, shallow networks might need an extremely wide single hidden layer with an inordinate amount of neurons, which will likely be nowhere near as computationally efficient as the deep alternative.

Another important type of learning associated with neural networks and deep learning is called *transfer learning*. Transfer learning is a very useful technique, and particularly effective when the labeled data needed for a given application is in short supply.

We discussed the concept of feature space earlier in the book, which refers to the number of possible feature–value combinations across all features included in a dataset being used for a specific problem. Not only do the values of each feature span a certain range of values (or space), each feature's values can also be characterized by some type of distribution.

Typically in machine learning applications, the training data should be representative of the data likely to be seen by the model in the real world, in terms of the feature space and each feature's distribution. Sometimes, it is very difficult to procure domain-specific data that meets these requirements, whereas data from another related domain is abundantly available and similar enough in the context of deep learning applications.

In this case, deep learning models can be trained on the widely available data, and then the knowledge learned can be transferred to a new model that fine-tunes the knowledge learned based on the less available, domain-specific data. Additionally, transfer learning is great for reusing knowledge learned for quicker training times.

Deep Learning Applications

There are many different general applications now possible with deep-learning model architectures and algorithms. Although a detailed discussion is beyond the scope of this book, following is a list of some of the more interesting ones; many more applications are discussed in *Deep Learning: A Practitioner's Approach*:[3]

- Audio-to-text transcription
- Speech recognition
- Audio and text analysis
- Sentiment analysis

---

3 Patterson, Josh and Adam Gibson. *Deep Learning: A Practitioner's Approach*. O'Reilly Media, 2017.

- Natural language translation
- Generating sentences
- Handwriting recognition
- Image modeling and recognition
- Synthesis of artificial images, video, and audio
- Visual question answering

Deep learning has also been used successfully in many specific applications, including:

- Reading lips from video (*http://bit.ly/2IZsOFs*)
- Voice recognition for cars (*https://zd.net/2XBeqwB*)
- Reading text from photos and videos (*https://zd.net/2XBeqwB*)
- identification of individual animals among thousands in a species (*http://bit.ly/2XlHDLR*)

Summary

Machine learning in general is truly powerful and amazing, particularly given the ability to learn from data and carry out tasks without requiring explicit programming. That said, the ability of deep neural networks to model very complex, nonlinear relationships and also automatically extract features from raw data to effectively "learn how to learn" is what sets deep learning models apart from the rest and is also why AI is most associated today with deep learning.

Despite the dominance of neural networks and deep learning specifically as a premier AI algorithmic technique, they are not the only advanced techniques in the AI toolbox. Nonneural network–based examples include algorithms associated with reinforcement learning and natural language, for example.

The AI Process

This chapter covers an AI and machine learning process model that I created called the *GABDO AI Process Model*. GABDO models the end-to-end process of actually preparing for, developing, delivering, and improving specific AI and machine learning tasks and projects.

There are other variations of this process that you might encounter such as CRISP-DM and knowledge discovery in databases, aka KDD. The existing process models are great and widely used. That said, I find that the majority of resources and content on AI, machine learning, and data science is geared primarily toward practitioners such as data scientists and machine learning engineers. As a result, my motivation in creating the GABDO model isn't to reinvent the wheel, but rather to reimagine the process in a way that I think is better suited to executives and managers.

With that, I introduce the GABDO AI Process Model. I refer only to AI in the model name because machine learning can be considered a subset of AI, so everything presented here applies to machine learning and other AI techniques.

The GABDO Model

Figure B-1 shows the GABDO AI Process Model.

The GABDO AI Process Model consists of five iterative phases—goals, acquire, build, deliver, optimize—hence, represented by the acronym GABDO. Each phase is iterative because any phase can loop back to one or more phases before. The typical duration of each phase is highly dependent on many factors, including the scientific, empirical, and nondeterministic nature of AI and scientific innovation. That said, some phases might require time on the order of days (e.g., identifying goals, identifying data), whereas others can be on the order of weeks (e.g., identifying opportunities, preparing data, exploring data), and others months and maybe even years (e.g., creating and optimizing machine learning models and complete production AI solutions).

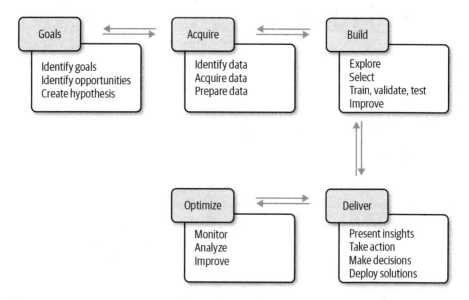

Figure B-1. GABDO AI Process Model

You might notice that the GABDO AI Process Model has some distinct similarities and seeming overlap as compared to AIPB. The GABDO Process Model can be used when executing the modular AIPB Methodology Component phases, especially build, deliver, and optimize. The key difference is that AIPB is a strategic framework intended to guide big picture, AI-based business initiatives, whereas the GABDO Process Model is a tactical-level model intended to guide specific AI and machine learning projects or tasks.

Let's discuss each GABDO phase at a high level, including the steps associated with each.

Goals

The first phase is used to identify high-priority goals and opportunities and to develop hypothesis around specific AI approaches and the data required to capitalize on the highest-priority opportunities to achieve intended goals.

IDENTIFY GOALS

The first step of this process is to identify key goals. These can be any stakeholder-specific goals that were discussed in this book or in general, and where stakeholders can be the business, customers, and/or users. Identifying key goals is typically handled at the executive level for top business goals, although more granular goals usually need to be created in order to identify and pursue specific opportunities and associated projects. Defining these goals, and potential opportunities as covered next, must be assisted collaboratively by business folks, domain experts, and AI practitioners.

IDENTIFY OPPORTUNITIES

The next step is to identify potential opportunities to use data and AI to achieve the highest-priority goals at the appropriate granularity; that is, create goal-aligned benefits and outcomes. This begins by first asking the right questions. Here are some examples:

- What AI opportunities could we pursue?
- What data is available or needed for these opportunities?
- What models and techniques could be experimented with for each opportunity?
- What potential time and effort is required for each opportunity (this might be very rough or not estimatable given that it's highly dependent on the scientific nature of AI, and also as a function of AI readiness and maturity as we've discussed)?
- What is the potential value and ROI of each opportunity?

Identifying relevant business and individual use cases should also be part of identifying opportunities. We looked at both earlier in the book.

CREATE HYPOTHESIS

After you have identified key goals at the appropriate granularity and a prioritized list of potential opportunities, the next step is to create a hypothesis to be tested as a project. This will help validate the opportunities and ensure that they're viable, feasible, and worth pursuing.

Example

Here is an example that we'll use throughout our GABDO discussion. Podcasts are gaining increasing popularity. Hypothetically, suppose that I also own a company built around a podcast listening platform that has both mobile and desktop interfaces for exploring, subscribing, and listening to podcasts. The platform also notifies users when new episodes of podcasts that they subscribe to are published. I intend for this platform to provide the best possible experience for podcast listeners, such that they'd be willing to pay a premium price for such a platform as compared to more common and free options.

Suppose that I have noticed that my current customer acquisition and retention (i.e., stickiness) levels are not being adequately met in order to satisfy my company's strategic growth goals. In this case my key goals are increasing customer acquisition and retention. Achieving these goals could certainly come from building a great product and highly delightful UX that could justify the premium price. In turn, this would ultimately help create a successful and profitable company.

Now that we've identified the primary goals of customer acquisition and retention, the key is to figure out how to achieve these goals specifically with AI and machine learning techniques—that is, how to identify opportunities to test and validate based on our available data and advanced analytics maturity.

Suppose that due to the explosion of podcasts across many different categories, users face choice overload (aka analysis paralysis) as a result of their being so many different podcasts available that span such a wide variety of categories, genres, and topics. A good question to ask is what if there were a better AI-based way to create highly personalized podcast recommendations that helps users quickly find new and interesting podcasts to listen to, all while serving up a best-in-class UX and design?

A specific AI-based idea and potential opportunity is attracting new users and helping to retain existing users (be more sticky) by making the platform more personalized, useful, and delightful. If Netflix is an apropos example, this should definitely be the outcome. We have now identified a very promising opportunity—increase customer acquisition and retention with a new and superbly designed podcast recommender system.

We might be making some risky assumptions here, however, in that we're calculating that this recommender system after it's built will have the desired user benefits and impact on our goals. Continuing with our thought process, providing personalized recommendations should remove a lot of the guesswork, labor, and search friction to finding new podcasts that the user will likely enjoy. It could also save a lot of time given that the user wouldn't need to click into each interesting-looking podcast to read more about it.

Given our idea, reasoning and logic, and some experience and expertise around specific data and AI techniques that we can try using, we now have a hypothesis that we can test to see whether we've identified a real opportunity that is worth pursuing to help achieve our goals. This will be our AI-based project. Next step, data.

Acquire

The next phase is to identify, acquire, and prepare AI-ready data for the build phase, and to test our hypothesis.

IDENTIFY DATA

The first step is to identify data. This means identifying the data sources that are available and that might be useful for the given project. This also includes identifying who "owns" these data sources (e.g., marketing, sales) and who to work with to get access, which can include getting access credentials and understanding the method required to obtain the data (e.g., BI tool, SQL, API). This also includes identifying any potential external data sources, as well, that can augment and/or be used alone for the application. Finally, this step might require identifying ways to generate and collect new data if the data required is not yet available (e.g., IoT).

ACQUIRE DATA

The next step is to simply acquire the data that was identified in the identification step, and this includes data ingestion and integration. This is the process of moving data from its source to another data store that is better suited for efficient preparation and advanced analytics (via ETL and ELT processes) and integrating (combining) data from different sources. Data can be acquired using queries, data dumps/exports, and APIs, for example. The final data store can be a local computer (e.g., a data scientists laptop), cloud computer/database, data warehouse, or data lake.

PREPARE DATA

The last step is to prepare the data for the AI project, which in our example is to create a recommender system. We discussed a lot of aspects of this step already in our discussion on the data powering AI earlier in the book. The list of potential steps includes data cleaning, data wrangling, feature selection, and feature engineering.

Example continued

With our podcast example, we need to obtain and prepare data for every platform user around their engagement metrics such as podcast subscriptions, categories listened to, episodes played, and frequency of listening activity. Ideally we also can obtain and prepare data from each user's preferences (which they've submitted voluntarily and purposefully for this application), and lastly, characteristic feature data for all podcasts that are distributed by our platform (e.g., podcast length, category, rating).

Build

For this phase, the appropriate data has been acquired and prepared for testing different hypotheses using AI techniques. Hopefully one of the hypotheses is validated and a deliverable can be built that will capitalize on the highest priority opportunity and achieve intended goals.

The build phase is used to explore acquired and prepared data, select models and performance metrics, determine initial model settings, train/validate/test models based on relevant hypothesis, and improve the AI models and applications. We'll assume machine learning techniques in the following discussion for simplicity, but note that not all AI techniques and applications are machine learning–based.

EXPLORE

The next step is to better understand the data being used to test hypotheses for a given AI opportunity (remember the TCPR Model data dependency?). This step is often referred to as exploratory data analysis (EDA). This step involves using tools like descriptive statistics, summary statistics, and data visualization. Summary statistics are values that summarize information about feature and target variables such as mean, median, standard deviation, variance, min, max, and range.

More generally, this step is intended to get a better understanding of potential relationships, correlations, and distributions of the data, feature and target data in the case of supervised machine learning, or just feature data for unsupervised machine learning applications. This information is very useful and can help make key decisions as the process continues. Exploration also helps expose any potential issues with the data, such as outliers (aka anomalies), bad values, and errors.

SELECT

The next step of the process is to make the appropriate selections to test each hypothesis. This is broken down into three steps: model selection, performance metric selection, and initial model parameter selection. Note that the word algorithm and model are often used interchangeably in this context (e.g., select an algorithm), although you can also think of an algorithm as being the technique by which a specific model is trained and optimized, and a model as the output of the algorithmic-driven learning, training, and improvement process for use in actual applications. For the purpose of simplicity and consistency, we use the term model.

Because our example involves a modeling step, our first step is to choose the appropriate model types to try. For recommender systems, options include collaborative-based and content-based filtering, but there are other approaches, as well (e.g., matrix factorization). One interesting thing to note is that the model chosen might not matter as much as other things discussed earlier in the book, such as data quality and feature selection.

Often, multiple models are chosen, tested, and compared to each other for best performance. One very important thing to note here is that a model that is ill-suited to represent the underlying relationships, correlations, and distributions of the data might never be successful, no matter how much data you have. An example would be trying to fit a straight-line model (e.g., $y = mx + b$) to data consisting of very highly nonlinear relationships. In those cases, neural network and deep learning methods might be better suited, assuming that they're applicable to the specific opportunities and application type.

Here are some things to take into account when choosing a model:

- Importance of transparency, interpretability, and explainability
- Importance of simplicity (aka parsimony) over complexity, when possible
- Importance of speed (training, testing, and real-time processing), costs, and resource requirements
- Importance of scalability

A good approach is to start with simple models and then increase model complexity as needed, and only when necessary. Generally, simplicity should be preferred unless you can achieve major performance gains by using increasingly complex models.

Model performance can be defined in many ways, but in general, model performance refers to how effectively the model is able to achieve the goals for a given problem (e.g., prediction, classification, anomaly detection, recommendation). Because the goals can differ for each problem, the measure of performance can differ, as well. Some common performance measures include accuracy, precision, and recall.

This step also requires choosing a performance metric that can be used to evaluate the performance of a given model but also to compare against other models, or even the same model tuned differently. It's almost always best to use a performance metric represented by a single value (e.g., F-score).

Just like a racecar can be made to go faster by tuning things like aerodynamic wing angles, front and rear spring rates, and static alignment settings, machine learning models can be tuned as well to increase performance. Many models include tunable configuration parameters that are often called *hyperparameters*, which allow the practitioner to tune various characteristics of how the model learns and arrives at a solution. Selecting the initial set of hyperparameter values is the final selection that must be made as part of the select step. We discuss this further in the next section.

TRAIN, VALIDATE, TEST

The next step is to train, validate, and test the model. Often the data used for model training is split into two or three subsets. These are training, validation, and testing data. The proportions of each from the original complete dataset can vary depending on practitioner's choice, but an example would be a 60/20/20 split, where 60% of the data is used for model training, and then 20% of the remaining data each for model validation and testing.

The training data subset is used by the model to learn—the predefined parameters in the case of parametric machine learning, or learning the model and parameters in general for nonparametric machine learning. The primary factors that affect potential performance during this step are data readiness and quality, modeling technique chosen, and initial model hyperparameter settings.

After a model has been trained, the validation data subset is usually used for two purposes: one is to validate the performance impact of tuning different hyperparameters, and the other is to make sure that the model is able to perform well with new and unseen data (i.e., data other than the data the model was trained on). The ability of a model to perform well with new and unseen data (i.e., generalize) is critical because models are meant to generalize to any data that it will encounter in the real world, which might differ from the data used during training. The final estimate of model performance is obtained by testing the model against the test data subset after training and tuning with the training and validation data subsets, respectively.

When a model has very good performance on the training data subset, but not with new and unseen data such as that used in the validation or testing datasets, the model is said to be either *overfitting* or *underfitting*, and sometimes this is referred to as the *bias versus variance trade-off* in more technical discussions of machine learning. This topic can easily be discussed in much greater detail, but we'll simply say that the overall goal is to build a model that performs equally well on both training data and new and unseen data (e.g., validation, testing, and real-world data).

IMPROVE

The final step is to improve a promising model's performance. This is done through processes such as additional hyperparameter optimization techniques, but also through fine-tuning with dataset refinement, feature selection, feature engineering, and other techniques.

Example continued

In our podcasting example, after exploring the data and testing many different approaches, we found a technique that works best given the available data and intended outcome. Assessing real-world outcomes from recommender systems is a bit difficult when in development, so we need to deploy it to our production platform so that real users can begin interacting with it, and we can begin to better understand its performance.

Deliver

The next phase of the process is to deliver results for a given AI project. Delivery can include a number of things depending on the specific scenario. The GABDO model defines four steps that are outcome specific and therefore might not all be relevant for a given AI project.

PRESENT INSIGHTS

For cases in which actionable insights are generated during the build phase, insights should be delivered to stakeholders. This can be as simple as communicating results either verbally, in written form, or both. Reports created manually or automatically could be another deliverable. Lastly, actionable insights can be presented in a digital format such as a dashboard or mobile app.

TAKE ACTION

Actionable insights are not valuable without taking action. Levers are meant to be pulled, and determining which levers to pull and by how much is an excellent application of advanced analytics. Take the actions suggested by your data and insights generated; this is a critical step to becoming more data informed and data driven.

MAKE DECISIONS

If insights suggest taking action, and taking action means making a decision, do it. Data-informed and data-driven decision making is a game changer, and a significant improvement over decision making based on historical precedent, simple analytics, and gut feel.

DEPLOY SOLUTIONS

Many applications using AI involve creating high-performing machine learning models that can be deployed as a standalone application, or integrated into a production solution. We covered deploying AI solutions to production in detail and in the context of AIPB earlier in the book. In the tactical, project-based context of the GABDO Process Model, we simply refer to the solution as the AI deliverable.

Example continued

In our podcasting example, we will take our best-performing recommendation engine and UX/UI design and deploy it to our platform so that users can begin receiving highly personalized recommendations that are served in a best-in-class, delightful UX.

Optimize

In the case of deployed AI deliverables, the final step is to improve and optimize over time. In AIPB, the optimize phase extends beyond just optimizing a single machine learning model, for example. It applies to the entire solution, and all aspects of it (e.g., impact on goals and business KPIs, UX and delight, customer retention and growth). The steps of the optimize phase are monitor, analyze, and improve.

MONITOR

A very important thing to consider is that a model that works well today might not work well tomorrow. This is a result of several things. First, things simply change over time. Changes commonly occur due to changes in trends (e.g., purchasing, trendy products), advancing technologies, the data collected (e.g., features, granularity), people's interests and behaviors, and seasonal and other time- and event-related effects. When this happens, the new and unforeseen data that a production model sees can be different from the data the model was trained and tested on, and the model's performance can degrade as a result. This is commonly referred to as *model drift*.

To catch model drift, it is highly recommended to develop and implement a performance monitoring solution. Ideally this solution would be able to report on model performance over time as well as alert on any significant drops in performance. Having this information would allow practitioners to train a new model and update the one running in production.

Another approach would be to regularly update production models according to an appropriately chosen cadence or as an automated process. This is a great option, as well. In general, monitoring should always be in place.

ANALYZE

There's not much point in developing an AI deliverable able to transform data into value if you're unable to determine whether any value was created or by how much and for how long (as some say, nothing lasts forever). This is where developing success metrics or KPIs to measure value, ROI, and lift is critical, along with the processes to regularly analyze them to gain insights and drive future actions and decisions for improvement and optimization. It's worth mentioning that success metrics can be both quantitative and qualitative.

Analytics and generated insights might also indicate that a product or feature should be abandoned, and that is a perfectly valid conclusion. Precious resources such as time and money shouldn't be wasted and are better spent on initiatives and projects that are able to help achieve intended goals and outcomes.

IMPROVE

After an AI deliverable has been deployed to a production environment, it should be continuously improved and optimized. Optimization is when the degree of improvement is maximized; that is, something is improved as much as possible at a given time.

Guidance and recommendations for potential improvements and optimizations will come from appropriate monitoring and analytics, as discussed, and also from ongoing collaboration with appropriate business folks, domain experts, and AI practitioners.

Example continued

Now we've developed and deployed a production recommender system for our podcasting platform and assume we have implemented monitoring, tracking, and analytics mechanisms to help us truly understand how our new recommender system is performing. Our analytics strategy includes manual (data science) and automated (predictive/prescriptive analytics) analysis. These analytics around deliverable performance will help make deliverable improvements and optimizations that are data informed and data driven.

Specifically, we need to understand whether our recommender has provided additional value (benefits) for users and has helped us achieve our acquisition and retention goals as a result. Let's discuss each of these in turn.

For customer acquisition, a simple metric we can use is new user registrations in a given time period. We will look at the number of newly registered users month over month since deploying the AI deliverable in particular to see the average increase in registered users. This should give us a fairly good idea of ROI, but it's worth noting that it will show more of an effect than a cause. With the goal of increasing customer acquisition, it might take marketing, UX, and UI updates and campaigns to inform potential users of this awesome new feature and its benefits—particularly in getting them to choose your platform over others. Increases in acquired users is not solely dependent on, or resulting from, building a cool, useful new feature.

Retention, on the other hand, has many more potential metrics to analyze. Examples include developing metrics around user engagement, such as frequency of platform usage, time on platform per session, finding and subscribing to new podcasts (conversion-related metrics), user behavior and flow while using the application, and churn reduction.

Summary

We have covered all phases and steps of the GABDO AI Process Model and presented a relevant example. The goals of the process are to prepare for, develop, deliver, and optimize AI projects that are aligned to high-priority goals and opportunities.

AI in Production

As briefly mentioned in Chapter 13, there is a very big difference between exploratory machine learning and AI development, as compared to creating production-ready AI solutions that require actually deploying, monitoring, maintaining, and optimizing.

This appendix covers many key considerations and differences associated with AI in production and development, including the concept of a computing environments, local versus remote development, the concept of production scalability, different types of AI learning for ongoing improvement, and AI solution maintenance.

PRODUCTION VERSUS DEVELOPMENT ENVIRONMENTS

The term "environment" refers to a physical or virtual computing machine that is characterized by its operating system, configuration, resources (e.g., RAM, CPU), data, and a specific set of installed software.

Development environments are either local or remote environments that are meant for a data scientist or machine learning engineer to write, test, and optimize deliverables (e.g., a predictive model, recommender system, scoring engine) before deploying into a real-world live solution.

After a deliverable is created and successfully meets all functional and nonfunctional requirements, and passes all tests where applicable, it is deployed (i.e., released) to a production environment. The production environment is where the software runs constantly and is generally available for use.

Hardware-wise, development environments run on machines such as laptops, desktops, and servers. In the virtual case, virtual computing environments run on actual hardware servers, usually in the form of virtual machines (VMs) or containers using a technology such as Docker. Machines are located either in a cloud, on-premises, or off-premises.

Software applications are usually developed and tested in phases before being integrated into a production solution and becoming available to all intended users as part of a production automation. The process of integrating software into production solutions is commonly referred to as a *software release, deployment,* or *continuous delivery.*

Data scientists, machine learning engineers, and software engineers write code to create software during the development phase, and software quality assurance and/or automated testing is performed on software following development in order to ensure that the software works as required and without bugs. When the software is verified to work as intended and is deemed bug free, it is deployed to production for use.

A different computing environment (again, physical or virtual) is typically created for each of these phases and named accordingly. Common environment names are *development, staging,* and *production.* The staging environment is used for testing chunks of software when ready, and before deployment to the production environment. For the remainder of this chapter, we focus on development and production environments, along with their differences.

Because production requirements and environments are different than those needed for development and prototyping, deploying code and AI/machine learning deliverables can be challenging due to the mismatch in environments. This is further complicated by the fact that production environments are often running larger applications (e.g., SaaS), and where the AI or machine learning-based components are a subset of the overall functionality and user experience.

Given this, there are a few options to consider when deploying AI deliverables to production. The first is to add functionality to the existing production system, using the same machine learning–specific languages and tools used during development. You can do this in a modular way; for example, as an API-based service or microservice hosted as an endpoint in the cloud. This option has the benefit of consistency and simplicity, although it might not be the most performant option.

Alternatively, you can translate code into a language and framework that is more compatible and performant with that already in use (e.g., Java). Keep in mind, however, that this option can be very costly and time consuming. It's also worth noting that in any of these scenarios, there can be a relatively significant amount of DevOps/DataOps and site reliability engineering–related work and talent required when deploying and maintaining AI solutions in production.

LOCAL VERSUS REMOTE DEVELOPMENT

Often in the development (preproduction) phase, typical machine learning tasks are carried out on a practitioner's local desktop or laptop computer. This can work well in many cases, although there are certainly situations for which development can or should be carried out on remote (e.g., cloud-based) machines.

Here is a list of some of the main reasons why it is not practical or desirable to perform all data science or big data–related tasks on your local development environment:

- Due to increasing concern and potential regulation around data security and privacy, it might be beneficial or required to store all data and perform all analytics tasks in a remote and controlled environment such as AWS or GCP.

- Datasets are too large and will not fit into the development environment's system memory (RAM) for model training or other analytics.

- The development environment's processing power (CPU) is unable to perform tasks in a reasonable or sufficient amount of time, or at all, for that matter.

- It is simply preferred to use a faster and more powerful machine (CPU, RAM, etc.) and not impose the necessary load on the local development machine.

When these situations arise, there are multiple options available. Instead of using the data scientist's local development machine, typically people offload the computing work to either on-premises powerful computing machines or cloud-based VMs. The benefit of using VMs and autoscaling clusters of them is that you can spin them up and discard them as needed, and tailor them on-demand to meet your computing and data storage requirements.

Other benefits of cloud-based computing include having the ability to use highly optimized hardware (e.g., GPUs) for model training, particularly in deep learning applications. Another benefit is being able to handle very large data processing, storage, and querying requirements using distributed processing, database, and querying systems such as Hadoop and Spark.

For situations in which the data required for a processing or learning task is larger than a single computer's system memory (RAM), you can use out-of-core, external memory, or incremental learning techniques and algorithms.

PRODUCTION SCALABILITY

Scalability—the ability to handle expected load on the system—is a very important consideration when building production AI solutions. Required scalability is usually accomplished by using servers that are either *scaled up* (scaled vertically) or *scaled out* (scaled horizontally).

Scaling up means to increase the memory capacity and processing power of a single machine (and sometimes disk storage, as well), whereas horizontal scaling means to add additional low-cost, commodity computing resources to distribute the workload. The latter is often referred to as *distributed computing*. Both options typically result in increases in cost.

Another technique for scaling out to handle a large number of concurrent requests that require processing data through a production model (e.g., make a prediction) is to deploy the same model to many different machines and distribute the requests through routing (e.g., load balancing), or to spin up ephemeral (temporary), on-demand, *serverless* workers using a technology such as AWS's Lambda. Serverless technologies such as Lambda are highly scalable and do not require the creation, maintenance, and general overhead of running a full and persistent server.

Other options include using a Platform as a Service (PaaS; e.g., Heroku) or Infrastructure as a Service (IaaS) provider like AWS or GCP. These platforms help abstract away many of the complexities associated with system and network administration, DevOps/DataOps, and site reliability engineering, for example. There also are a growing number of scalable, specialized APIs being made available as a service that provide various AI, machine learning, and other advanced analytics-related functionality.

LEARNING AND SOLUTION MAINTENANCE

Lastly, AI solutions are trained, as discussed, in a local or remote development environment. After you develop and test them, a deliverable is then deployed to a production environment where new and unseen data passes through it in order to produce the desired benefits and outcomes. This can be handled offline in a batch process, in real-time (minimal time delays), or near real-time (e.g., acceptable delay of several seconds or minutes).

Offline learning (aka batch learning) is when deliverables are trained outside of production on an entire dataset or on a subset of the data (minibatch). Part of this involves storage and access of data from data stores such as a relational database, NoSQL database, data warehouse, or data lake.

Online learning, on the other hand, refers to when retraining and recreation of the deliverable, along with performance assessment, occurs online in a production environment with production data. This process is usually carried out on a recurring interval (cadence) that can be minutes, days, or longer.

Online learning is intended to address maintenance and upkeep of target performance based on changing data, as in the batch learning case, but it also is designed to incrementally update and improve deployed solutions without retraining on an entire dataset. This requires performant and available data storage and access and is dependent on factors such as network communications, latency, and availability of network resources.

Online learning is associated with the concept of online algorithms, in which algorithms receive their input over time and not all at once, as in the offline case. Online learning is also associated with incremental learning techniques, which is when models continue learning as new data arrives while also retaining previously learned information.

Because data, and the underlying information on which AI solutions are based, can change over time due to trends, behaviors, and other factors, the solutions should be updated on a recurring interval. This allows them to capture these changes and maintain the desired level of performance. Without doing this, performance degradation or drift is common, particularly with predictive models.

Manual deliverable training and optimization iterations are typically carried out before deploying the new and optimized deliverable to production. Alternatively, automated learning is another method for automating these deliverable updates. Automated learning is when model training, validation, performance assessment, and optimization are automated on a regular cadence, and then new and improved models are deployed to replace existing models in production. The deployment process can be either automated or manual (for an additional safety check).

This approach should include some form of model performance tracking and comparison framework to determine whether automatically generated and validated models are an improvement relative to a previous or base model.

Bibliography

- Coppenhaver, Robert. *From Voices to Results - Voice of Customer Questions, Tools and Analysis: Proven techniques for understanding and engaging with your customers.* Packt Publishing, 2018.

- Domingos, Pedro. The Master Algorithm: How the Quest for the Ultimate Learning Machine Will Remake Our World. New York: Basic Books, 2015.

- Drexler, K.E. (2019): "Reframing Superintelligence: Comprehensive AI Services as General Intelligence", Technical Report 2019-1, Future of Humanity Institute, University of Oxford.

- The Future of Jobs Report 2018, World Economic Forum, Switzerland, 2018.

- Hawkins, Jeff, and Sandra Blakeslee. *On Intelligence:* Times Books/Henry Holt, 2008.

- Horowitz, Ben. *The Hard Thing About Hard Things: Building a Business When There Are No Easy Answers.* New York: HarperCollins, 2014.

- Hu, H. (2015). Graph Based Models for Unsupervised High Dimensional Data Clustering and Network Analysis. UCLA. ProQuest ID: Hu_ucla_0031D_13496. Merritt ID: ark:/13030/m5oz9b68. Retrieved from *http://bit.ly/2X1gRss.*

- Krug, Steve. *Don't Make Me Think, Revisited: A Common Sense Approach to Web Usability.* 3rd ed., New Riders, 2014.

- National Commission on Technology, Automation and Economic Progress, Technology and the American Economy, Volume 1, February 1966, pg. 9.

- Olsen, Dan. *The Lean Product Playbook: How to Innovate with Minimum Viable Products and Rapid Customer Feedback.* New Jersey: Wiley, 2015.

- Patterson, Josh, and Adam Gibson. *Deep Learning: A Practitioner's Approach.* O'Reilly Media, 2017.

- Pearl, Judea, and Dana Mackenzie. *The Book of Why: The New Science of Cause and Effect.* New York: Basic Books, 2018.

- Sinek, Simon. *Start with Why: How Great Leaders Inspire Everyone to Take Action.* New York: Portfolio/Penguin, 2009.

Index

About the Author

Alex Castrounis is the founder, CEO, and principal consultant of InnoArchiTech. An expert in business, analytics, and product management, Castrounis has nearly 20 years of innovation experience. His primary areas of expertise are data science and advanced analytics.

Alex has helped companies of all sizes and in many industries to benefit from technological innovation and digital transformation, and to build great data products. Alex is also an experienced speaker and teacher who has helped thousands of people grasp the details and benefits of data science and advanced analytics. Alex lives in Chicago with his wife and their cat.

Colophon

The cover illustration is by Karen Montgomery, using an image from Adobe Stock. The cover fonts are Gilroy Semibold, Guardian Sans, Bebas, Nexus Mix, and Oswald. The text font is Scala Pro; the heading and sidebar font is Benton Sans.

CPSIA information can be obtained
at www.ICGtesting.com
Printed in the USA
BVHW042153070719
552783BV00013B/23/P

9 781492 036579